COMPANY LAW

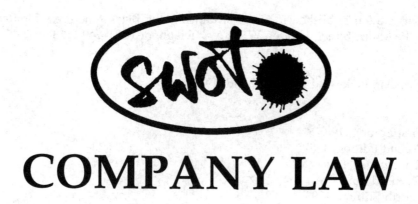

COMPANY LAW

Fifth Edition

Allan Blake

Deputy Dean, Leeds Metropolitan University

and

Helen J. Bond

Principal Lecturer in Law, University of Central Lancashire

Series Editor: C.J. Carr, MA, BCL

This edition published in Great Britain 1996 by Blackstone Press Limited, 9–15 Aldine Street, London W12 8AW. Telephone 0181–740 1173

© Allan Blake and Helen J. Bond, 1985

First Edition, 1985
Second Edition, 1987
Reprinted, 1989
Third Edition, 1990
Fourth Edition, 1993
Fifth Edition, 1996

ISBN: 1 85431 478 5

British Library Cataloguing in Publication Data
A CIP catalogue record for this book is available from the British Library

Typeset by Montage Studios Limited, Tonbridge, Kent
Printed by Bell and Bain Limited, Glasgow

CONTENTS

PREFACE

A lot of things have changed since 1985 when the first edition of this book was published, Mrs Thatcher is no longer Prime Minister for one thing and many degree courses no longer consist of year long courses assessed solely by an end of year examination. Structural changes in higher education mean that semesterisation, modularisation and the introduction of in-course assessment have all had an impact on the way in which students study, learn and are assessed. We have attempted in this edition to take these issues on board in the advice we provide in Chapters 1 and 2 on studying and assessment. Additionally, we have tried to integrate these new approaches and advise on how to handle them in the remaining ten substantive chapters.

Further changes to the rules on insider dealing in the form of the Criminal Justice Act 1993 and the current debate on corporate governance have involved major re-writing of those sections of the text. Chapter 9 on Loan Capital has also been subject to major revision, but this time in a backward direction. The provisions in the Companies Act 1989, Part IV which were to alter fundamentally the law relating to the registration of charges were never brought into force; consequently the provisions contained in the Companies Act 1985 have been re-introduced into this edition as it represents the current position.

We would again like to thank our families for their support, good humour and patience during the preparation of this edition and all the staff at Blackstone Press, especially Kieran Falconer, for their truly professional support.

Allan Blake
Helen Bond
January 1996

PREFACE TO THE FIRST EDITION

The main reason why we wrote this book stems from an awareness in tutorials in company law that students were having difficulty in pulling the various strands of the subject together. The sheer volume of the statutory provisions is formidable, now consolidated into four main Acts, the main Act being the Companies Act 1985 which runs to 747 sections, 25 schedules and 600 pages. When it comes to revise for the inevitable examination, where does the student start? This book will hopefully provide a basis for the successful study of company law throughout the year's studies, from taking notes in lectures, understanding the main issues involved in each area, through to the examination itself and how to use the material you have compiled throughout your studies.

Every author has people to thank for assisting in the preparation of a book. We should like to thank our typists, Lesley and Madeleine; may their word processor never crash again. Also, thanks to Heather Saward for some constructive and incisive comments on the draft. Finally, it is undoubtedly the case that this book would have been impossible to write without the help of all the students to whom we have taught company law, and whose examination scripts and assessments we have marked. It is through the problems in the subject that we have seen them face, and usually overcome, and the various experiments we have tried in order to convey some of the more difficult points of company law, that much of the style and content, and indeed the genesis of this book, is based.

Allan Blake
Helen Bond
School of Law, Lancashire Polytechnic, Preston

ABBREVIATIONS

STATUTES AND STATUTORY INSTRUMENTS

Where appropriate 'CA' represents the Companies Act of the stated year.
CC(CP)A 1985 — Companies Consolidation (Consequential Provisions) Act 1985
CDDA 1986 — Company Directors Disqualification Act 1986
CS(ID)A 1985 — Company Securities (Insider Dealing) Act 1985
FSA 1986 — Financial Services Act 1986
IA 1986 — Insolvency Act 1986
 Table A — Companies (Tables A to F) Regulations 1985 (SI 1985 No. 805)

LAW REPORTS

The references to less frequently used law reports include:

ALJR — Australian Law Journal Reports
BCC — British Company Cases
BCLC — Butterworths Company Law Cases
Com LR — Commercial Law Reports
CMLR — Common Market Law Reports
DLR — Dominion Law Reports
F — Federal Reporter
F Supp — Federal Supplement
IRLR — Industrial Relations Law Reports
LEd — Lawyers Edition Supreme Court Report
LT — Law Times

NI — Northern Ireland Law Reports
NY — New York Court of Appeals Reports
NZLR — New Zealand Law Reports
P & CR — Property, Planning & Compensation Reports
SEC — Securities and Exchange Commission Decisions and Reports
TLR — Times Law Reports
US — United States Supreme Court Reports
VLR — Victorian Law Reports

ARTICLES

Articles from the following journals are referred to:

Am J Comp Law — *American Journal of Comparative Law*
CLJ — *Cambridge Law Journal*
Co Law — *Company Lawyer*
Conv — *Conveyancer and Property Lawyer*
Crim LR — *Criminal Law Review*
ILJ — *Industrial Law Journal*
JBL — *Journal of Business Law*
LQR — *Law Quarterly Review*
LS Gaz — *Law Society Gazette*
MLR — *Modern Law Review*
SJ — *Solicitors Journal*

TABLE OF CASES

1 STUDY AND REVISION TECHNIQUES

INTRODUCTION

Company law can be dry and boring. There are very few students who go into ecstasies about the rule in *Foss* v *Harbottle*; hardly surprising. If company law is dry, a book that has as its aim the dissemination of guidance on how to study, prepare coursework and pass examinations in company law runs the danger of being positively arid. Hopefully we have overcome this danger and, at the same time, taken away some of the mystery that appears to surround assessments and company law examinations in particular. All too often it can appear that the subject is so complex with the many different statutory provisions, 'authoritative' cases and expressions of academic opinion, that you can never get to grips with it sufficiently to pass the course. You can, and this book will try to cut through some of these complexities to provide at least a basic guide to how to study and pass a company law course. We will not swamp you with information about cases and statutory provisions; your textbook can help you there. We will cover the basic company law areas and put them into the context of answering examination questions and preparing coursework. It is for you, the student, to judge whether we are successful. We do not guarantee that you will pass after reading this book. We do guarantee that studying company law will be easier; to say that it would be enjoyable would perhaps be stretching the book's credibility.

This book is designed to be your companion to the company law course you are studying this year. This chapter will show you how to study efficiently and effectively throughout the course and ensure that when the assessment or examination time arrives you have a useful set of notes to revise from; it will also deal with effective revision techniques. Chapter 2 will explain how to put this all into practice in preparing coursework and on the day of the examination. The remaining 10 chapters take different substantive areas of company law and try to assist in the study, and revision, of these areas so as to produce a sound examination performance. The book is not intended as merely a revision aid. We believe you will find it helpful throughout the year when preparing seminars, assessments and in your general understanding of what can at times be seen as a maze of legislation and case law, interspersed with academic articles that seem to make the maze even more difficult to escape from.

PLAGIARISM

Plagiarise is defined in the *Concise Oxford Dictionary* as to 'take and use (the thoughts, writings, inventions, etc. of another person) as one's own'. All universities and colleges treat plagiarism seriously. It is absolutely forbidden and will usually render a person liable to proceedings under the institution's disciplinary procedures. It is essential therefore to be clear about what constitutes plagiarism and to avoid falling foul of the rules.

Most institutions will consider a variety of activities as constituting plagiarism. These are discussed in detail and advice given on handling academic writing in chapter 2.

STUDY TECHNIQUES DURING THE YEAR

It is our experience that the majority of you spend a great deal of time at the end of the course rewriting your lecture and tutorial notes in order to produce a set of notes of manageable size to revise from. This is a time-consuming exercise and is usually of little use. If you can produce a set of notes of manageable size during the year, a substantial amount of time can be saved at the revision stage and your energies can be devoted to actual learning rather than rewriting lecture notes. Poor study techniques will produce a poor set of notes which are usually too long and treat everything with the same degree of importance. It is important to acquire good study habits during the year as these will ultimately aid your attempt to succeed in assessments and the examination.

STUDY TACTICS: LECTURES AND TUTORIALS

Law, on whatever type of course, is usually taught via a traditional lecture and tutorial programme. It is important for you to ascertain at the beginning of the course what your tutor or tutors perceive to be the function of each element of the programme in order for you to approach the study of company law in an efficient manner. For example, lectures may be used to expand and explain the basic principles which make up a particular topic and tutorials to explore more fully the difficult, interesting and important aspects of a particular topic. This is the more common practice.

The other method is to use lectures to give a fairly detailed account of the particular topic to be covered and to use tutorials to deal with topics that it is not intended to deal with in lectures. Depending on the method that is adopted on your course your approach to study and note preparation should be structured accordingly. The following advice may be useful.

Lecture Notes

(a) Where the lecturer intends to use the lecture to explain the basic principles which make up the topic your notes should reflect this. Do not attempt to write down every word he utters. Be prepared to listen to his explanation of the law and write down the salient points of what has been said. Remember, much of what has been said will be reinforced via the programme of tutorials. Your understanding of what has been said is far more important at this stage than beautiful, neat, copious, and sometimes meaningless notes! Write legibly, keep your notes short and to the point, and try to re-read them the lunch-time or evening after the lecture. Always read through your notes before preparing the tutorial on the topic. One thing that should be avoided at all costs is the rewriting of lecture notes after lectures. Many students do this. It is a complete waste of time and should be unnecessary if you have followed the advice above and produced a useful set of notes in the lecture. Where your lecture adopts this approach you will find it useful to take a copy of *Butterworths Company Law Handbook* into the lectures with you. This will enable you to refer to the sections being dealt with easily and relieve you from the pressure of writing them down, which will mean that you can devote more energy to listening and understanding what is being said.

(b) Where the lecture is designed to provide a detailed coverage of the topic, your notes will have to reflect this. Often lecturers who adopt this method use lecture hand-outs to aid the process. These hand-outs can vary from a basic skeletal outline which will consist of the main headings and cases, to a full-blown thesis on the topic. If you are presented with the former you will be required to take relevant notes to fill in the gaps left by the hand-out. Be sure to remember to keep your notes legible and to the point, although the finished product at the end of the lecture will probably be longer than that produced by the method described earlier which, of course, is what is intended by the lecturer.

If you are presented with a very detailed hand-out to accompany the lecture *do not* use it as an excuse to miss the lecture altogether or to take what you consider to be an hour's well-earned 'catnap' during the lecture. The fact that you have a detailed hand-out does not mean that you *understand* its contents. The best course of action to adopt in this situation is to listen to what the lecturer says while following the hand-out. Make a practice of underlining the important or difficult aspects and points which are emphasised by the lecturer. There are substantial advantages if the system is used correctly by the lecturer and the student: you can listen to what is being said without the pressure of taking notes. You should feel more free to ask questions and, in short, be more likely to understand what has been dealt with at the end of the lecture.

Any discussion of lectures would be incomplete without referring to some of the more unusual variants that you may come across.

The 'wanderer' of a lecturer does just that, wandering through the lecture room sometimes checking to see that you are noting accurately the gist of his performance. Your task is not made any easier by this journeying to and fro, especially when the lecturer ends up at the back of the room, gazing out of and talking to a window, thinking of his forthcoming summer vacation touring around Europe. Try to be sympathetic; perhaps jogging was too strenuous and walking up and down a lecture room is the only exercise he gets.

The 'dictator' could be replaced by a photocopying machine. He just reads his notes and intends that your notes will be exact duplicates. This is not lecturing, it is dictation, and is to be deplored. Your understanding of the subject is advanced very little because too much time is spent on ensuring that a 'good set of notes' (i.e., the lecturer's) are provided. You will have to do a lot of background reading to make up for this deficiency in lecturing. Students are fairly quick to see what is happening and it has been known for a few nominated scribes to attend these dictation classes and, for a small fee, provide copies to the large number of absentees, especially if the lecture is early in the morning.

There are complex variants on the 'wanderer' and the 'dictator'. One such variant combines both (mal-)practices. This involves the lecturer who establishes at the outset that when he stands to the left of the room the assembled students are expected to take down every word that issues forth; when he stands to the right, then there is no need to take any notes. This is an extremely subtle method of avoiding 'pure' dictation and does avoid the problem encountered by some students of identifying the parts of a lecture that should be noted. However, total confusion erupts when the lecturer who has established this procedure starts talking from the middle of the room.

There is also the 'academic dictator' who has had books or articles published and proceeds to read them in the lecture like a bedtime story. If you come across one, buy the book and skip the lecture. The 'not-so-academic dictator' reads out other people's books or articles. Identify which ones they are, buy them, and then skip the lecture.

The one lecturer that remains to be discussed is the 'optimist'. The optimist asks his students, at the beginning of the course, to read the appropriate chapters of the set textbook before the lectures are delivered on any given topic. This is a common request made by many lecturers and, if complied with, does help the student to identify the problem areas in advance and so be more aware of the importance of particular parts of a lecture. However, the optimist actually believes that his students have followed this instruction. The lecture may, therefore, be punctuated by such comments as: 'You have already noted . . .', or 'I don't need to go into this area in any great detail because you will have already read . . .'. An abbreviated lecture of this sort can be difficult to follow if the student has not in fact read the text in advance. We have called this lecturer the 'optimist', but he may be well aware that you have not read the appropriate sections in advance and yet still lecture as if you had. In which case you may wish to devise your own term to describe him. However, be generous; it could be an attempt to persuade the students to read in advance of the lecture so that they will not waste inordinate amounts of time taking lecture notes and later recopying them. With some prior understanding of the area the students should be able to identify more easily the main points and the difficult points from the lecture and make abbreviated notes accordingly.

Tutorials
Bearing in mind what has been said earlier about the purpose of the tutorial, and therefore the kind of and amount of material you should be aiming to produce for use in the tutorial, this section will be divided into two parts. This first part will give advice on the way in which the tutorial should be prepared to fulfil the purpose intended by the tutor. Part 2 will give general advice on the way in which statutes, textbooks, cases and academic articles should be used to aid in the preparation of tutorial notes which can be used for revision purposes at the end of the year.

Part 1: Preparation

Where the tutorial explores more fully points discussed in lectures
There are two important points to bear in mind when preparing a tutorial. Both involve your consideration of the uses to which you will be putting the material: In the tutorial at the end of the academic year. In the tutorial your tutor is likely to be looking for two things: an understanding, in more depth than was given in the lecture, of the law and also a willingness on your part to 'discuss' some of the more controversial aspects of the law. The material you prepare must reflect this aim. At the end of the academic year you will want to use your notes for revision. Accordingly you must bear this in mind when preparing the tutorial.

In our experience a typical hard-working student prepares far too much material for the tutorial. This produces three undesirable results:

(a) He cannot remember it all, and when he is asked a question by the tutor he has to resort to turning over page after page of copious notes to find the case, article or point in question. This is obviously not conducive to stimulating group discussion and can give rise to tutors banning files of notes from tutorials altogether to avoid this practice.

(b) By preparing such copious notes he will often find it difficult to see the 'wood from the trees' and be unable to answer a question put to him, or appreciate the arguments on a particular aspect of the law.

(c) The material will be utterly useless when he comes to use it to revise from for the end-of-session examinations and will involve him in preparing 'revision notes'.

The issues raised or questions asked on a tutorial sheet are likely to reflect in no small way the kind of approach adopted by the examiner in the assessments and end-of-year examinations on a particular topic and these should form the standpoint from which you prepare your seminars. Your aim should be to cover all the necessary material in order to understand and discuss the issue raised but to *avoid* straying into minuscule points of detail and general background information. Thus a typical seminar covering 'the section 14 contract' under the CA 1985 (the cases and articles referred to will call this the section 20 contract as that was the appropriate section in the CA 1948) may require you to 'discuss the extent to which the section forms a contract between the company and its members'. You will have to state the accepted interpretation as propounded by Astbury J in *Hickman* v *Kent or Romney Marsh Sheep-breeders' Association* and the views put forward by academic writers on the accepted interpretation of the law. The preparation of an answer to this question involves a discussion of statute, case law, textbook writers' opinions as well as those expressed by academics via articles in legal journals. How, and how much should you prepare to achieve the aims set out above for the tutorial, and produce a set of notes useful and compact enough to revise from? Part 2 of this discussion attempts to explain this.

Where the tutorial is intended to deal with a topic not dealt with in lectures
Where the topic you are preparing for the tutorial has not been dealt with in the lecture programme you will have to act as your own lecturer. We would advise you to prepare a basic set of notes from a textbook, preferably an introductory text. This will allow you to pin-point important cases and statutory materials to read and to highlight difficulties which form part of the topic and give you a sound basis from which to prepare the tutorial. The

tutorial sheet should direct you to the important aspects of the area if it has been prepared properly by the tutor. When doing the work, bear in mind what is said in part 2 of this discussion regarding cases, textbooks and articles.

Part 2: Handling Statutes, Case Law, Textbooks and Academic Articles

Statutes

Most examiners now provide you with the necessary statutory material you will need in the examination. Bearing this in mind, when you prepare your notes you should attempt to write down the essence of what a particular section sets out to do, paying particular attention to key words and phrases. It is usually pointless writing down the section verbatim because you will have to explain its meaning, not just recite what it says. So to answer a question on CA 1985, s. 14, your notes should look something like this:

> Covenant has been signed and sealed by each member (*but no mention of the fact that the company is deemed to have signed*). The section states that the members and the company are bound.
>
> Section also states that *all* the provisions of the memorandum and articles must be observed.

You have extracted the important points from the section and this is really all you need. As most company law students purchase a *Butterworths Company Law Handbook* or a copy of the Companies Act 1985 you will usually be in a position to refer to the actual wording used in these. If in a seminar you are asked by your tutor to explain the *literal* meaning of the section the short note you have taken will be more than adequate to do this.

Textbooks

The textbook you have been advised to purchase will provide you with all the basic information you need to appreciate the law on a particular topic and should also raise any issues which are difficult or controversial. A good textbook which is used correctly is an invaluable aid to you. For your tutorial you will want to make some notes from the textbook. How should you do this? The first thing to say is that it is pointless writing verbatim from the textbook. This is a complete waste of time as you already have the textbook, and notes written in this fashion tend to be meaningless.

You must ensure that when you make notes you take down only the salient points. This will enable you to recognise what is important and what is not so important. To be able to pick out the salient points you will have to read the relevant part of the textbook three times. Each reading has a different purpose.

Reading 1 — this allows a general reading of the material to achieve an understanding of the topic.

Reading 2 — you should try to recognise the important points which make up the topic.

Reading 3 — make notes on the important points.

Thus a typical set of notes on CA 1985, s. 14, from Gower's *Principles of Modern Company Law* might look something like this:

Fact that full account not taken of vital new factor, namely fact that incorporated company was a separate legal entity and words 'as if . . . signed and sealed by each member' did not have added to them 'and by the company'. This oddity has survived into the modern Acts.

Accepts the following as established points:

(a)   Memo. and arts constitute a contract between the company and each member. But this contract has various special characteristics:

(i)   Terms of contract (memo. and arts) are alterable by special majority voting at a general meeting.

(ii)   Normal remedies for breach of contract not available, e.g., un-liquidated damages.

(b)   Contract under s. 14 enforceable among members *inter se*. Issue may arise, e.g., where arts confer on members a right of pre-emption or first refusal when another member wishes to sell his shares a *direct* action between the shareholders concerned is possible.

(c)   Section 14 gives memo. and arts contractual effect only insofar as they confer rights or obligations on the member in his capacity as member. This is also the case where the contract between him and his fellow members is concerned. Discusses *Eley's* case, *Hickman's* case and *Beattie* v *E. & F. Beattie Ltd.*

Important to note that s. 14 affords the basis on which members may be able to restrain corporate irregularities notwithstanding the rule in *Foss* v *Harbottle*.

Discusses articles written by Wedderburn and Goldberg.

Wedderburn says — no reason why a member should not, despite rule in *Foss* v *Harbottle*, be allowed to sue in a personal capacity to restrain any breach of the articles even if indirectly, that has the effect of enforcing rights conferred on him or anyone else otherwise than as a member. Wedderburn relies mainly on *Quin & Axtens Ltd* v *Salmon* for this.

Goldberg argues that Wedderburn's view involves overruling innumerable weighty dicta in a number of cases: the proposition should be reformulated thus — that a member has the right under s. 14 to have the affairs of the company conducted by the particular organ of the company specified by the company's memorandum and articles even if this indirectly enforces outsider rights. This proposition he argues would reconcile all the decisions. In addition, articles by Prentice, Gregory and Drury broadly support the view expressed by Wedderburn but seek to refine it in different ways (see chapter 3).

Gower's view of this proposition — it is not the basis of the reported decisions and there is no authority that s. 14 would bear such an interpretation.

At the end of the section, Gower calls for either a review of all the relevant authorities by the House of Lords or a revised version of s. 14. He points out that the latter would probably be desirable even if there were a definitive ruling by the Lords since, on the present wording of the section, it is difficult to see how any interpretation could cure all its imperfections.

Cases

At this stage in your 'career' as a law student you must be prepared to read cases. Company law is a substantive case law subject so it is probable that you will need to read a number of cases during your course.

As a general rule it will not be enough for you to read only the headnote of a case. This is because it is too brief and, in some circumstances, can give the wrong impression. Consequently unless your tutor says that reading the headnote is enough (because the case is of minor consequence) you will have to read the whole case.

Reading judgments

If the case has one judgment then your task is relatively simple — you should read it. However, if the case is a Court of Appeal or House of Lords decision it is very likely that you will be faced with a multiple judgment. To read the whole case in this situation will be time-consuming and much of what you read useless at the end. The following are a few general guidelines which should be borne in mind when faced with a multiple judgment:

(a) If there is an obvious leading judgment, read it, and leave the others if they just give short supporting judgments in agreement with the main one.

(b) If you are faced with three or more judgments of roughly equal length then it is quite probable that although the judges reached the same conclusion they did so for different reasons. In this situation it is important that you read all the judgments.

(c) If there is a dissenting judgment read it. This will be valuable in order to look at an alternative approach to the problem considered by the court.

Remember, because of the way in which the doctrine of precedent works, a dissenting judgment represents uncertainty in that particular area of the law. Consequently you may be able to use the dissenting judgment to argue an alternative approach in the tutorial.

Taking Notes

(a) Always start by reading the headnote because this will give you an overview of the case. It is useful to use the headnote to make a note of the facts as it will give the gist of things.

(b) Read the judgments you have to read twice, if not literally at least in your mind as you go through the judgment. The first time to get an idea of what has been said. The second time to make notes. Look for three things:

  (i)   The *ratio decidendi.*
  (ii)   *Obiter dicta.*
  (iii) Any other reasons why the conclusion was reached.

To take an important case on CA 1985, s. 14, and make some notes let's look at *Hickman* v *Kent or Romney Marsh Sheep-breeders' Association* [1915] 1 Ch 881.

It will be necessary to note the salient facts of the case. This can often be done from the headnote. However, in an important or complicated case you will be wise to take notes from the judgment as these will be the facts that the judge has based his judgment on.

The *ratio* should always be noted. In the present case it can be found at p. 903:

. . . article 49 . . . creates rights and obligations enforceable as between the plaintiff and the association respectively. . . . general articles dealing with the rights of members 'as such' [should be] treated as a statutory agreement between them and the company as well as between themselves *inter se.*

Obiter comments are also useful to note. For example, at p. 897:

An outsider to whom rights purport to be given by the articles in his capacity as such outsider, whether he is or subsequently becomes a member, cannot sue on those articles treating them as contracts between himself and the company to enforce those rights. Those rights are not part of the general regulations of the company applicable alike to all shareholders and can only exist by virtue of some contract between such person and the company.

Reason for the decision
Astbury J bases his argument mainly on *Eley* v *Positive Government Security Life Assurance Co. Ltd* and feels that no right other than a right given in a capacity as a member can be enforced. Note his comments at p. 896.

Articles
Articles divide into two distinct groups and will be dealt with accordingly.

   (a)   *Case notes.*   These are short notes, usually 1,000 to 1,500 words, giving you an insight to the case. They are useful as a short cut to reading a case. If you are short of time it is better to have read the case note rather than nothing at all. They may also provide you with an explanation of a particularly difficult or complex decision and point out the implications that the decision may have for the future. In this situation it will be useful to read the case note before you tackle the case in the law report.
   (b)   *Articles in legal journals.*   These can vary greatly in their approach and depth. Those which appear in journals like the *Modern Law Review*, the *Cambridge Law Journal*, or the *Law Quarterly Review* are usually very academic and of a high standard. Some can be difficult to understand for a law undergraduate and even lecturer. Those which appear in journals like the *New Law Journal* or the *Company Lawyer* are orientated towards practitioners and adopt a practical approach to explaining the law. Both types, if used correctly, are very helpful in that they will provide you with both an insight to the law and a different interpretation of it.

Taking notes
Read the article to determine whether it will be of use to you and to understand what the writer is saying. Read it a second time and note the salient points of argument. Remember this will be the most you can expect to reproduce in the tutorial and the examination.
   Thus your final notes of an article for your tutorial on s. 14 may look like this:

Gregory (1981) 44 MLR 526

This proceeds on a historical footing and points out that prior to 1915 when *Hickman's* case was decided a significant number of rights and obligations under the articles which did not affect members qua member had been enforced under s. 14, e.g., *Imperial Hydropathic Hotel Co., Blackpool* v *Hampson* (1882) 23 ChD 1 where the company wished to dispense with Hampson's services as director before his period of office *under the articles* had expired. Jessel MR and Bowen LJ expressly used the s. 14 contract to enforce Hampson's right to remain in office.

In *Hickman's* case his counsel pressed Astbury J to hold that s. 14 did not create a contract between the company and its members on the basis of dicta in *Eley* and other cases. Astbury J, in order to get around this, adopted his analysis of rights under s. 14 as enforceable only if they affect the member in his capacity as member. This analysis has received widespread support, e.g., Pennington and Gower.

In *Hickman* counsel for the Sheep-breeders' Association cited *Imperial Hydropathic* as authority for the proposition that the 'articles constitute a contract between a company and its members in respect of their ordinary rights as members'. Astbury J, accepting this, quoted Bowen LJ's judgment but omitted to refer to the majority judgment (above) which enforced Hampson's tenure of office as director under s. 14 as a contract between the members *inter se*. On this basis and on the basis of Astbury J's treatment of *Browne* v *La Trinidad* Gregory demonstrates the weakness of the *Hickman* analysis. He concludes that the proposition that 'outsider' rights in the articles are beyond the scope of s. 14 is wrong since it is flatly contrary to all those cases where such rights have been enforced.

Much of the controversy stems from the argument that s. 14 creates no contract between the company and its members — a controversy arising from the draftman's oversight. But this has always been countered in the House of Lords, e.g. *Salmon's* case, where it is clearly settled that there is such a contract.

Gregory concludes: 'Even if we may, on occasion, be compelled to accept that *Parliament* does not mean what it says, how can we, in the face of clear wording, adopt a novel canon of statutory interpretation that the *statute* does not mean what it says?'

PREPARING COURSEWORK

If your company law course is assessed partly by coursework then it will be important to achieve the highest possible mark in this element. Read the coursework instructions carefully to ascertain the tutor's expectations. Some coursework questions will contain information about the marking criteria that will be used. Such criteria could include some or all of the following:

(a)   Style and organisation of the work.
(b)   Understanding of the issues raised by the question.
(c)   Evidence of wide reading and use of research skills.
(d)   Clarity and consciseness of expression within the available word limit.

These criteria will form the basis for marking the work, together with the accuracy of the legal material discussed. For one example of different instructions, see chapter 12, question 2.

It is important to address these criteria when preparing your coursework. Each one will be considered in turn.

Style and Organisation of the Work

It is essential to dissect any question you are given to identify the issues raised and plan how and in which order they occur in the question. It will not always be best to deal with the issues in the order they occur in the question. A well planned answer is easier to produce than one which is constructed 'on the hoof'.

Understanding of the Issues Raised by the Question

This relates to your ability to identify the issues raised, locate the relevant legal rules applicable to the issues, apply those rules and come to a conclusion. It may also be the case that issues raised by a particular question interrelate with each other and your ability to deal with this aspect of the question will earn you credit.

Evidence of Wide Reading and use of Research Skills

The academic writings of other lawyers will form the basis of much of the material that you will study in preparation for writing your coursework. It is important to demonstrate to your tutor that you have read and researched widely around the subject matter of the question. In this context you might want to consider a trip into the management and accountancy section of the library and look at the materials available particularly in respect of issues relating to corporate governance. Indeed throughout this book we will refer you to materials not normally cited in the more traditional company law textbooks. It is also important to ensure that academic writings used as part of the answer are properly referenced to avoid falling foul of the rules on plagiarism.

Generally speaking *all* materials read in preparation for the coursework should be included in the bibliography even though they are not actually used in the written answer.

Any quotation or passages taken from any text or law report must be acknowledged and properly attributed in footnotes or endnotes.

Remember you will be assessed on your understanding of the issues. Over–reliance on extensive quotations from the works of other writers at the expense of your own discussion or explanation of the law will result in poor marks and, in bad cases, a failure.

Clarity and consciseness of expression within the available word limit

The ability to write clearly and concisely is important in any field of work but particularly so for lawyers. Bear this in mind when dealing with the facts of cases. Is it really necessary to go into great depth or can you isolate the salient points? You will need to be selective when using quotations from texts and law reports. Have you chosen the shortest and most appropriate quotation? The examiner wants to see your work, not Pennington's, or Gower's, or Blake and Bond!

Advice on answering particular types of coursework questions is given in chapter 2.

REVISION

Examinations and the revision involved in preparing for them are viewed by the majority with dread. To those few brave souls who do not become anxious at the thought of examinations they are, to say the least, a tedious process. The situation is further compounded by the fact that the whole ghastly business is carefully timetabled by lecturers to coincide with other important events like Test Matches, Wimbledon and occasionally even the Olympic Games or World Cup football. The only consolation we can offer is that it doesn't last for ever. At this stage in your education you should hopefully only have to go through this on a few more occasions. In any event look on the bright side, it's better to be successful now than have to spend the rest of semester 2 or the summer swotting for resits!

Before we develop a revision programme it is important to establish just what the purpose of the examination is. To do this you must look at the situation from the examiner's, rather than the student's, viewpoint.

Basically it is fair to say that examiners want you to pass the examination. What you *do* know is more important to them than what you *don't* know. For example they will give you marks for making a particular point but will not take marks away because you haven't made it. They will not try to catch you out by examining on obscure aspects of the law. They are much more interested in finding out whether you have understood the principles of law, can apply them to a given factual situation and make some critical analysis if required.

If you have studied sensibly during the year your task now will be a lot easier than that of the person who finds himself with an incomplete set of notes because he has not attended classes regularly or the person who has noted down everything he can get his hands on. The former will not have enough material to revise from, the latter too much. Both are faced with a great deal of work before they can even begin the revision process properly.

If you have followed the advice given earlier on study techniques then you should be ready to plan your revision programme immediately.

If you have not then you will find it necessary to check all your lecture and seminar notes to ensure that you have a complete set. You may also find it necessary to rewrite parts of your notes in order to reduce them to a manageable size for revision purposes. Try to ensure that if this process is necessary, it is done as early as possible in your revision programme. It is a time-consuming process and does little to advance your revision programme.

Planning your Revision Programme

Length of the revision period
It is obviously vital that you start your revision programme early enough to allow for unforeseen difficulties and to prevent the whole exercise becoming a last-minute cramming session. There is no ideal length of time. You will usually be governed by outside factors, e.g., when the teaching programme ends. The best way to divide up the amount of time you have allocated yourself is to draft a 'revision timetable'. This timetable should cover the whole of the revision period and the time you may have between the actual examinations. This will force you to concentrate your mind on the amount of work ahead and enable you to divide your time between various subjects and concentrate more on weaker areas. A well-drafted timetable should give you confidence in knowing that if you stick to it you will go into the examination having done the necessary amount of revision to pass.

Drafting your Revision Timetable

(a)   Your first step is to note the number of examinations you will have to sit and the place, date and time that these examinations will take place. These should be carefully entered on your timetable.

(b)   You should then consider which topics you are going to revise not only for company law but for the other subjects which will make up the diet of examinations. Having done this draw up a list of these topics and mark the ones you consider to be your weakest with an asterisk. In order to draw up such a list some basic assumptions need to be made.

(i)   An *internally* set and marked examination (and nearly all degree examinations fall into this category) will reflect fairly accurately what has been taught during the year. Topics which have been singled out for special treatment in the tutorials, for example, are strong candidates for examination questions. Remember the examiner is not trying to catch you out and is very unlikely to examine on something that has not been given a fairly thorough treatment during the year.

(ii)   For an *externally* set and marked examination the situation is a little more uncertain because you will usually not have been taught by a person involved in the setting of the paper. Consequently your lecturer may have emphasised topics or aspects of a topic which the examiner may not see fit to examine on for this particular paper. Your best course of action in this situation is to go through past papers and work out what is likely to appear on the paper.

Having done this you should have a core of topics on which you believe you will be examined. You then have to decide which ones and how many you are going to revise. Most degree examinations will involve a straight choice of four or five questions from nine or ten set. It is to counsel perfection to suggest you learn everything you have been taught during the year, but in reality for most people this is not practical and neither is it in our view desirable. The student who covers everything is unlikely to know anything in sufficient depth to achieve an upper-second standard of answer unless he is brilliant.

We suggest that if you have to answer five questions in an examination, you learn seven topics and if you have to answer four questions, six topics. This should ensure that you are not 'caught out' in the examination whilst minimising revision.

Thus a typical revision list would look like this:

(i)   Incorporation. Lifting the veil especially with regard to groups and multinational companies.

(ii)   The company's contractual capacity.

(iii)   The alteration of the articles and the s. 14 contract.

(iv)   Directors' duties.

(v)   Insider dealing.

(vi)   Share capital.

(vii)   Minority protection.

(viii)   The division of powers between the shareholders in general meeting and the directors.

(ix)   Liquidations.

(x)   Corporate governance.

You will have ticked seven topics and also asterisked those which you consider to be your weakest.

When choosing the topics to revise remember that a paper which is internally set and marked will usually reflect topics which have been concentrated on in lectures and seminars. For a paper which is externally set it may be advisable to pick topics which are your best and anything which has received the attention of Parliament or the courts recently, e.g., have there been any recent important decisions or legislative changes?

(c)   There are two ways you can proceed at this point:

(i)   Subject-by-subject revision — which involves the revision of the whole subject in one sustained effort. This has advantages for subjects where topics tend to be interrelated, e.g., the law of evidence, criminal law and to some extent company law, because you will be in a position to see clearly this interrelationship at an early stage. You will also have the satisfaction of having got one subject out of the way. This method also has distinct disadvantages. The main one is that it is boring studying the same subject for a sustained period of time. It may also unnerve you because you have not dealt with any material from any of the other subjects you have to revise.

(ii)   Topic-by-topic revision — this in our opinion is a preferable method because its advantages outweigh the disadvantages. The main disadvantage is the advantage pointed out in the method described above, in that topics are learnt in isolation and sometimes it may be difficult to see the interrelationship at the end. (However, we believe that this can be remedied, see *post*.) The advantages are that:

(1)   Revising contrasting subjects will make the revision process less boring: the old cliché a change is as good as a rest, would certainly apply.

(2)   You can follow the revision of a topic that you don't like with one that you do like.

(3)   You will be making progress on a number of subjects at the same time which should give you confidence that you will not be weak in one particular paper because of lack of revision.

Your daily timetable

Once you have decided which approach will suit you best you can think about drafting your timetable. Before drafting your timetable you should bear in mind the following points:

(a)   Rest periods — effective revision can only be sustained for approximately two hours. Therefore, it is pointless timetabling a revision slot for any longer than this period. You should ensure that adequate 'rest periods' are included. During these periods you should try to do something completely different, e.g., go for a walk, have a cup of coffee with a friend, do your shopping, even play a game of squash. Another advantage of timetabled rest periods is that they are quite legitimate — you won't feel guilty at having sneaked out and so should enjoy them more.

(b)   Set realistic targets — each revision session should seek to achieve some sort of target. The important thing is not to set an unrealistic target which you are unlikely to achieve. This will only serve to undermine your confidence. If your target is slightly less than you think you can achieve you should always achieve it and this will build confidence. As your revision progresses and you become more used to it, your later targets may be raised to higher levels. This will again build confidence. (The type of things which can be set as targets will be illustrated later.)

(c)   Weak topics — should be given special consideration at an early stage. We suggest you incorporate them into the early stages of your revision. This will allow you to seek advice or clarification from your tutor of any point which you find unclear or difficult and if things are very bad you may decide to delete it from the programme and substitute it with a different topic from the same subject. You should also plan more revision slots for your weaker topics to ensure you are prepared when it comes to the day of the examination.

(d)   Wind down in the evenings — you will all have heard of the 'chap' who revises from 8 a.m. to midnight day in and day out for weeks before the examinations and who does not get a 'first' at the end. He has undoubtedly overworked himself or his time has not been spent properly. In the final analysis we are human beings not machines and cannot revise at that sort of pace all the time. We have already talked about rest periods being important, the other thing which is equally important is to unwind at the end of the day's revision and to get a good night's sleep. There is nothing wrong with ending work at say 9.30 p.m. and watching TV or going to the pub for an hour or so. In fact, if you do not do this you will probably find yourself reciting cases on company contracts in your sleep because your mind will be overactive and you will not get a good night's sleep. This in the end is bound to be counter-productive.

In our experience there are two different types of student. The one who works late, the 'night-owl', and the one who 'rises early' and goes to bed early. There is nothing wrong with this so long as you remember to ensure that you do get enough sleep if you work late and do not 'overdo it' if you are an early riser.

The following timetable is an example of the way in which a day might be divided up and can be adjusted to suit the 'night-owl' or 'early riser' as they see fit.

Thus a typical timetable could look like this:

(a)   Company law.
(b)   Law of evidence.
(c)   Family law.
(d)   Revenue law.

MONDAY
8.30 a.m.	Alarm — Breakfast.
9–11 a.m.	*Revise* — company law (company contracts).
	Target — to understand basic principles contained in the legislation.
11–11.30 a.m.	Coffee break.
11.30–1 p.m.	*Revise* — evidence.
1–2 p.m.	Lunch.
2–4 p.m.	*Revise* — family law.
4-6 p.m.	Tea.
6–7.30 p.m.	*Revise* — revenue law.
7.30–8.00 p.m.	Coffee and snack.
8–9 p.m.	Practise examination question on topic revised earlier in the day.
9 p.m.	FREE TIME.

This represents a typical working day with $7\frac{1}{2}$ hours of revision time spread out through the day, with each subject you will be examined on being covered. It also allows an hour to do something slightly different, like practising an examination question which is an important part of the revision process. Remember to change the order of subjects around each day to allow for the fact that the longer periods of revision occur in the morning when you are fresher.

Having decided how you want to allocate your time for a typical day you should be able to plan a programme for several weeks to cover the total revision period. Remember to allow yourself the odd afternoon off by cutting out the 2 p.m. to 4 p.m. revision slot. Try to use this time to do something different and relaxing.

LEARNING THE MATERIAL

It has already been pointed out that more time should be devoted to those topics you consider to be your weakest to allow you to bring them to the same standard as the others in your revision programme.

Most legal subjects are taught by being subdivided into a number of topics. Often these boundaries are artificial and drawn merely for the convenience of the lecturer teaching the subject. A similar pattern will often follow in the examination, especially when the paper is internally set. However, some examiners regard it as quite legitimate to mix topics in one question and it is not unusual to see one or two questions on company law papers where this has happened. For example, minority protection and the rule in *Foss* v *Harbottle* regularly appear in questions alongside a consideration of directors' duties. This must be borne in mind when you revise a particular topic.

It will also be important to remember the amount of time you will have available to you in the examination to produce your answer, usually 35 minutes. This should affect the amount of material you attempt to learn on a particular topic. This is where lecture and tutorial notes which are of a manageable size are important.

REMEMBERING THE MATERIAL

There is no ideal way to sit down and learn and remember information. Everyone has a different level of ability when it comes to remembering material they have read. A very few fortunate people have the enviable photographic memory and can commit large amounts of information to memory with very little effort. For most of us, learning is a time-consuming and laborious process. However, one thing must be emphasised: you will not pass the examination unless you have adequate factual knowledge of the material you expect to be examined on. This will provide a firm foundation for some critical analysis of the legal issues you have studied.

As we have already said there is no ideal way to sit down and learn, but the following dos and don'ts may be borne in mind:

Do:

(a) Try to recall what you have learnt by writing it out (the evening revision session is useful for this type of exercise). It is only by doing this that you will really find out if you have learnt something.

(b) Practise answering past examination questions under examination conditions. Remember to hand as many of these as possible to your tutor for marking. This is a very good yardstick to judge your progress by.

(c) Sit at a desk when revising. It's no good sitting in an easy chair just reading a book, because it is likely that you will fall asleep.

Don't:

(a) Sit in a room with other people when you are trying to revise. You will be distracted and find it difficult to concentrate.

(b) Have the TV or radio on (there are exceptions for those who find it impossible to revise in total unnerving silence).

(c) Revise at all hours of the day and night.

PREPARING FOR THE DAY OF THE EXAMINATION

Four to five days before the first examination go into the institution where you will sit the examination and recheck the date, time and place of the examination. Every year students turn up for the wrong exam or turn up at the wrong time. This is totally unnecessary and a real pity after the work you have put in.

The night before the examination check that you know where you should be and the time you should be there the next day. Ensure that you have all the necessary equipment including a spare pen! If you are allowed to take any materials into the examination make sure that they are to hand.

Finally, finish your revision early, even if you are a 'night-owl', at about 8 p.m., do something relaxing and try to get a good night's sleep.

FURTHER READING

Clinch, Peter, *Using a Law Library* (London: Blackstone Press, 1992).
Holland, J. A., and Webb, J. S., *Learning Legal Rules* (London: Blackstone Press, 1993).
Rylance, Paul, *Legal Writing and Drafting* (London: Blackstone Press, 1994).

2 THE ASSESSMENT

The aim of this chapter is not to try to impose any procedures or particular style on the way you handle yourself in the examination room or in preparing assessments; it is an attempt by us, both as invigilators and examiners, to provide a guide to how you could confront some of the problems you may encounter and to provide an insight into the expectations of examiners and what you can do to improve your performance. The biggest problem, of course, is company law itself, and the next 10 chapters will hopefully be of assistance in your attempt to comprehend, remember, recognise and revise some of the main principles of company law which could appear in your examination paper or assessment question.

Assessments can take a variety of different forms. The examination is still a favourite, although it is rare to find a course that is assessed solely in this way. It is more usual to see an examination and some form of coursework, the combined result leading to an overall determination of your final mark for company law. The weightings given to each component of the assessment should have been explained in the course or module documentation. This should also explain if there is a minimum mark required for each part of the assessment. Sometimes you may sail through the examination but have just failed your coursework, or vice versa. The examination regulations may allow for a failure in one part of your assessment to be compensated by a pass in another component of your assessment, but they may not. If the documentation that you have received does not explain the relationship between different parts of your assessment and what happens if you pass one part and fail another, or the relative weightings, then ask your tutor. An assessment question that also requires a seminar presentation is another variation and is illustrated in chapter 12, question 2. The dissertation or project is another form of assessment that can be either a one-year (double-module) or one-semester (single-module) undertaking. These are designed to test your research skills to a far greater extent than the examination or coursework and may or may not be accompanied by a viva (oral assessment) to test if you really understand what you have written. This chapter looks at:

(a)   How you can approach planning and writing an answer as there are common features that an examiner is searching for in a good examination script, piece of coursework or project; and
(b)   Some guidance on the procedural and presentational aspects of the different forms of assessment.

PLANNING AND WRITING AN ANSWER

The planning and writing of answers to assessment and examination questions is a skill that has to be learnt if you are to achieve good performances. The content is obviously important but if it cannot be presented in a logical, clear and focused manner then all your research skills will have been wasted. The examiner only has a relatively short period of time to make a judgment about your capabilities; the way the evidence is presented will influence that judgment. If the argument that you are making flows clearly and logically and is supported by appropriate citations of authority, this will undoubtedly score higher than a disjointed response where the examiner has to pull different sections of the answer together for you to ascertain what you are really trying to say. There are some components of the skill of planning and writing which apply equally to examination answers, coursework assessments and projects or dissertations. These will be dealt with first. This will be followed by some specific features that apply to the different forms of assessment. Although you can learn the skills involved in planning and writing an answer, your approach will of necessity be an individual one. This chapter can offer suggestions and tips, but you should and will evolve your own style of planning and writing answers that you are happy with. But remember that there is an examiner out there who is going to have to read and assess the end result.

Reading the Question Carefully

It is trite to ask you to read the question carefully, but there are always examination scripts and assessments which indicate that a proper analysis of the questions has not been undertaken. Certain words or phrases appear to trigger a reaction in some pens that cannot be stopped. For example, if the phrase 'reduction of capital' appears somewhere in a problem this could start a reaction which involves the regurgitation of all the provisions on reduction of capital in the Companies Act 1985 when the question might be totally unconnected with any of these provisions (see question 2 in chapter 5).

If it is a problem question you need to identify and make a note of the following:

(a)   The parties involved and their status (e.g., creditor, shareholder, director, etc.). In an examination, you can note this quickly in simple diagram form on your script including who holds shares and how many.

(b)   If some event occurs, such as the transfer of shares from one party to another, establish the situation both before and after the event; is the proportion of shares held by each party relevant to your answer?

(c)   Which organs of the company have made any decisions: the board of directors, one director (is he a managing director?), the general meeting or a class meeting (were they properly convened and conducted?), the liquidator?

(d)   Are there any minority shareholders who might be able to take advantage of the various common law and statutory provisions available for the protection of minority shareholders?

(e)   Is there any reference to the constitution of the company, the memorandum or articles of association; if there is, to what extent does it vary from the normal provisions of Table A; if there is not, are there any provisions of Table A that it could be useful to include or refer to in an answer?

(f)   Whether this is a question that involves various areas of company law: the 'mixed' question. These are popular company law questions (for the examiner or assessor to set, not necessarily for the candidate to answer). You may not identify all the areas involved or may identify some that you are unable to answer. In an examination, whether you should answer the question in this latter situation depends upon the nature of the issue involved: is it a main part of any answer or only an ancillary issue? If it is only ancillary then your omission of a discussion on that particular point will not be penalised too heavily. If it is a main part of the answer involved, is there a better question that you could choose? Chapters 10 and 12 look at the treatment of this type of problem in greater detail. These two chapters deal with the protection of minority shareholders and the governance and management of the company, the two areas which arise most frequently as part of 'mixed' questions.

(g)   The instruction, normally to 'advise' one or more of the parties mentioned in the question.

Essay questions usually involve the citation of an extract from a judgment, academic, official report or, less frequently, a statute. Sometimes a statement is not attributed to any of these sources. This means that the examiner has concocted his own statement to test you with. Although essay questions appear to be easier to comprehend than some problems, you should still approach them with care. The temptation is to read the question quickly and not to refer to it again until your answer has been completed. Then you realise that you have misread a vital word, or the instruction, or even missed out a complete line in your rush to get on with the answer. Read every essay question at least twice before starting to answer it.

The source of the extract that you are asked to discuss can sometimes be of assistance. If it is an extract from a decided case, was there a dissenting judgment and does the extract come from that judgment? Are there any cases that contradict the extract? Does the extract give the full flavour of what the judgment was in that case: were any caveats added later in the judgment (see question 1 in chapter 3)? Each of these situations will point to an area which your answer can expand upon.

If the source of the extract is an academic it is highly likely that there is at least one other academic who disagrees with him. It is also likely that the extract is critical of a statutory provision, or the judicial treatment of a statutory provision (see question 1 in chapter 5). The question therefore calls for a discussion of why this criticism has arisen, and the case law and statutory provisions involved. This would also apply if the extract was taken from some official report such as those emanating from Royal Commissions or other committees set up by the Government of the day. These committees are really only established so that their reports will provide examiners with material for examination purposes. Other official reports which are used include reports of the Law Commission, White Papers, Green Papers, consultative documents, research reports and reports that are compiled by non-governmental bodies such as the Cadbury Committee on Financial Aspects of Corporate Governance. Your tutor should have brought your attention to these reports, and they will generally be critical of the law in some respect and suggest some reforms. You will need to identify the criticisms in greater detail and, if possible, the proposals for reform put forward in that report and in any others that might have appeared. The report might even have given rise to a change in the law which you could refer to, although this is a fairly rare occurrence (but see chapters 3 and 9 and the partial implementation of the Cork Committee's report in the Insolvency Act 1986 and Professor Diamond's report into the CA 1989).

In examinations, beware of what some examiners refer to as the 'mug question'; these tend to be essay-type questions. The phrase 'mug question' is an unfortunate expression which describes a common, but suspect, practice. Candidates of all abilities sit the same examination paper but, unless there is no choice, they will answer a variety of different questions. In practice candidates tend to merge towards what are perceived as the more straight-forward questions and supply solid, but usually not brilliant, answers to these questions. The 'mug question' is there to stretch the ability of the better candidate and will usually require an answer that shows a very good academic overview of, and brings together various areas of, company law. You should be aware of your own abilities in the subject by the time of the examination. If you think you can handle such a question have a go, because if you know your company law well enough the examiner should be prepared to be more liberal in the allocation of marks for this question and a high mark might be obtained. The reason why the practice of including such questions is suspect revolves around the very expression given to these questions. Some candidates fail to recognise the complexities involved in the question and often misinterpret what the examiner is after. If this is not what the examiner was looking for then the marks awarded would be low. The desire to stretch the better candidate more often than not ends up in penalising the 'mug' who has failed to identify the nature of the question or, at best, leaves a significant proportion of candidates with one less question to choose from. So beware of these questions and read all essay questions as carefully as you should read the problem questions.

The last part of any question should tell you what the examiner wants you to do. A variety of 'stock' phrases are used by examiners ranging from 'discuss', 'critically analyse', or 'critically appraise' in essay-type questions to the usual 'advise X and Y' in problem questions. Don't ignore the instruction when compiling your answer. The instruction to 'discuss' leaves you to dissect the preceding extract with a fair amount of freedom, although be careful to look for particular slants in the extract whilst undertaking your dissection: does the extract refer to judicial or statutory treatment of a problem or imply a contrast between the two? The instructions which ask you to 'critically analyse' or to 'critically appraise' will have a tail-end to them which will tell you what you have to critically analyse or appraise; not surprisingly it is usually the preceding extract. If the extract is taken from a judgment, the case from which it is taken may be cited as well. If you know the case, all well and good, but note that the question will probably ask you to critically analyse the statement not solely the case from which it was taken (see question 1 in chapter 3). The facts and legal principles involved in the case will no doubt be of use but the examiner will be anticipating a far wider appreciation of the area identified in the extract than just that one case. The extract has only been chosen as a method of seeking your overall comments on the points raised in it. For this reason you could even answer the question and achieve a satisfactory mark without any, or only a little, knowledge of the case referred to as long as you can direct your answer to the issues raised in the extract. However, bear in mind that the judgments from which extracts are taken usually come from one of the major cases in that area of company law; your revision and knowledge of that area of law could be in question if you do not recognise the case.

Planning the Answer

Everyone has their own method of planning answers: in their heads, on the examination paper or, preferably, in the answer book. In examinations, some candidates go to extraordinary lengths in formulating a plan which, having been meticulously crossed out, sometimes seems better and in far greater detail than the actual answer. On occasions a plan is made and promptly ignored, for the answer appears to bear little relationship to it.

The aim of a plan is to give the answer some coherence and structure, to ensure that all the main points are covered, and that you do not get carried away on one point leading to 'overkill' or, even worse, repetition. In problem questions the plan often writes itself as you work your way through the legal issues raised in the problem; at least you have something to work around. The planning of answers to essay questions is more difficult. If it is not undertaken carefully then a phenomenon known as 'aerial bombing', which is discussed later, can result.

A good plan will lead to a coherent and structured answer by:

(a) identifying the legal issues involved in the question — the beginning;

(b) breaking those issues down in greater depth identifying the common law principles involved; statutory provisions and academic arguments — the middle and heart of the answer;

(c) identifying some concluding comments, including suggested reforms and even your own appraisal of the authorities — the end.

If you can, identify some 'golden threads' which could run through your answer and try to link the various sections of your answer. This is better than what could otherwise be a series of unconnected paragraphs. Planning an answer can and should be time-consuming, so be careful with your time in an examination situation, but a well-constructed answer will be rewarded with more marks than an answer comprising a hotchpotch of unconnected statements. Hopefully, the next 10 chapters will assist you in developing the mechanics of planning answers to company law questions. When you have read these chapters you can practise making plans using questions from past assessment or examination papers; it is a useful revision exercise.

The Answer

The first part of your plan, which identifies the legal issues involved in the question, would usually be useful as the opening of any answer. It tells the examiner where the answer is going to lead and that you have identified the main issues. In an examination, this would be the first paragraph which could suffice as the only plan you need, especially if you are short of time. In an

assessment you could allocate more space although you have to be careful
not to repeat what will be appearing later in the answer or exceed your word
limit. You can even provide a brief summary of what your conclusion is.

Reference has already been made to the problem of 'overkill': that is, going
overboard in making a particular point, trawling in every conceivable
authority to support a single proposition. This means that in an examination
you will not be able to spend as much time on the other aspects of the question
or, if you do, you run out of time to answer the required number of questions.
In an assessment you will have exhausted your word limit and will not have
contested properly for the marks that are available for raising these issues.
This is unlikely to be compensated by the limited number of marks available
for, and awarded in, the area of 'overkill'.

Another technique referred to earlier is that of 'aerial bombing'; the real
thrust of the question has not been grasped and, in what is often a vain hope
of hitting the target, all but the kitchen sink is thrown into the answer. It is
not really an answer to the question, more of a 'blitzkrieg' attack upon it.
Sometimes a lucky hit on target will result, but the marks awarded will in no
way reflect the time and usually vast quantities of ink deployed in this form
of exercise.

In the heart of your answer use the art of common law methodology that
should have been nurtured by your tutors over your years of legal training:

(a)   Cite relevant cases.

(b)   Apply the principles adopted in those cases to the facts or statement
in the question.

(c)   Where appropriate, distinguish these cases from each other and the
facts of the problem, commenting upon whether or not that distinction could
affect the application of any principles identified with those cases. For
example, are there certain principles of company law that appear to apply
only to small family companies or 'quasi-partnerships' (e.g., *Ebrahimi* v
Westbourne Galleries Ltd [1973] AC 360 — see chapters 10 and 11, *Clemens* v
Clemens Bros Ltd [1976] 2 All ER 268 — see question 1 in chapter 12, *Coleman*
v *Myers* [1977] 2 NZLR 225 — see chapter 7).

Where appropriate cite and apply the relevant statutory provisions and the
model articles in Table A using the rules of statutory interpretation. Use any
academic articles or texts that you may have read to support your
interpretation and application of the cases or statutory provisions. If you read
articles or texts that put forward a particular view or critique of the law and
its application, then you should cite them where it is relevant to your answer,
as long as you attribute that particular point of view to the appropriate
author. You might even want to criticise that author's particular stance
yourself; this is perfectly legitimate as long as your argument is supported by

authority in some way, and it is perhaps preferable to leave such criticisms to your concluding comments on the question.

Do not forget the question in this middle section of your answer, particularly if it is a problem that you are answering. Bring the facts of the problem into your discussion of the major legal issues involved quite clearly, remembering that you may have been asked to 'Advise X and Y'; therefore you should start to formulate your conclusions on the application of the relevant legal principles as such advice. Evidence of your legal research skills, which will include the ability to sift the relevant from the irrelevant, must come through in this part of your answer if you are to obtain a good grade. If you have read more widely than the traditional legal text and incorporated a contextual approach to the answer this will also be rewarded. These two factors, which relate directly to the content of your answer, are the most common ones that distinguish a very good answer from an average one.

The concluding part of your answer should tie your answer together, preferably with the 'golden threads' that you have managed to take through the answer. The conclusion is also an opportunity to offer your opinion on the legal situation if you have formulated one that can be supported with authority. Be brief in this part of the answer; the main arguments should have been discussed already in the heart of the answer. Try not to include new substantive material in this part of the answer, although if in an examination you do suddenly remember an important case or statutory provision that should have been included earlier insert it if time permits, or add an addendum after the answer with an appropriate indication for the examiner at the relevant point in the main body of the answer.

Write your answer in paragraphs. Limit each paragraph to a consideration of the issues you have identified in your plan, or even a part of one of those issues. For example, a statutory provision like CA 1985, s. 127, can be split into its component parts in one paragraph while another paragraph is allocated to comment on the judicial interpretations of the expression 'variation' that appears in that section (see chapter 5 and question 2). The use of paragraphs and clear identification of the issues that each paragraph is attempting to discuss adds to the clarity of your argument and therefore helps the examiner to follow your argument.

THE EXAMINATION

Find a desk to sit at. Sometimes you will have no choice of where to sit, but if you do you might want to avoid the wobbly table or chair that appear at most pizzerias. You might also want to avoid sitting too close to an invigilator either because you intend to cheat or, a more likely possibility, because you have already encountered the invigilators who find it impossible not to talk for the normal three-hour examination period. Taking a company law examination is bad enough without such distractions, although there is little you can do about the 'perpetual stroller' of an invigilator who struts up and down the examination room in what sounds like a pair of clogs. However, by carefully choosing your seat, every time you raise your head from its downward gaze at the examination script you can avoid the sight of either the front page of the *Guardian*, the invigilator marking a set of examination papers, one of which could even be yours, or the company law tutor writing detailed answers to the questions that you are struggling with.

Having positioned yourself suitably, if you haven't got a watch can you see a clock? You must attempt all the questions required of you and this requires you to be aware of the amount of time you spend on each answer. Some examination candidates use the new electronic bleeper alarms that appear on some watches to warn them when they should be thinking of moving on to the next question. The only problem with these is that if everybody used them, every 35 minutes there would be 200 bleeper alarms going off in the examination room, which might even drown the sound of the clogs.

In front of you should be an examination script to write your answers in and the company law examination paper. There was one occasion when a student revealed to the invigilators at the end of a three-hour examination that he was not expecting an examination in that particular subject, but that he had tried to answer it nevertheless; he had been given the wrong paper but had not said anything.

Enter your details (e.g., name or number, course etc.) on the script as required, and remember to do this on any additional paper you need as well. It gives you something to do while waiting for the 'all clear' and also serves the useful purpose for the examination board of revealing that it is your script.

If you can see the rubric on the examination paper, read it before the 'all clear' is given. The chief invigilator will be going through all the information that he is required to tell you before the examination begins: when you can leave the room, raising your hand to obtain the attention of an invigilator if something is needed, the prohibition on cheating and when the examination will end. He may also advise you to read the rubric carefully; it is good advice. The rubric tells you the structure of the examination that you are about to sit: how many questions to answer, whether there are compulsory questions and, in the case of a split examination paper, how many questions should be answered from each section. You should have established what the rubric is well in advance of the examination. If the rubric you are confronted with is different to that which you expected (e.g., answer five questions not four), then ask if there is a mistake; it has happened before in a company law examination. A mistake may be due to a drafting or typographical error. If there is no mistake and you were not informed that the rubric had changed from previous years or you were misinformed as to what was expected in the examination, then you may have grounds for an appeal against your examination result if you fail or perform less well because of the error. Raise the possibility of a mistake with the invigilator and then start to answer your first question. If you are not satisfied with the invigilator's response and feel that your result has been jeopardised in some way, inform the examination board of the mistake in writing after the examination and the effect it had on your performance. If you are not satisfied with their response there will be an appeal machinery which the students' union or college authorities should tell you about; but act quickly because there could well be a time-limit within which you are allowed to appeal.

Students are often advised to read the whole examination paper before starting an answer, and we would not want to suggest that this advice is anything but sound. There may be a period allowed for reading the paper. If this is not the case some company law papers are quite lengthy and a thorough reading of the questions could take 15 minutes. Meanwhile, pen has not yet been put to paper and the nerves are probably getting worse with the reading of each question. A compromise is to find, fairly quickly, an essay question that you can answer well and to get on with it. By the time you have finished this question your stomach will have settled and you will be in a better frame of mind to read the rest of the paper with the knowledge that one question at least is behind you. However, you should check briefly to see if the correct number of questions are on the examination paper. There are some examination papers that arrive back from the printers with pages missing, blank pages, printed back-to front or upside down. The invigilators should spot this type of error before the examination begins but there could be just one rogue copy that has got through.

Mistakes in the actual content of examination questions are far more frequent than those in the rubric or structure of the examination paper, but your reaction upon the identification of a mistake or an ambiguity in a question should be the same: inform the invigilator who will check with the examiner to see if there is a mistake or to clarify any ambiguity. Don't be hesitant in taking this action if it concerns a question you want to answer; this is one of the duties of invigilators, who resolve more mistakes or ambiguities in papers than they find cheats. If the mistake is fundamental and affects the answer considerably then inform the examination board. Very few candidates adopt this course of action, probably because they are unaware of its existence. If, when it comes to the examination, your success is jeopardised in any way through some typographical or drafting error you, the consumer of the examination paper, should attempt to seek some redress. The best way is to ask the examination board to exercise whatever discretion they may have, and it is usually considerable, in your favour because of the unfortunate error.

If you are taken ill during the examination, truly ill not just nausea at the sight of the questions, then inform the invigilator and, if the illness is so bad that you cannot carry on, see a doctor immediately. Ask the doctor to give you a letter addressed to the chairman of the examination board informing the board of the nature of your illness and how it affected your ability to complete the sitting of the examination; being carried out of the examination room by stretcher and taken away by ambulance is only prima facie evidence that you could not complete the examination. If you are able to complete the examination you should still see a doctor immediately and obtain a similar letter relating how your illness could have affected your examination performance. The same would apply if you were ill or suffered a close bereavement in the run-up period to the examination. These letters should be taken into account by the examination board when they make a decision on your final set of marks.

The endless stream of candidates waiting to go to the toilet never ceases to amaze invigilators, and the actual number who disappear to perform this bodily function, or retrieve waterproof notes from the cistern, is sometimes the subject of a sweepstake. Nerves, the opportunity for a smoke or just a break no doubt account for some of these visits. If you must go, just raise your hand and you will be accompanied to a greater or lesser extent depending on the vigilance and curiosity of the invigilator.

If you need extra (writing) paper, just raise your hand. Do not wait until you are on the last line of the last sheet of paper. The invigilator may take some time to spot your raised arm, so write with the other one while waiting.

Although there are financial cut-backs in higher education it is permissible to allocate one side of paper to a brief sketch of a plan for your answers. You will probably not need all of this space but start your answer on a clean page. Leave plenty of space, even a clear page, between your answers. This is better than suddenly remembering that you have left something important out of a question and then having to search for a space to leave a message for the examiner to let him know that the rest of your answer is at the back of the answer book. The other common practice is to cram the forgotten point in minute writing into a margin that states 'leave this margin clear'. However well you plan an answer, you will always remember a point that you could have included in one of the answers after you have moved on. If you leave some space you allow for a remedy to this possibility.

There is normally a limited amount of time available in an examination. It is therefore surprising the number of occasions that candidates use this valuable time to rewrite the question, or a substantial part of it, in their scripts. Contrary to popular belief, no marks are awarded either for spelling your name right or for copying the question out.

You must attempt all the questions required of you. The failure to follow this golden rule of examination technique leads to more failures or substantially lower marks than any other deficiency. It could be that you are unable to answer the correct number of questions. That is unfortunate and illustrates a need to work on your revision technique. However, if you fail to answer the required number of questions because of timing difficulties, that is poor examination technique and stupid. You are throwing away valuable marks that could make a substantial difference in the standard of your pass and, very often, the difference between a pass or fail. Unless you have supplied some brilliant answers to the questions that you have completed, the vast majority of candidates are far more likely to pick up more marks by starting a new question than could be obtained through overindulgence in the others.

If you find that you are reaching your time-limit for an answer, leave a couple of blank pages and move on to the next question; you can always come back later to finish the question if you have sufficient time. As a last resort, when time has virtually run out, you can fill in the blank pages with brief notes of what you would have included had time permitted. This is a last resort though, and is a poor substitute for a proper answer. When you revise and plan your answers you have to take into account the time that is available in an examination for any one answer. Relevance and applicability to the question become crucial factors, as well as a sufficient knowledge of the area to enable your answer to be authoritative yet succinct.

THE USE OF STATUTORY MATERIALS PROVIDED IN THE EXAMINATION ROOM

Some examinations allow statutory materials to be referred to during the examination and the consolidation of the main statutory provisions into a single Act may make this practice even more popular. This does alleviate, to a certain extent, the need to memorise the numbers of the various sections and model articles, as well as their specific content. It also makes it totally pointless to reproduce the whole of a statutory provision in an answer if the examiner knows that you have it in front of you during the examination. There is no need for this total reproduction even when statutory materials are not supplied in the examination. Where materials are provided, you will still need to cite specific parts of the statutory provisions and model articles when using a particular phrase in the section or article to support your argument. For example, you would still need to state in any answer on CA 1985, s. 459, that it applies to 'unfairly prejudicial' conduct which is unfairly prejudicial to 'the interests of its members generally or of some part of its members'. You would then need to apply that particular part of the section to the facts in the question (see chapter 10). Some other statutory provisions and model articles may require a similar treatment.

The apparent advantage of having materials present in the examination is that it leaves you more time to dwell on the application, and interpretation, of those materials, rather than having to waste time on the regurgitation of particular sections or articles. In practice you still need to cite selectively from these materials, as we have seen with s. 459, and a good candidate would do this whether or not the statutory materials were at his elbow. One real advantage is that at the revision stage of your preparation for the examination there is no need to concentrate too heavily on memorising statutory provisions, although this gives rise to the disadvantage when in the examination room of having to spend time in finding the relevant provisions and using time which could be used in writing your answer. Some candidates, when provided with materials, seem to spend an inordinate amount of time browsing or flicking through them during the examination as if it is the first time they have seen them. If you can, try to treat these materials as a last resort which you can refer to should your memory fail you. There is no compulsion to look at them at all.

'Open-book' examinations are less common and vary considerably as to the materials that the candidate is allowed to use during the examination and the time allowed to complete the examination. They are a hybrid between the 'closed-book' examination and assessment, but still require a structured answer at the end of the day. The same applies to 'seen' examinations where candidates have prior knowledge of the content of the examination paper. At the moment these forms of examination are still relatively rare in company law.

COURSEWORK ASSESSMENT

Many courses now allow for some form of coursework assessment provision whereby a set number of pieces of work completed throughout the year will be credited towards a final mark. This may even be the only form of assessment. Where there is coursework assessment, a certain proportion of the total marks should therefore be in the bag before you even enter the examination room. This alleviates some of the pressure from the written examination, but replaces it with some periods of pressure at other times during the academic year. If you have performed badly in your pieces of coursework then the pressure on a good examination performance will be even greater than if there had been no coursework provision. It is more usual however for a coursework mark to lower the mark required in the examination to obtain a pass rather than to increase it although some examination regulations have a minimum requirement in both coursework and the examination.

Most of the procedures already seen in the context of examinations (e.g., on illness or bereavement etc.) apply equally to coursework. As far as the answer is concerned, there is more time to consider and research, for example by using LEXIS or a study of company reports. However, you are more likely to stray into the areas of 'overkill' or 'aerial bombing' because the pressure of time is not as great, although there is likely to be a limit on the length of the answer. You may have to state the number of words contained in the coursework either on the coursework itself or on a separate cover sheet that is completed when you submit the assessment. This needs to be a fairly accurate figure. You will not be penalised if your stated figure is slightly inaccurate, but if it is quite a long way of the actual figure then some institutions may see this as an attempt to gain an unfair advantage, otherwise known as cheating. Examiners do not count every word, but if it is blatant that the word limit has been exceeded and you have misled the examiner as to the number then you could be disciplined and marked at zero. Apart from the consequences this could have on your overall degree classification you may want a reference, possibly to effect entry into the legal profession, so any action that could reflect on your honesty is not advised. Another approach by examiners where the word limit has been exceeded and there is no attempt to hide this fact is for the coursework to be marked up to the point of the limit, the excess being disregarded. The rules that apply are normally fixed in the examination regulations, and you should be able to obtain access to these through your course tutor or the library.

Cheating is easier in coursework but examiners are on the look-out for the ardent plagiarist, some of whom have even been known to incorporate into the submitted answer the footnotes as well as the text from an out-of-date textbook. Any substantial duplication or edited summary of a textbook, article or other source must be acknowledged. The source should appear in the bibliography. If you are quoting directly put the extract inside quotation marks. There are also the answers from different students that bear a remarkable resemblance to each other, even down to the misspellings. The rise of coursework assessment as a technique for testing ability has seen a corresponding increase in the black market in good answers. Different authorities take different attitudes to these sorts of practices ranging from expulsion to a severe downgrading of the mark, the severity depending on the extent of the cheating. Therefore, do not be foolish enough to allow anyone to borrow or have sight of your piece of work. Do not lend your computer disks to friends if they have your completed essay on them. If you are writing your assessment on a computer laboratory screen, remove your file from the computer after taking your disk copy. The examiner will not know who was the copier.

Most institutions have a system of penalties for late submission of coursework. When submitting your work keep a copy and either note on the copy the date you submitted it, or put a note in your diary. Sometimes receipts will be provided for courseworks, but this is not always the case.

It is good practice in coursework, and sometimes compulsory, to provide a bibliography of the materials that you have used in answering the question. But please don't include 'lecture notes' in the bibliography.

Many coursework questions are taken from old examination papers. Even if they are not, they resemble the questions that you are likely to find in an examination paper. The following chapters therefore apply equally when trying to answer a coursework assessment just as they apply to examinations.

Oral Delivery of Coursework

Some courses require that you not only have to prepare a piece of coursework, but that you also have to deliver a presentation of your work, usually in one of the seminars in front of your peers. The examiner is testing your ability to present a detailed legal argument within a time limit in an environment where you are under pressure. The pressure will be there, however well you have prepared. If you are not the first victim of this process you will have observed how some of your colleagues have performed and learnt something from them. You will need to clarify some of the ground rules with your tutor. How much weight is given to the presentation as opposed to the written piece of work? Can you use an overhead projector (and will there be one in the room)? Can you use the whiteboard or blackboard (make sure you get the correct pens)? How long do you have?

Why might you want to use the projector or boards? People absorb information through different media. If you can provide a stimulating visual medium it helps the audience to follow what you are saying. This is particularly the case if there is a corporate structure or complex line of thinking that you wish your audience to understand which can be portrayed visually and diagrammatically. Try not to put too many words on to the projector or board unless it is an important quotation. A written outline of your argument is better left to a one-page handout that you can distribute. In presenting your answer, you will need to get to the core of the problem as quickly as possible. You should illustrate the breadth of your research and highlight the contextual points. It is good practice to finish the presentation by leaving your audience with some questions that will open up the debate during the rest of the seminar. Some students have been known to plant these questions in advance with members of the audience. You will have considered your response in advance whether or not the questions are planted.

PROJECTS AND DISSERTATIONS

You may choose to undertake a final-year project on a topic that involves company law. Alternatively, your company law course may be assessed by a long piece of work that has to be researched by you. You will normally be asked to consider which area of work you wish to work upon, and are in effect given the opportunity to design your own question which you then have to answer. The earlier section on planning and writing an answer applies equally to these longer pieces of work, the planned paragraphs of an essay evolving into planned chapters of a project or dissertation. However, there are some additional points that you need to consider.

The whole point of assessing your knowledge in this form is to test your legal research skills to a much greater extent than the shorter coursework or examination essay. This should be reflected in the choice of your topic. Choose an area of law that you know you can find material on. A dissertation on some obscure area of law may have the advantage of being unique, but it may also leave you with the problem of having very little data to call upon. Your choice should enable you to widen the area of study to include some context into the final piece of work. This could include corporate governance (see chapter 10), insurance and directors' liability (see chapter 6) or accountancy practice and the treatment of loan capital (see chapter 10). If you can, try to build a LEXIS search into the project, if possible widening the search to include a European or international perspective. Examiners, including external examiners, place a particular emphasis on project marks, which is usually looked at when any exercise of discretion relating to the borderline between degree classifications is exercised.

The final date for submission of the project may seem a long way off at the beginning, but the academic year will disappear before your eyes once you get into the routine of lectures and tutorials. You will have other deadlines to meet and the project may get pushed to one side. Don't let this happen. A lot of marks will normally rest on this piece of work, although this does depend on the structure of your course. Find out how important this project is to your degree classification. It is usually very important and for part-time students may be the element that decides your degree classification. Give it the attention that it deserves. Plan a schedule of work and stick to it. Get into the library to secure the books you need early in the year. Put your requests for inter-library loans in early. If you have difficulty in obtaining relevant information talk to your dissertation supervisor or the law librarian. Discipline yourself to achieve targets for completing various stages of the project by set times, providing sufficient time at the end for the dissertation to be typed, if you are not doing it yourself, and proof read.

You will normally have a project supervisor. Use them: test them out with the title for your project; write a couple of pages explaining the structure of the project and ask for their comments; make sure that you schedule a series of meetings that coincides with your planned deadlines for each part of your project; try to get some feedback on the level of your work; ask if there are other sources of references that you should try. Your supervisor will have been given some time to supervise you, so you need to ensure that you use their expertise to help your performance. In the rare cases where you are unhappy with the supervision that you are receiving, don't wait until you have failed the project or received a lower mark than you were hoping for. Raise the issue directly with your supervisor and if you are still not happy go to the course leader. As a last resort if you feel that the supervision has been poor put your grievance in writing and submit it to the examination board. However, you cannot expect your supervisor to write the project for you or to be available every week. You can expect to get reasonable feedback and to have meetings at critical stages of your work. These need to be agreed very early on in the project and adhered to. If your supervisor does not take the initiative in establishing this, you should.

The project will require an extensive bibliography. Examiners require it and it is good evidence of your legal research skills. In *Using A Law Library, A Student's Guide to Legal Research Skills*, ch. 6 provides some valuable advice on this.

STRUCTURE OF THE REMAINING CHAPTERS

Having looked at some research and revision techniques, and the mechanics involved in planning and writing an answer, you are now confronted with the problem of applying all this to the substantive areas of company law. The following chapters are an attempt to help you in this task and look at the areas of company law that are likely to occur in any company law assessment. Each chapter is divided into five main sections:

(a)   An *introduction* to the area of the company law involved including an attempt to put that area into the context of company law as a whole.

(b)   The *main issues* involved in that area of company law.

(c)   Special points to look out for when undertaking *research* and *revision* of that area of company law.

(d)   *Identification of the questions* that usually arise connected with that area of company law.

(e)   *Questions,* normally two, which are stated and followed by a commentary which explains the possible methods of answering those questions, and also looks at the pitfalls that are to be avoided in any answer.

FURTHER READING

Clinch, Peter, *Using a Law Library* (London: Blackstone Press, 1992).

3 CORPORATE PERSONALITY

INTRODUCTION

In 1897, following the collapse of Mr Salomon's boot-making company, the House of Lords recognised that Parliament had permitted the creation of corporations as distinct legal entities separate from the individual shareholders. If seven shareholders decide to establish a company and take one share each, they would have created an eighth legal person — the company itself. It is the treatment of the corporate personality or 'corporate veil', judicially recognised in *Salomon* v *A. Salomon & Co. Ltd* [1897] AC 22, that is the subject of this chapter.

The existence of a separate corporate personality is at the heart of company law and can be raised in connection with various questions. For example, chapter 8 looks at the company's share capital. Because the company is a separate legal entity it is the company that incurs liabilities, although personal guarantees may be taken from the directors. Therefore, creditors of the company can only look to the company's assets for payment of their debts. Part of those assets comprise the capital the shareholders invested in the company, and the statutory provisions looked at in chapter 8 try to ensure that these capital accounts are protected from dissipation, particularly for public limited companies, so that the creditors, in theory, have some assets to look to as security for their debts.

Chapter 10 deals with the protection of minority shareholders and will include a discussion of how the rule in *Foss* v *Harbottle* (1843) 2 Hare 461 can be used in questions involving minorities. This rule is an extension of the corporate personality theory. If you were punched on the nose you would not expect your neighbour to bring a civil action against your assailant. The same applies to a company: if a wrong is done to a company then the company itself is the proper plaintiff. This is the essence of the rule in *Foss* v *Harbottle* and, although there are 'exceptions' to the rule, exceptions also exist for individuals who are either unable or prevented from looking after their own affairs (e.g., because of infancy, mental illness) just as they exist in a similar situation for companies (e.g., where those who control the company perpetrate a fraud on the minority).

These are just a few examples illustrating how the separate corporate personality lies at the centre of company law (see also the dissenting judgment of May LJ in *Multinational Gas & Petrochemical Co.* v *Multinational Gas & Petrochemical Services Ltd* [1983] Ch 258 discussed in chapter 12). Thus, the existence of the separate corporate personality can be used in answers to various questions, always ensuring that it is put into the context of the particular subject area a question is aimed at.

MAIN ISSUES

Lifting the 'Veil' of Incorporation

The standard question in this area is to ask the candidate to analyse the principles adopted by the courts or the legislature when deciding whether or not to 'lift the veil' of incorporation or to 'peek' behind it. A discussion of an extract from a judgment is frequently called for and the treatment of this sort of question will be looked at in question 1.

Groups of Companies

The commercial world has changed rapidly since 1897 with the growth of groups of national and multinational enterprises. The extent to which a legal principle developed in 1897 can cope with this development is another fertile area for questions, particularly in light of some recent case law (e.g., *Multinational Gas & Petrochemical Co.* v *Multinational Gas & Petrochemical Services Ltd* [1983] Ch 258 and *Adams* v *Cape Industries plc* [1990] Ch 433) and European developments. These include the 7th EC Directive on group accounts now implemented in the CA 1989, the Vredeling Directive and the application of the Treaty provisions on competition by the European Court of Justice in *Imperial Chemical Industries Ltd* v *Commission of the European Communities* (case 48/69) [1972] ECR 619 and *Viho Europe BV* v *Commission of the European Communities* (case T–102/92) [1995] ECR II–7.

It is interesting to note the extent to which the legislature, prompted by European Union harmonisation provisions, has intervened to regulate financial disclosure of groups of companies replacing professional control by accountants. Napier and Noke have commented (1991) 54 MLR 810 at p. 829 that:

> . . . the changes of CA 1981 appeared to grant regulatory control to the accountants in accounting for businesses combinations, but at the same time the general provisions of this Act represented a quantum leap in the volume of regulation of financial statements by law. This 'juridification' of accounting has been expanded through CA 1989, which provides detailed rules on accounting for business combinations. Despite all protestations to the contrary, the accountancy profession has recognised that it cannot regulate accounting independently of the law.

Most of these detailed rules will be examined in question 2 but the importance of the treatment of groups of companies by national and international legislatures cannot be underestimated. According to Wedderburn (1993) 109 LQR 220 at p. 222:

> There is no legal issue more urgent for the legislature than that of company groups.

Although Wedderburn continued to focus on the British courts' inability to reopen the *Salomon* decision when confronted by these large concentrations of capital operating as a single economic entity through the medium of various subsidiary legal entities, this is a multinational not a national problem. Wheeler comments that:

> National regulation is hampered by the absence of a business form for corporate groups which is either nationally or internationally based; each national jurisdiction has to make the decision whether it will recognise the economic reality of the group situation and accord enterprise entity status to the group or whether it will confer separate legal personality on each member of the group (*The Law of Business Enterprise*, p. 40).

The 'Alter Ego' of the Company

The company is a legal fiction and, despite the increase in technology, human individuals acting through corporate structures, such as a board of directors, or as authorised individuals must act and think for the company. There is a difficulty in distinguishing between when the actions and thoughts of these human individuals are their own personal actions and thoughts, and when they are the actions and thoughts of the company. This causes particular problems in the case of the 'one-man company' where the main shareholder, director and employee can be the same person (as in *Lee v Lee's Air Farming*

Ltd [1961] AC 12), and that person could also be the main creditor (as in *Salomon* v *A. Salomon & Co. Ltd*). What are the actions and thoughts of the company, particularly in respect of tortious and criminal activity? What person or organ of the company has sufficient status that their actions and thoughts are deemed to be those of the company? This requires an identification of those individuals or governing bodies within the company who can be adjudged to have the capacity to bind the company, which can be assessed by looking at the company's constitution or by application of the principles of agency and vicarious liability. It is important to understand the complexities of the legal rules involved in the determination of the *alter ego* or 'directing mind and will' of the company so as to identify what are the actions and intentions of the company. The vicarious liability test involves consideration of the 'contractarian model' of the company, which analyses the various contracts that underpin the company so as to reach a conclusion on the identification of the appropriate individual. This model portrays the company as a range of contracts between the various stakeholders in the organisation: employees, managers, shareholders, consumers, creditors:

> Thus, it no longer makes sense to think of the firm or company as a thing, capable of being owned or controlled. One simply has a web of contractual relationships between human actors. Similarly, the company disappears as an actor; understanding 'its' behaviour involves understanding the behaviour of a variety of *human* actors and the relevance to that behaviour of the contracts into which such actors have entered. (Riley (1995) 58 MLR 595 at p. 597).

However, although you may identify some evidence of this contractual approach being adopted (see chapter 5), it is not generally applied (see *Director General of Fair Trading* v *Pioneer Concrete (UK) Ltd* [1995] 1 AC 456). Wells has noted the judicial confusion as to which test should be applied to establish which individual embodies the conduct and intent of the company, and when this intent is separate and distinct from their individual conduct and intention for which they could be personally liable (see (1994) 57 MLR 817). Decisions made by the Privy Council in *Meridian Global Funds Management Asia Ltd* v *Securities Commission* [1995] 3 WLR 413 and the Court of Appeal in *El Ajou* v *Dollar Land Holdings plc* [1994] 2 All ER 685 indicate that the courts are adopting a pragmatic approach to the issue. Whether a company can be liable, and which organ of the company or individual within the company provides the relevant attribution of knowledge or actions for the company depends on the interpretation and policy inherent in each particular statutory provision. The phrases 'alter ego' and 'directing mind and will' derive from the judgment of Viscount Haldane in *Lennard's Carrying Co. Ltd* v *Asiatic Petroleum Co. Ltd* [1915] AC 705 at p. 713:

[A] corporation is an abstraction. It has no mind of its own any more than it has a body of its own; its active and directing will must consequently be sought in the person of somebody who for some purposes may be called an agent, but who is really the directing mind and will of the corporation, the very ego and centre of the personality of the corporation.

The courts will determine who is the responsible officer or organ of the company that represents the ego or directing mind and will of the company according to the provisions and policy of the relevant statute and it is not necessarily confined to the board of directors (see *Moore* v *I. Bresler Ltd* [1944] 2 All ER 515, but compare this to *Tesco Supermarkets Ltd* v *Nattrass* [1972] AC 153; *Tesco Stores Ltd* v *Brent London Borough Council* [1993] 1 WLR 1037).

Although the contractarian approach would look at the constitution of the company to identify these individuals, it is clear that the courts do not always adopt such a strict approach in establishing which officer of the company represents the ego or directing mind and will of the company.

Once it is ascertained which person or organ within the company does have sufficient status, the question still arises as to when they are thinking or acting personally and when their thoughts and actions are to be treated as those of the company (e.g., what is the situation where the sole directors and shareholders sign a cheque payable to themselves for £20,000 each to pay for their holidays — see *Attorney-General's Reference (No. 2 of 1982)* [1984] 2 All ER 216 and Griew [1986] Crim LR 356).

Advantages of Establishing a Company

Because the corporation is a separate legal entity it possesses several advantages over other forms of business organisation, such as the partnership or sole trader, that encourage trade and investment. This was eventually recognised in 1844 when the first standard form of incorporation was introduced; limited liability was made available for the registered company in 1855. With limited exceptions any business consisting of more than 20 persons must now trade as a registered company (CA 1985, s. 716). This brings a large proportion of commercial organisations within the considerable bulk of statutory provisions that regulate a company's affairs. There were 956,700 companies registered on 31 March 1992, and 1.4% were public limited companies. A regulatory price has to be paid for attaining corporate status and this also includes a considerable amount of form-filling to keep the Companies Registrar (and therefore the public) informed of financial performance and any one of numerous possible alterations in the company's affairs. A question could ask the candidate to identify the relative advantages of a company compared to those of a partnership; a common response is to list the advantages of establishing a company to carry on a commercial activity, usually concentrating on limited liability, with little or no comment on the following:

(a)   Some of the difficulties relating to the establishment of a company if there are only a few individuals involved: the problem of drafting a constitution that prevents the majority excluding the minority from the management of the company (as in *Ebrahimi* v *Westbourne Galleries Ltd* [1973] AC 360); the illusory nature of limited liability if personal guarantees are required by creditors from those individuals running the company, and the burden of the disclosure requirements under the Companies Acts. Freeman has identified that, in a survey of 429 firms, 66% stated that they were incorporated to attain the benefit of limited liability but 54% had personal guarantees over the debts of the company ((1994) 57 MLR 555). The individuals who established these companies were therefore not really achieving the main benefit that they incorporated for, Freeman commenting (at p. 563) that 'some firms may be incorporating in order to obtain the unattainable'.

(b)   The development of the company from the partnership, the consequences of which are still apparent in some areas of company law, particularly where small family 'quasi-partnership' companies are involved (see *Ebrahimi* v *Westbourne Galleries Ltd*; *Clemens* v *Clemens Bros Ltd* [1976] 2 All ER 268 and the historical introduction to company law in your textbook). The CA 1989 envisaged the development of a 'partnership company', a company whose shares are intended to be held by the company's employees, but this provision is not in force (CA 1985, s. 8A [CA 1989, s. 128]). According to research undertaken by the Institute for Management Development in Lausanne 75 per cent of companies in the United Kingdom are 'family businesses'. This compares with 80 per cent in Spain, 90 per cent in Switzerland and 99 per cent in Italy! The life expectancy of such companies is low compared to other types of company with most failing in the first five years. Only one in 10 of these survivors makes it to the third generation.

(c)   The difference between small private companies and large private and public companies, for the advantages of incorporation may also vary in importance according to the size of the company. For example, the transferability of shares will usually be of far greater value to the public company than to the private company (see question 1). The Law Commission has been looking at the possibility of a new legal form for small businesses to overcome the perceived concern regarding the burden of disclosure and bureaucracy surrounding the establishment and maintenance of the corporate form. The DTI, having issued a consultation paper back in 1981, have now asked for views on the Law Commission paper which doubts whether a new corporate form would be of any great assistance (*Company Law Review: The Law Applicable to Private Companies* (DTI, 1994)). It is unlikely that there will be any changes. It is now possible to establish a private company with one member as a result of the Companies (Single Member Private Limited Companies) Regulations 1992 (SI 1992/1699), which implements a European Council Directive of 1989.

(d)   The relationship between the various advantages of trading through a company and the establishment of a separate corporate personality: most of the advantages stem from the existence of a company separate and distinct from its members (e.g., perpetual succession, holding property, suing in the corporate name, transferability of interests, corporate liability for debts). It is possible to apply the contractarian model to some of the relative advantages of adopting the corporate form. All of the contractual relationships that exist within the corporate form could exist outside of the corporate form. However, the corporate form offers what is in effect a standard-form contract for those who want to pool their assets in a collective economic enterprise. For example, the 'transaction cost' of agreeing and enforcing the terms upon which capital is provided into a business from numerous individuals could be much higher if the corporate form was not used, where the articles of association provide a standard but adaptable contract. If the transaction costs of establishing and maintaining a company increase, perhaps because of greater regulation, then the economic justificaton for using the corporate form may diminish.

(e)   The growing concern about the governance of companies, particularly plcs and listed companies, and the interests they seek to promote. The interests of the various stakeholders in the company — shareholders, creditors, senior managers, employees, customers and society at large — may all differ and sometimes conflict. This is dealt with further in chapter 12 but is relevant to this topic as it illustrates that the regulatory framework that companies operate within protects a variety of interests. Once a certain size of membership is reached businesses are forced into corporate regulation (CA 1985, s. 716), although why the criterion is number of members and not turnover is difficult to discern. Some interests need statutory or judicial protection backed up by sanctions against the company, its senior managers or both. Such legislative and judicial interventions do not necessarily deny the existence of the company as a separate entity; they confirm that the company is an entity that has a wide range of stakeholders, different to those of a partnership or a sole trader.

(f)   The prestige and credibility offered through trading under the corporate form are also important reasons why individuals establish companies, despite the reality that the corporate form advertises to the world that the liability of the members is limited. Freeman identified that 50% of the firms she surveyed stated this as one of the reasons for adopting the corporate form.

To summarise, there are five main areas that could surface as questions relating to the corporate personality:

(a) Judicial attitudes to lifting the 'veil' of incorporation (see question 1).
(b) Statutory lifting of the 'veil' of incorporation (see question 1).
(c) The legal treatment of groups of companies (see question 2).
(d) The alter ego doctrine.
(e) The relative advantages of a registered company compared to those of a partnership.

REVISION AND RESEARCH

You must research and revise this topic. You will have difficulty understanding the rest of company law if you do not have a basic grasp of the legal materials and principles surrounding the existence of the separate corporate personality. You will also be throwing away marks that could be accumulated in answers to questions that are not aimed specifically at a discussion of the separate corporate personality. This can be achieved by astute citation of the *Salomon* principle as illustrated at the beginning of this chapter.

One method of tackling research and revision for this topic is to divide the task into the five main areas already indicated. There are also some special points to look out for:

(a) The provisions contained in the IA 1986, s. 214, are intended to introduce the Cork Committee's concept of 'wrongful trading'. The slightly strengthened provisions relating to the disqualification and personal liability of what the Cork Report referred to as 'delinquent directors' are to be found in the CDDA 1986. The wrongful trading provisions are intended to supplement the provisions affecting the civil liability of directors found in the IA 1986, s. 213, which deals with 'fraudulent trading', and can be a fertile area for examination questions in connection with the duties of directors of an insolvent company (see *Insolvency Law and Practice: Report of the Review Committee*, Cmnd 8558, 1982, chs 44, 45 — Cork Report).

These provisions can provide a useful input to any question on corporate personality. Although the provisions on wrongful trading do not pierce the corporate veil they can lead to personal liability for the debts of an insolvent company. There is also an issue as to whether a holding company can be liable for the debts of its subsidiary under this provision. You should include reference to the paragraphs of the Cork Report that led to the statutory implementation of some of these suggested reforms (Cork Report, chs 44, 45, 51; *A Revised Framework for Insolvency Law* (Cmnd 9175, 1984); IA 1986).

(b) The 7th EC Directive's complexity is only matched by the provisions in the CA 1989 that implement the Directive. Pennington's article (1984) 5 Co Law 66 is probably the best guide to the European background of the provisions which amongst other things attempt to define when a 'group' situation exists for the purposes of producing group accounts. Also, when researching the control of groups of companies, include Schmitthoff's arguments in his article on the 'theory of the enterprise' [1972] JBL 103 and make notes on the critical survey carried out and conclusions reached by Tom Hadden in *The Control of Corporate Groups* (London: Institute of Advanced Legal Studies, 1983).

It is with regard to questions dealing with the corporate personality in particular that answers seem to lack any sense of direction and tend to be just a rehash of rote-learnt cases. This is always a danger when confronted with essay questions, but questions on the corporate personality seem to attract this sort of answer more than any other essay question. This is unfortunate and means that you are missing out on a higher grade that could be awarded for an application of the material to the specific points that are raised in the question as well as any attempt to show a wider appreciation of the points raised by the question. Therefore, when researching and revising, use the materials to support and counter the various arguments that arise in this area of company law. The main areas have already been identified and the two questions that follow illustrate the different emphases that may take place, and how they can be dealt with.

It has already been noted that the different principles of company law may apply with varying degrees of relevance according to the size of the company. When it comes to each area of company law, not just that relating to the corporate personality, you can establish in your research and revision the following factors.

Does the practical effect of the various principles of company law vary according to the size of the company? For example, limited liability may be illusory for small private companies when personal guarantees are required from the directors who will usually also be the shareholders. The duties a director owes to the company become slightly irrelevant when the sole director owns all but one share which is in the name of his or her spouse (but see *Re Neptune (Vehicle Washing Equipment) Ltd* [1995] 3 WLR 108 which found that a sole director must still comply with the disclosure provisions of CA 1985, s. 317). Since July 1992 even the need to have two members has disappeared (CA 1985, s. 1, as amended by SI 1992/1699). Who is going to take up any breach of duties? The creditors may, but there is some debate about whether duties are owed to creditors and, if they are when any duty starts to operate (see *post* at p. 116). In a large public quoted company the control of the company by the shareholders becomes difficult in practice when share ownership is vested in either a multitude of individuals or financial institutions who rarely exert combined pressure on the management (see question 1; Farr and Russell (1984) 5 Co Law 107, and chapter 12).

To what extent does the actual application of various common law principles or interpretations of statutory provisions vary according to the size of a company? The size of a company can vary enormously from the private company with just one member to a public quoted company with millions of members. Company law does distinguish between different sizes of company in that stricter statutory requirements are in force, for example, as regards the issue and maintenance of share capital for public companies (see chapter 8). There are also special statutory concessions relating to the disclosure of financial information according to whether the company is a small or medium-sized company (dependent on criteria of turnover, balance sheet total and average number of employees — see CA 1985, ss. 217–50). These are statutory admissions that not all companies are the same and some need different rules. You need to be aware of this as you revise the various areas of company law. The most recent example is the amendment to the CA 1985 introduced in July 1992 that makes it possible to form a company with only one member. This will be of use to the sole trader wishing to incorporate and to those companies wishing to establish subsidiary companies who now no longer need to find another nominee shareholder. Is a similar distinction, in terms of the size of the company, made by the judiciary? The test for wrongful trading under CA 1985, s. 214 also varies in its application according to the size of the company (*Re Produce Marketing Consortium Ltd (No. 2)* [1989] BCLC 520; see chapter 11). In *Ebrahimi* v *Westbourne Galleries Ltd* [1973] AC 360, the House of Lords was considering whether it was 'just and equitable' to wind up a company under IA 1986, s. 122(1)(g). In considering the phrase Lord Wilberforce commented (at p. 379) that:

> The words are a recognition of the fact that a limited company is more than a mere legal entity, with a personality in law of its own: that there is room in company law for recognition of the fact that behind it, or amongst it, there are individuals, with rights, expectations and obligations *inter se* which are not necessarily submerged in the company structure.

These individual rights, expectations and obligations are more likely to accrue in a small private company that possibly existed as a partnership before seeking out the advantages of incorporation, as in *Westbourne Galleries* itself. However, Lord Wilberforce went out of his way to state that the fact that a company is a small one is not enough to give rise to the equitable considerations that the House of Lords imposed in *Westbourne Galleries*. Also required, according to Lord Wilberforce, are:

(a) a personal relationship, involving mutual confidence, arising from the association which could be evidenced by a pre-existing partnership;

(b) an understanding that participation in the management of the company would continue (a principle of partnership law); and

(c)   restrictions on the transfer of shares in the company so that if a member is removed from management he cannot take his stake out and go elsewhere, his capital being locked into the company (this would apply to a considerable number of private companies in practice).

Although Lord Wilberforce commented that size is not the only factor, the other three criteria considered would invariably occur only in a small private company. Are there special rules for small companies or 'quasi-partnerships' which could surface in other areas of company law? Once incorporated, the participants are involved in a company not a partnership or 'quasi-partnership', but it does appear that different rules may apply in certain situations involving small companies where a 'legitimate expectation' has been raised (*Murray's Judicial Factor* v *Thomas Murray & Sons (Ice Merchants) Ltd* [1993] BCCC 1437). In your research and revision for all the areas of company law watch out for these situations and look back at past assessments to see whether the problem questions are specifically concerned with small family companies or partnerships converted into companies. Are there special restrictions on voting rights (*Clemens* v *Clemens Bros Ltd* [1976] 2 All ER 268, cf. *North-West Transportation Co. Ltd* v *Beatty* (1887) 12 App Cas 589)? Are the civil remedies as a consequence of insider dealing different (*Coleman* v *Myers* [1977] 2 NZLR 225, cf. *Percival* v *Wright* [1902] 2 Ch 421)?

Is it possible that the directors of the company could be criminally liable for the actions of the company as well as the company itself? The size of the company is also a factor in the application of the test to attribute the directing mind and will of the company and in assessing whether or not the directors are personally liable for any criminal misconduct. In small companies it will be easier to show the personal involvement of directors and managers that is necessary to incur personal criminal liability, whereas in large companies this will not be easy to prove (see Gobert (1994) 14 LS 393 at p. 401).

Therefore, in the area of corporate personality as in all areas of company law do not blindly apply the various principles you are learning without regard to the size and nature of the company.

IDENTIFYING THE QUESTION

Questions on the corporate personality are not difficult to identify, but you do need to be careful in identifying any particular slant in the question, emphasising your answer accordingly.

The questions are normally essays rather than problems. If there is to be a problem it will usually be one part of a two-part question and will centre around the alter ego and vicarious liability doctrines, the judicial treatment of groups of companies or the wrongful and fraudulent trading provisions contained in the IA 1986 and the imposition of personal liability on the management of the company for some of the company's debts.

An essay question may link the judicial and statutory treatment of the corporate 'veil' as question 1 does. Alternatively, the judicial and statutory treatment could be split into a two-part question. The legal treatment of groups of companies requires analysis of both judicial and statutory attitudes with particular reference to the group situation.

The two questions on corporate personality that are considered in this chapter have some overlapping material. It is therefore important to identify the main issues in each question and to emphasise the answer accordingly. In the first question the examiner is looking for an appreciation of the nature of the corporate personality and the different judicial and statutory treatment of the separate legal status that is conferred on companies. The second question is far more specific, requiring detailed analysis and critique of the treatment of groups of companies.

QUESTION 1

'... in view of its *raison d'être* and its consistent recognition by the courts since *Salomon* v *A. Salomon & Co. Ltd*, one would expect that any Parliamentary intention to pierce the corporate veil would be expressed in clear and unequivocal language' (per Lord Diplock in *Dimbleby & Sons Ltd* v *National Union of Journalists* [1984] 1 All ER 751). Critically analyse this statement.

Because the statement is taken from a case where the company law consideration was whether two subsidiaries of a holding company could be treated as the same employer under the Employment Act 1980, the tendency could be to jump straight into all the cases and other authorities on the judicial and statutory treatment of groups of companies. That does form part of the required answer, but only a part.

The question asks you to 'critically analyse this statement', not the case from which it was taken, although *Dimbleby* [1984] 1 All ER 751 will need to be referred to in order to place the statement in some sort of context. If you do analyse the statement, three main areas become apparent which could appear in many questions on the corporate personality:

(a)   What is the *raison d'être* of the corporate veil? Why has the legislature created a legal fiction for the purpose of carrying on a business?

(b)   Have the courts consistently recognised the corporate veil, or do they 'pierce' the veil or 'peep' behind it on occasions?

(c)   In what situations, if any, has the legislature expressed itself clearly in its intention to pierce the veil? What was the situation in *Dimbleby*?

Having established the main issues, and at the same time written the first paragraph, the examiner knows in which direction you are heading. The first paragraph can become a brief plan for the rest of the answer.

It is sometimes useful to identify some 'threads' which can carry through the whole answer and be consolidated in a conclusion. In this and most questions involving corporate personality there is a 'thread' which could be used to sew the whole answer up: this would require comment on what is meant by 'piercing' the corporate veil and the extent to which the judiciary or legislature can really be seen to have done so on various occasions. A clear statement as to the nature of the corporate veil needs to be made at an early stage; it is common to see answers which consist almost entirely of the judicial and statutory techniques of piercing the veil with no prior statement as to the exact nature of the separate corporate personality.

Consideration will now be given to the main issues that have been identified.

The Nature of the Corporate Veil

The nature of the corporate personality can be analysed by reference to *Salomon* v *A. Salomon & Co. Ltd* [1897] AC 22 and to the advantages of trading as a company. These advantages can be linked to the existence of the corporate personality, the encouragement to trade and invest, and their relative importance according to whether the company is a large public company, a small private company or part of a group of companies comprising a holding company and subsidiary companies. The large public company can obtain substantial amounts of share capital to invest in projects for the advantage of its members. These members have a relatively liquid asset, more so if the shares are 'listed' and traded on the Stock Exchange, because of the transferability of shares. The company exists independently of any change, death, insanity or bankruptcy of membership, and the transferability of interests in the company encourages such investment. There is hardly any market for shares in a private company except through trading with the other shareholders (see CA 1985, s. 81) or the company itself (see chapter 8), and the ability to transfer interests in the company, and not affect the status of the company in any way to the outside world, is therefore of less importance compared to a large public listed company whose shares are a readily marketable asset.

The small trader, who might otherwise have been a sole trader or in a partnership, may establish a company primarily to separate the assets and liabilities of the company from those of its members. The managers and owners are often the same people and they may well want to restrict transferability of interests to prevent unknown outsiders from intruding, although if they do wish to sell out, the transferability of shares does allow for an easy take-over, the party taking over the company merely buying their shares. The company lives on, only the shareholders have changed. The principle of the separate corporate entity means that it is the company that incurs liabilities and then calls on its members according to their obligation to pay on liquidation, which in the case of a company with limited liability would only apply if a share was partly paid. Thus, for the small trader, the availability of limited liability (CA 1985, s. 13(4)) might be an important reason for adopting the corporate form as identified by Freeman. However, remember that limited liability and the attainment of a corporate personality have not always gone together, and it is still possible, although rare, to have corporate status with unlimited liability for the members of the company.

In the answer to this question, as opposed to the one which asks a candidate to contrast a company with a partnership, it is not necessary to identify all of the advantages of using the corporate form; the question does not ask for them. It is necessary to identify the main legal reasons for obtaining a corporate identity:

(a)   The transferability of shares and the ability to combine capital from a large number of organisations and individuals in a corporate framework that can cater for varying interests. This encourages trade ventures which any one of those individuals would either be unable or unwilling to take on alone. If these individuals combined their capital outside of the corporate framework the 'transaction costs' of so doing would probably be more expensive than forming a company.

(b)   The separation of the liabilities and assets of the company from those of its members, which in modern practice includes the availability of limited liability upon corporate insolvency (CA 1985, s. 13(4)).

Judicial Treatment of Corporate Veil

In *Salomon*, the House of Lords accepted the corporate entity in the form of the registered company. Lord Diplock refers to the 'consistent recognition by the courts' of the separate legal entity since *Salomon*. *Salomon* does provide certainty but some decisions could be interpreted as having 'lifted the veil' to reveal the mere human (or holding company) culpability, nationality or residence. It is difficult to ascertain any clear principles of judicial intervention in this area, although for an interesting attempt you should look at the article by S. Ottolenghi (1990) 53 MLR 338, where the categories range from 'peeping behind the veil' to 'penetrating', 'extending' and 'ignoring' the veil. Most company law texts do attempt to categorise the circumstances where the corporate veil has been lifted in one form or another. You must be careful not to duplicate these categories without any discussion of the uncertainties that do exist. These categories include:

(a)   Where the corporate veil is used for some fraud, illegality or improper purpose — cases that could be cited in this area include *Gilford Motor Co. Ltd* v *Home* [1933] Ch 935, *Jones* v *Lipman* [1962] 1 WLR 832, *Wallersteiner* v *Moir* [1974] 1 WLR 991 and *Alec Lobb (Garages) Ltd* v *Total Oil (Great Britain) Ltd* [1985] 1 WLR 173. A recitation of the facts with a statement that the corporate veil was pierced in these cases is not enough. Do these authorities really ignore the separate corporate personality? Some of the colourful language used by the judges would seem to suggest that this is the case, describing the company variously as a 'cloak', 'sham', 'device', 'mask' or 'puppet'. However, a closer analysis of some of the cases can reveal that the decisions could have been arrived at by the application of normal legal principles without calling the corporate personality into question. For example, Lord Denning's marionette analogy in *Wallersteiner* v *Moir* is clearly indicative of an agency relationship which requires distinct and separate legal entities not their 'piercing'.

(b)   The alter ego doctrine — where the court needs to ascertain some physical or mental attitude then it is necessary to look at the human management involved in the governance of the company. In attributing physical or mental characteristics to a company, reference must be made to the corporate structures or specific human individuals involved. Although the company is a separate legal entity it can only act and think either through corporate structures which are defined in the company's constitution as having authority, such as the board of directors or a committee of the board, or through individuals who have the requisite authority through principles of agency or vicarious liability. Lord Hoffmann referred to these alternatives as the 'rules of attribution' in *Meridian Global Funds Management and Asia Ltd* v *Securities Commission* [1995] 3 WLR 413. However, he considered that these rules could not always apply where a statutory provision required a state of mind expressed in terms of a natural person, which is generally the case in criminal law. He concluded (at p. 419) that the court had to develop rules of attribution according to the particular requirements of the statute:

> This is always a matter for interpretation: given that it was intended to apply to a company, how was it intended to apply? Whose act (or knowledge, or state of mind) was *for this purpose* intended to count as the act etc. of the company? One finds the answer to this question by applying the usual canons of interpretation, taking into account the language of the rule (if it is a statute) and its content and policy.

This is why the internal compliance steps taken by Tesco Supermarkets were deemed to be sufficient and the acts and defaults of the local manager of one shop were not attributed to the company so as to make it liable for misstating a price under the Trade Descriptions Act 1968 (*Tesco Supermarkets Ltd* v *Nattrass* [1972] AC 153), but were attributed to the company when it came to interpreting legislation governing the sale of videos to under-age children

(*Tesco Stores Ltd* v *Brent London Borough Council* [1993] 1 WLR 1037). In *Director General of Fair Trading* v *Pioneer Concrete (UK) Ltd* [1995] 1 AC 456 the conduct of the senior managers of the company was not imputed to the company but the conduct of local managers was. The senior managers instructed local managers not to infringe orders made by the Restrictive Trade Practices Court relating to the supply of ready-mixed concrete. This was not a defence to a contempt charge against the company for the actual breach of the orders by local managers. Lords Templeman and Nolan stated that a company falls to be judged by its actions not by its language. Compliance procedures initiated by senior management in this case were not a defence, unless the statute expressly provided so, even if the local manager was acting outside his authority or had no authority. It is clear from this case that the court was concerned that the policy behind the Restrictive Trade Practices Act could be undermined if companies could avoid liability for breaching orders because a member or organ of higher management identified as the 'directing mind and will' of the company had forbidden other employees to breach those businesses.

In cases like *The Lady Gwendolen* [1965] P 294 and *Lennard's Carrying Co. Ltd* v *Asiatic Petroleum Co. Ltd* [1915] AC 705 there was a judicial search for the 'directing mind and will' of the company so that the correct attribution could be made. The Privy Council in *Meridian Global* considered that although this phrase was probably an accurate description of the individual or corporate organ to whom attribution was attached in those cases, the actual location of attribution, if any, will vary according to the statutory provision and the rule in consideration:

> It is a question of construction in each case as to whether the particular rule requires that the knowledge that an act has been done, or the state of mind with which it was done, should be attributed to the company. Sometimes, as in *Director General of Fair Trading* v *Pioneer Concrete (UK) Ltd* and this case, it will be appropriate.... On the other hand, the fact that a company's employee is authorised to drive a lorry does not in itself lead to the conclusion that if he kills someone by reckless driving, the company will be guilty of manslaughter. There is no inconsistency. Each is an example of an attribution rule for a particular purpose, tailored as it must always be to the terms and policies of the substantive rule. (Per Lord Hoffmann at p. 423.)

A similar approach was adopted in *El Ajou* v *Dollar Land Holdings plc* [1994] 2 All ER 685, where the Court of Appeal declared that the location of the 'directing mind and will' of the company may vary according to the activities that are in question. A strict contractarian position, identifying where the 'directing mind and will' is by analysing the constitution of the company, is not always adopted. However, as Jefferson points out ((1995) 16 Co Law 146) the smaller the company the easier it is to attribute a 'directing mind and will'.

An attribution of characteristics does not necessarily contradict the *Salomon* principle and lift the corporate veil; it could be said to enhance the personality of the corporation as any statement about what a company has or has not done or thought must include a reference to some rule of attribution. The company can only act or think through its corporate structures and authorised individuals.

(c) Consideration of the holding company and subsidiary company relationship — this area can be used to portray various inconsistent judicial attempts and techniques to bring *Salomon* into a modern economic context. These techniques include establishing a trust or agency relationship between the companies or by referring to them as a single 'economic entity'.

To illustrate judicial consideration of an agency relationship between a holding company and subsidiary company, you can contrast the case of *Smith, Stone & Knight Ltd* v *Birmingham Corporation* [1939] 4 All ER 116 (note the six guidelines laid down in this case by Atkinson LJ, considered in question 2), and *Ebbw Vale Urban District Council* v *South Wales Traffic Area Licensing Authority* [1951] 2 KB 366. The *Ebbw Vale* case required an express agency agreement before such a relationship could be considered, a view supported by Kerr LJ in *J. H. Rayner (Mincing Lane) Ltd* v *Department of Trade & Industry* [1989] Ch 72, where he commented that 'in my view no conclusion of principle can be derived from [*Smith, Stone and Knight*]', a case which could be seen as an attempt to derive an agency relationship from various control factors. This decision was upheld in the House of Lords in *Maclaine Watson Ltd* v *Department of Trade and Industry* [1990] BCLC 102, where Lord Templeman reaffirmed the vigour of the *Salomon* principle commenting, at p. 111, that: 'Since *Salomon's* case traders and creditors have known that they do business with a corporation at their peril if they do not require guarantees from members of the corporation or adequate security'. In *Adams* v *Cape Industries plc* [1990] Ch 433, a decision of the Court of Appeal that is discussed further in the next question, Slade LJ stated that there is no presumption of an agency relationship between holding and subsidiary companies, nor could there be a presumption that the subsidiary is the parent company's alter ego for, 'If a company chooses to arrange the affairs of its group in such a way that the business carried on in a particular foreign country is the business of its subsidiary and not its own, it is, in our judgment, entitled to do so' (at p. 537).

The possibility of a trust relationship can be supported by *Littlewoods Mail Order Stores Ltd* v *CIR* [1969] 1 WLR 1241 (note Lord Denning's comment that the statutory provision for group accounts provides the precedent for the courts to look at a group of companies as a whole).

Judicial consideration of the group of companies as an economic entity in its own right was supported by dicta to this effect in *DHN Food Distributors*

Ltd v *Tower Hamlets London Borough Council* [1976] 1 WLR 852. However, the decisions in *Woolfson* v *Strathclyde Regional Council* (1979) 38 P & CR 521 and *Adams* v *Cape Industries plc* were critical of this approach as a rule of general application. The specific statutory provisions in question need to be assessed, the rule of general application being the principle laid down in *Salomon*. In the *Cape Industries* case Slade LJ responded (at p. 536) to the concept of treating groups as a single economic unit with the following restatement of *Salomon*:

> Our law, for better or worse, recognises the creation of subsidiary companies, which though in one sense the creatures of their parent companies, will nevertheless under the general law fall to be treated as separate legal entities with all the rights and liabilities which would normally attach to separate legal entities.

This statement has all the attributes of a good quotation that could be used by examiners in an examination question.

The more recent cases of *Woolfson, Dimbleby, J. H. Rayner (Mincing Lane) Ltd* and *Cape Industries* prefer the certainty of *Salomon* and a stricter interpretation of legislation in line with the corporate entity theory. In *Woolfson* Lord Keith of Kinkel, commenting upon the *DHN* decision, stated: 'I have some doubts whether in this respect the Court of Appeal properly applied the principle that it is appropriate to pierce the corporate veil only where special circumstances exist indicating that it is a mere façade concealing the true facts' (at p. 526).

The *Dimbleby* case concerned whether two companies with the same shareholders and same holding company could be treated as the same 'employer who is a party to the dispute' within s. 17(3) of the Employment Act 1980 which deals with secondary action. The Lords held that it was 'quite impossible' to construe the section in this way, although Lord Diplock did go on in his judgment to add a caveat to the statement in question 1; he did not wholly exclude the possibility that even though there might not be express statutory language a 'purposive construction' of a statute may lead the courts to find that Parliament did intend to pierce the corporate veil and treat one company as sharing the personality of another. Was it a 'purposive construction' of the statutory provision in *DHN* or *Re Bugle Press Ltd* [1961] Ch 270? Lord Diplock's rider to the initial reaffirmation of *Salomon* can be used to illustrate an occasional willingness to acknowledge the economic realities of the situation as opposed to the legal fiction. But this is one of a number of tests that the courts seem to apply. The 'special circumstances' test was used in *Woolfson* and has been applied in *Pinn and Wheeler* v *National Dock Labour Board* (unreported, CA, 15 March 1989) although May LJ also stated that, 'one should look at the realities of the situation, rather than the legal niceties'. He continued to find that there were no special circumstances in the case, there being commercial and historical reasons for the retention of four separate companies.

The question does not deal with groups of companies specifically, but this group of authorities can be used to illustrate that it is difficult to identify clear and certain rules as to when the corporate veil will be pierced. Slade LJ commented in the *Cape Industries* case (at p. 543):

> From the authorities cited to us we are left with sparse guidance as to the principles which should guide the court in determining whether or not the arrangements of a corporate group involve a façade within the meaning of that word as used by the House of Lords in *Woolfson*. We will not attempt a comprehensive definition of those principles.

It is absurd not to have clear rules laid down in this important area of economic activity, either through the common law or by statute. The Court of Appeal in *Cape Industries* has abandoned this role, leaving the courts and potential litigants trapped between the certainty that *Salomon* encourages and the desire to recognise the economic realities and justice of individual cases.

Statutory Treatment of the Corporate Veil

There are a wide range of statutory provisions in the area of revenue law and elsewhere that could be cited as examples of an express intention by Parliament to breach the corporate veil. One example that could be drawn from constitutional or European law is the Merchant Shipping Act 1988, which attempts to look behind the company and proscribe nationality, and therefore eligibility to draw upon the United Kingdom's fishing quota, with regard to the nationality of the company's shareholders. This statutory attempt to look behind the corporate veil to attribute nationality was subject to review in the European Court of Justice and has been suspended following a successful application by the European Commission to the European Court of Justice (*Commission of the European Communities* v *United Kingdom* (case 246/89R) [1989] ECR 3125; *R* v *Secretary of State for Transport ex parte Factortame Ltd (No. 2)* (case C–213/89) [1991] 1 AC 603 at pp. 641–2; see also *Re FG (Films) Ltd* [1953] 1 WLR 483).

The statutory examples that can be construed as illustrating inroads into the *Salomon* principle include:

(a) CA 1985, ss. 226–231, 258–260 [CA 1989, ss. 4–6, 21–221 (disclosure of group accounts)

(b) CA 1985 ss. 736–736B [CA 1989, s. 144] (definition of subsidiary and holding company for a variety of purposes).

(c)   CA 1985, s. 24 (personal liability if the number of members of a plc falls below two).

(d)   IA 1986, ss. 213 and 214 (personal liability for fraudulent or wrongful trading).

(e)   CDDA 1986, s. 15 (personal liability upon contravention of a disqualification order or if, as a director, a person acts on the instructions of a person so disqualified).

(f)   CA 1985, s. 349(4) (personal liability for the non-use of the company name in certain circumstances).

(g)   CA 1985, s. 117(8) (personal liability for failure to comply with share capital requirements in a public company).

In considering these statutory provisions you will need to assess whether they do pierce the veil or merely impose additional liability or requirements in certain special circumstances. A brief recitation of the contents of the provisions by itself is not enough. It is possible to retain the corporate entity yet by statute impose some liability on the members or management. The company still exists but, by imposing liability on the members or the management to contribute towards the debts of the company or to take over an obligation of the company, is this a statutory 'peep' behind the veil? It depends on how you define the attributes of a corporate personality and whether the statutory provisions do encroach upon them. The extent to which the group disclosure provisions are really an inroad into *Salomon* and affect its *raison d'être* may also be called into question. Does disclosure by a holding company of some of the subsidiary's financial affairs affect the subsidiary's separate legal status?

Any question on corporate personality will require a discussion as to the attributes of that personality and the inconsistent judicial statements as to when that personality must be put aside in favour of looking at the members of which the company is composed, its management, or its holding company. The inconsistencies can be exploited in any answer which should also assess whether the various cases and statutory provisions do 'pierce' the corporate veil.

QUESTION 2

'English law has not yet begun to grapple with the legal problems raised by the wholly owned subsidiary and the controlled company' (C. M. Schmitthoff). Discuss.

This question is still concerned with the principle of the separate corporate personality but is directed at the artificial nature of this principle when dealing with groups of companies and the failure of the law to deal with some of the problems that arise. Although some of the material used in question 1 could be used again in an answer to this question, you must be careful to slant your answer towards consideration of groups of companies. It is fairly common to see assessments or examination answers where the writer appears to have forgotten the question altogether, just writing all that they know about the separate corporate personality, ignoring the fact that the question above is not the same as question 1. They could do this for two reasons:

(a)   The material on groups of companies has not been revised for an examination but the material that has been revised is close enough, there being no other question on the paper to answer. This is fair enough, although an illustration of bad planning of revision. But it is still not an excuse for totally abandoning the direction the question is aimed at; at least try to merge the material you do know into the context of the question wherever possible.

(b)   The question has not been read properly or there is a failure to interpret what the examiner is really seeking as an answer to the question.

There is a third reason, but in that you have been astute enough to either borrow or even buy a copy of this book we will assume that it could not apply to you.

Any answer to this question should cover the following points:

(a)   The identification of the legal problems the question refers to relating to the treatment of groups of companies. Try not to concentrate on one issue only, forsaking the marks that are available for the others.

(b)   The extent to which legislation has been introduced particularly through the CA 1989 to deal with those problems.

(c)   The judicial reaction to these problems.

(d)   Both the judicial and statutory intervention, or lack of intervention, can be contrasted with each other and with European intervention in this area and even the various international codes of conduct for multinational enterprises.

Coverage of these four areas would give a fairly complete answer, although care must be taken in timing the writing of the answer because the temptation is to dwell on a few issues to the exclusion of a 'complete' and fuller response.

The Legal Problems of Groups

The 1896 decision in *Salomon v A. Salomon & Co. Ltd* [1897] AC 22 still applies even when one company controls 100 per cent of the shares of various companies which may even have common boards of directors and common board meetings. The commercial reality that these companies constitute a single economic group is not reflected in English law which recognises each of the companies as a separate entity. Multinational enterprises have created a new economic order which often transcends national legal controls and includes such activities as transfer pricing by companies in a group so as to organise their affairs to incur a high proportion of the group's tax liability in the country where the tax rate is most favourable. Commercial reality has outgrown the 19th-century principle of *Salomon* and this is a recurring 'thread' that can be used in questions on groups of companies.

The various legal problems associated with groups of companies include:

(a)   The difficulty in defining when a group situation exists.

(b)   The occasions when holding companies carry out ventures through subsidiary companies, in particular the more risky enterprises, allowing the subsidiary to incur substantial debts or other liabilities with the knowledge that the holding company has limited liability if the venture fails.

(c)   Disclosure of group information to employees and investors.

(d)   The effectiveness of national legal controls over multinational enterprises trading in various legal forms.

(e)   Corporate governance issues as supplied to group situations.

These legal problems can be analysed by looking at the way 'English law' has dealt with them or may be required to react after European prodding.

Statutory Provisions

The main statutory provisions on groups relate to the disclosure of financial information and the definition of when group accounts are required. These provisions have been substantially altered by the CA 1989 which was prompted by the need to implement the 7th EC Directive on group accounts. It is an underlying principle of company law that companies which take advantage of limited liability should provide full financial disclosure of how the directors have managed the company to shareholders and creditors. This is reflected in the requirement that accounts must portray a 'true and fair view of the state of affairs of the company' (CA 1985, s. 226(2) [CA 1989, s. 4(1)]). Where a number of companies have interlocking shareholdings and/or a common management, as in figure 3.1, or a more common vertical relationship based on shareholdings, as in figure 3.2, a 'true and fair view' taking into account any transactions that may take place between the different companies can often only be portrayed through group accounts as opposed to individual company accounts. Of fundamental importance to the required production of group accounts is the definition of the relationship between two or more companies, or even between a company and an unincorporated body, that requires them to be treated as a single entity for accounting purposes. Prior to the CA 1989 a fairly simplistic definition in CA 1985, s. 736, provided the test. The new definitions introduced by the CA 1989 are more exacting and complicated, perhaps indicating a greater willingness to grapple with some of the problems. A table indicating the statutory sources of the various definitions is provided in table 3.1.

One method of approaching the question would be to identify the main differences between the old definition contained in CA 1985, s. 736, and the new definitions contained in the new CA 1985, s. 258 [CA 1989, s. 21] and the amended CA 1985, s. 736 [CA 1989, s. 144]. These are:

(a)   there are two definitions introduced by the CA 1989:

(i)   'subsidiary undertaking' and 'parent undertaking' are the more exacting definitions for establishing when group accounts are required, and this includes unincorporated bodies;

(ii)   'subsidiary company' and 'holding company' are defined for all other purposes within companies and other legislation.

(b)   the old definition in CA 1985, s. 736, referred to controlling the composition of a board of directors, a test based on actual number of directors, whereas both new definitions refer to the ability to appoint or remove a majority of the directors, a test based on the attribute of power rather than its exercise.

(c)   The old definition in CA 1985, s. 736, referred to one company holding more than half in nominal value of another company's 'equity share capital', which is defined in CA 1985, s. 744. The new definitions both refer instead to the control of 'voting rights'.

(d)   Both new definitions now include the ability to control the majority of voting rights through a voting agreement.

(e)   A 'subsidiary undertaking' also exists where there is a right for the parent undertaking to exercise a 'dominant influence' over it by directing the operating and financial policies of the company, either through the company's constitution or a control contract, or where a 'participating interest' is held and a dominant influence is actually exercised or the subsidiary and parent undertakings are managed on a unified basis.

This last definition is now wide enough to include the group situation illustrated in figure 3.1. Of particular relevance is the definition of 'participating interest' which is presumed where there is a holding of 20% or more of an undertaking.

Table 3.1

parent/subsidiary undertaking	CA 1985, s. 258 [CA 1989, s. 21(1)]
undertaking	CA 1985, s. 259 [CA 1989, s. 22]
dominant influence/control	CA 1985, sch. IOA, para. 4
contract	[CA 1989, sch. 9]
participating interest	CA 1985, s. 260 [CA 1989, s. 22].
subsidiary/holding company	CA 1985, s. 736 [CA 1989, s. 144]

Figure 3.1

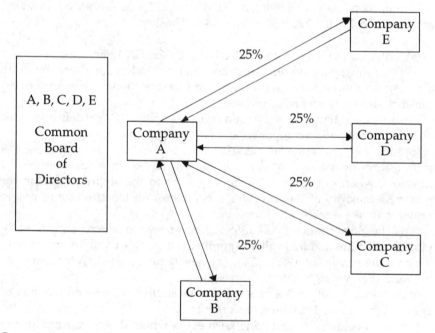

Company A owns 25 per cent of the shares in the other companies. Each of the other companies holds similar cross-shareholdings but no company owns more than 25 per cent of any other company's shares.

Figure 3.2

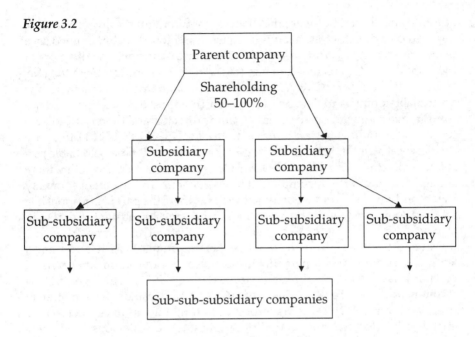

You should also refer to CA 1985, s. 458, and the provisions in the IA 1986, s. 213. CA 1985, s. 458, provides for criminal liability at any time for any person involved in the management of a company where the company's business is being 'carried on with intent to defraud creditors of the company'. The IA 1986, s. 213 includes provisions that impose civil liability to contribute towards the debts of the company incurred during such a period of 'fraudulent trading' but only when a company is being wound up. However, fraud is difficult to prove (see, for example, *Re Sarflax Ltd* [1979] Ch 592, a case immediately in point because it concerned a group situation where assets of a subsidiary company were sold to meet debts owed by the subsidiary to its holding company). This gave rise to the Cork Committee's suggestion of a less severe objective test of 'wrongful trading' for the imposition of civil liability, and to its enactment in the Insolvency Act 1986, s. 214. You will need to know what the test for 'wrongful trading' is (see *Re Produce Marketing Consortium Ltd (No. 2)* [1989] BCLC 520), when it applies (note that civil liability under ss. 213 and 214 only applies when the company is in the course of a winding up, cf. CA 1985, s. 458), and the background to its existence. Chapter 11 goes into further detail on the test for wrongful trading. For the purposes of this chapter you would need to establish whether a parent company could be liable for wrongful (or fraudulent) trading where it has exercised managerial functions in a subsidiary company. To answer this question you should be aware that liability for wrongful trading can only be imposed on a director but that this includes a 'shadow director' defined as 'a person in accordance with whose directions or instructions the directors of the company are accustomed to act' (IA 1986, s. 251). In *Re a Company (No. 005009 of 1987), ex parte Copp* [1989] BCLC 13, the court thought that there was an arguable point as to whether a bank which imposed restrictions under a fixed charge could be construed as a 'shadow director' and therefore be liable for wrongful trading. In *Re Hydrodam (Corby) Ltd* [1994] 2 BCLC 180, there are unequivocal *obiter* statements that a holding company can be held liable as a shadow director under s. 214. The Cork Committee considered whether there should be a statutory presumption that instructions from a parent company lead to any wrongful trading of the subsidiary where the parent is responsible for the appointment of the board of the subsidiary, or a substantial part of it, or where the boards of the two companies are virtually the same. However, the Committee backed down on any concrete proposals as it could affect 'entrepreneurial activity' (para. 1940) and have ramifications in other areas of company law, such as directors' duties (para. 1951). However, it did recommend that a review of the situation be undertaken 'as a matter of urgency' (para. 1952). Whereas wrongful trading only applies to directors, civil liability for fraudulent trading applies to 'any persons who were knowingly parties to the carrying on of the business' in a fraudulent manner. You should refer to *Re Augustus Barnet & Son Ltd* [1986] BCLC 170, a case decided under the predecessor to IA 1986, s. 213, to establish whether the wrongful trading provisions would have applied had they been in force.

Judicial Treatment

The judicial treatment of groups of companies was looked at in question 1. Note in particular the six guidelines laid down by Atkinson LJ in *Smith, Stone & Knight Ltd* v *Birmingham Corporation* [1939] 4 All ER 116 at p. 121, as to when the courts could treat a holding and subsidiary company as a single legal unit:

(a)   Were the profits of the subsidiary treated as profits of the parent company?

(b)   Were the persons conducting the business of the subsidiary appointed by the parent company?

(c)   Was the parent company the 'head and brain of the trading venture'?

(d)   Did the parent company have control over the venture and decide what capital should be employed?

(e)   Did the subsidiary make the profits through the parent's 'skill and direction'?

(f)   Was the parent company in 'effectual and constant' control of the subsidiary?

In many cases an answer would just list these six factors with a varying degree of accuracy. To pick up further marks you should apply the six points to any details you are given if it is a problem question. In an essay question you could raise, and possibly answer, the question as to how many of those guidelines relate to management control and how many to the financial interrelationship between a holding and subsidiary company. However, as well as looking at the general area of the judicial consideration of groups of companies, question 2 requires an additional input.

Multinational Gas & Petrochemical Co. v *Multinational Gas & Petrochemical Services Ltd* [1983] Ch 258 provides a useful link to the other parts of this answer and is perhaps an example of the 'entrepreneurial activity' that the Cork Committee recommended should be reviewed urgently. *Multinational* illustrates how holding companies can establish subsidiaries to run a risky venture and, if it goes wrong, escape without paying all the subsidiary's creditors. This type of situation prompted Templeman LJ to comment that 'English company law possesses some curious features, which may generate curious results' (*Re Southard & Co.* Ltd [1979] 1 WLR 1198 at p. 1208). Even undertakings by holding companies to pay a subsidiary's debts, referred to as 'letters of comfort' have a doubtful legal status in that if they are entered into in furtherance of purposes not authorised by the holding company's memorandum they will be beyond the powers of the directors of the company and the subsidiary will not be able to rely on the undertaking if it knew of this lack of authority (see *Rolled Steel Products (Holdings) Ltd* v *British Steel Corporation* [1986] Ch 246). If the memorandum does not authorise the giving of guarantees at all then such 'letters of comfort' could be *ultra vires* the company (see chapter 4). In *Re Augustus Barnett & Son Ltd* [1986] BCLC 170, a parent company that provided such 'letters of comfort' for the auditors of its subsidiary was not held personally liable under IA 1986, s. 213, for the £4.5 million of debts that the subsidiary owed to unsecured creditors. However, this was only because there was no carrying on of the business with an intent to defraud creditors by the directors of the subsidiary and it was not pleaded that the holding company actually carried on the subsidiary's business fraudulently. Hoffmann J did echo the Cork Report's conclusions regarding the unfortunate state of the law with respect to the liability of holding companies for their subsidiaries' debts. In *Kleinwort Benson Ltd* v *Malaysian Mining Corporation Bhd* [1989] 1 WLR 379 it was held that a letter of comfort from a parent company relating to £12 million of debts accruing to its subsidiary only created a moral responsibility on the parent company to pay the money when the subsidiary collapsed, not a legal responsibility. Given that the parent company had no legal responsibility to pay the bank, it would be difficult to justify the payment, even if the parent company had a strong sense of morality, in that a benefit to the parent company would have to be illustrated to allow such a payment to fall within the ambit of the directors' duties.

Reference should be made to the various calls for reform in this area suggesting that groups without independent subsidiaries acting as a group should be liable for the subsidiaries' debts as partially happens in Germany via the concept of integrated groups and control contracts. The Consultative Committee of Accounting Bodies recommended in 1979 that a UK parent should be liable as guarantor for the debts of the UK subsidiary unless it publicly declared otherwise. It changed its mind in 1981 at the same time as the Law Society Standing Committee on Company Law made recommendations similar to those made by the Consultative Committee in 1979. The 9th Draft EC Directive broadly followed the provisions of German law whereby creditors of subsidiaries could look to the holding company for payment except where the limited liability of the subsidiary was publicly proclaimed and independent accounts maintained (see Wooldridge, *Groups of Companies, The Law and Practice in Britain, France and Germany*, 1981).

Corporate groups may seek to protect some companies within the group from a range of liabilities through the creation of subsidiaries. In *Adams v Cape Industries plc* [1990] Ch 433, Cape Industries, based in South Africa, established a range of subsidiary companies for the marketing and production of asbestos. Asbestos dust is obviously a hazardous substance, and the employees of the American subsidiary's factory in Owentown, Texas were successful in the American courts in obtaining judgments for injuries arising from exposure to asbestos dust. However, the American courts awarded the judgments against the South African holding company and its English subsidiary, not against the American company because the plaintiffs were targeting the companies which they considered had the assets to pay the damages. The case arose in the English courts through an attempt to enforce the American judgment. This takes us into the realm of conflict of laws explored fully in the judgment of Slade LJ, and there is a question regarding the extent to which the jurisdiction issue tilts the main judgment on the corporate entity. However, the key question was the extent to which a group of international companies could use the corporate entity principle in association with national boundaries to avoid legal liability for particular activities of the group. It is an indictment of the international regulation of corporate affairs that the Court of Appeal held that liability could be avoided, Slade LJ stating (at p. 544) that:

> . . . we do not accept as a matter of law that the court is entitled to lift the corporate veil as against a defendant company which is the member of a corporate group merely because the corporate structure has been used so as to ensure that legal liability (if any) in respect of particular future activities of the group (and correspondingly the risk of enforcement of that liability) will fall on another member of the group rather than the defendant company. Whether or not this is desirable, the right to use a corporate structure in this manner is inherent in our corporate law.

One further legal problem that can be raised in respect of the wholly owned subsidiary and controlled company concerns the role of nominee directors. These are directors nominated on to the board of a subsidiary by the holding company. Such directors do not occupy any special position and are subject to the normal duties that directors owe to companies. However, where the holding company and subsidiary are competing, as in *Scottish Cooperative Wholesale Society Ltd* v *Meyer* [1958] 3 All ER 66, the nominees of the parent company are placed in a 'difficult and delicate position' (per Lord Simonds at p. 71). It is difficult to see how they can operate in this situation without being unfair to the minority shareholders who could have a good claim for unfairly prejudicial conduct under CA 1985, s. 459. Where the businesses do not compete such a claim would be more difficult to make either against a nominee director or the holding company directly (see *Nicholas* v *Soundcraft Electronics Ltd* [1993] BCLC 360). Holding companies are entitled to conduct their business as best they can in order to survive. No director can sacrifice the interests of the company of which he or she is a director for the interests of another, albeit closely associated, company. In many cases it will be clear that the interests of both holding company and subsidiary company will coincide, and the directors do not need to give formal and separate consideration as to the respective benefits of all actions. However, it is equally clear that it is not sufficient for directors just to look at the benefit of the group as a whole as regards the benefit of any particular action for:

> Each company in the group is a separate legal entity and the directors of a particular company are not entitled to sacrifice the interest of that company … The proper test, I think, in the absence of actual separate consideration, must be whether an intelligent and honest man in the position of a director of the company concerned, could, in the whole of the existing circumstances, have reasonably believed that the transactions were for the benefit of the company. (*Charterbridge Corporation Ltd* v *Lloyds Bank Ltd* [1970] Ch 62 at p. 74 per Pennycuick J.)

This potential for conflict is recognised in the New Zealand Companies Act 1993, where a director of a wholly owned subsidiary may: 'act in a manner which he or she believes is in the best interests of that company's holding company even though it may not be in the best interests of the company' (s. 131(2)). In subsidiaries that are not wholly owned, directors can act in this way if permitted by the company's constitution and the independent shareholders (s. 131(3)). In *Dairy Containers Ltd* v *NZI Bank Ltd* (1995) 7 NZCLC 96–609, the New Zealand High Court considered that this provision adjusted the form of fiduciary duties that directors owe and went on to make the holding company, Dairy Containers Ltd, liable for the negligence of its executive directors in respect of the performance of their duties as directors of a subsidiary company. This shows another legal avenue that could open up to make holding companies liable for the actions of their subsidiaries; it would be a radical shift in the approach to directors' duties as the Department of Trade and Industry estimate that only 30 per cent of registered companies are independent and not subsidiaries or sub-subsidiaries of other companies.

European Treatment

Any answer in this area will require a knowledge of the European reforms which include the 7th EC Directive, the 9th Draft EC Directive mentioned above, the European Economic interest grouping (EEIG), and the draft statute for a European company under art. 235 of the Treaty of Rome.

The creation of a European Company or Societas Europaea was a radical initiative. Professor Pieter Sanders of the Netherlands has been credited as the author of the proposal, although the French claim some responsibility (Farrar et al., *Farrar's Company Law*, 2nd ed., p. 647; Gower, *Gower's Principles of Company Law*, 5th ed., p. 67). The first draft statute for the European company was submitted to the European Council in 1975, but the proposals have been stuck ever since, the latest revisions to the proposals having been issued in 1991. The intention was the creation of a corporate form that broke down national barriers and had a European identity. This could be achieved through merger, the creation of a joint holding company or a joint subsidiary. In the latest version of the proposals a single public company could transform itself into a European company as long as it had a subsidiary or branch in another member State. At first glance this seems to be a visionary example of European legislation attempting to catch up and deliver a structure that partially matches the real world of multinational business. However, the vision is shattered upon discovery of the requirement of a registered office in a member State and the prevalence of national law in certain key areas, including taxation. It may well be that the taxation issue is the driving force behind the retention of a national link, the leap to requiring companies to pay tax directly to the European Union being too large to make. It was originally intended that European Companies would be registered in the European Commercial Register at the European Court. The current proposals for the European Company require national registration instead which will defeat the whole purpose of the original concept: to create a European corporate structure with one set of rules, thus side-stepping the harmonisation of company law via the slow progress of 'salami tactics'. These tactics, involving legislating for discrete areas of company law slice by slice, have led to many changes but the process has inevitably been lengthy and piecemeal. If sufficient incentives had been made available, particularly through the tax regime, then the European Union could have created an organisational structure that would have been very attractive to multinational business, and enhanced the opportunities for their expansion within the Member States. The proposals would have narrowed the gap between economic realities and legal structures.

Appropriate and timely structures can be an important boost to commercial confidence. At the moment the European Company is an opportunity that has been lost. An illustration of the absurdity of the situation is the tailor-made measures that had to be taken to realise the partnership between the French and English companies involved in the building and operation of the Channel Tunnel. Eventually a 4th Protocol to the UK-French Tax Treaty was employed to resolve the taxation of the partnership between Trans Manche SA and Channel Tunnel Group Ltd, the joint operators of Eurotunnel. For smaller ventures this is just not an option and complex dividend access plans have to be designed to ensure that tax is not paid twice by an application of the imputation principle where the business pays tax not just on its own profits but also on behalf of the members to whom it distributes those profits.

The European Company in its original guise deserves the accolade of a visionary proposal. The European Economic interest grouping (EEIG) does not, although the structure has been used widely in France since 1967. Following a Council Regulation adopted in July 1985 (No. 2137/85), EEIGs could be established from 1 July 1989. Member States have passed their own legislation which elaborates on the Regulation and provides the national process for registration. In the United Kingdom this has been undertaken by delegated legislation in the European Economic Interest Grouping Regulations 1989 (SI 1989/638). The EEIG is a form of joint venture operation which is based on a contract between the parties and the provisions of the Regulation, providing a vehicle for the provision of common services to its participating members. It is an incorporated partnership at European level, each member retaining its autonomy yet having unlimited joint and several liability for the debts of the EEIG. It is not intended that the EEIG will carry on the activity of each of its members or any new activity. Indeed, art. 3(1) of the Regulation expressly prohibits their establishment for the purpose of trading and making a profit. Where profits are made they are apportioned to the members in the proportion laid down in the contract for the formation of the group and taxed in the normal way by the relevant member State Arts 21 and 40). The key activity is cooperation between the members for their mutual advantage, possibly for research and development purposes or marketing. It does not appear to have been widely used, although some providers of services have used it as a mechanism for international collaboration where there are professional barriers inhibiting European collaboration.

There are also various international codes of conduct for multinational enterprises drafted by the European Economic Community, United Nations, including the United Nations Conference on Trade and Development (UNCTAD), International Labour Organisation and the Organisation for

Economic Cooperation and Development (OECD). These codes impose no legal obligations but are seen as part of the 'new economic order' (Sanders (1982) 30 Am J Comp Law 241).

The reforms coming from the EEC can be used to illustrate a recognition that multinational enterprises need to be encouraged and controlled by multinational laws. Schmitthoff prefers the extension of national law through the 'theory of the enterprise' in order to subject such enterprises to UK company law whatever form they adopt if they carry on substantial business in the UK (Schmitthoff [1972] JBL 103). Hadden sees the main problem as being the complexity of group structures: to have effective legal controls some external controls must be imposed on the internal accounting and decision-making structures of such enterprises (Hadden, *The Control of Corporate Groups*, 1983). If you have looked at the 7th EC Directive and the definitions of 'subsidiary company' and 'subsidiary undertaking' introduced by CA 1989, you may sympathise with the view that groups of companies should be compelled to adopt certain structures which are carefully monitored by legal safeguards that actually work rather than having to establish complex definitions of what a 'group' of companies consists of which will inevitably be scrutinised for loopholes through which some 'groups' will try to escape regulation. In a way the former approach, compelling groups to adopt certain structures, is similar to the approach of the Bubble Act in 1720 when all business organisations trading as 'companies' without a charter were declared illegal and were forced to use the unincorporated partnership instead. The problem with the Bubble Act was that it failed to provide a convenient structure through which businessmen could trade, whereas any reform of the laws relating to groups of companies could provide a legal structure under which groups conforming with that structure could exist, all others being outlawed. However, although this is a possibility for reform on an international basis the provisions introduced by the CA 1989 are clearly not directed towards this method of reform. Certainly 'English common law', based as it is on a principle established in 1897, has not kept pace with commercial developments. The present judicial treatment can be used to illustrate this, the structural tests for control advanced in *Smith, Stone & Knight* contrast sharply with the 'holding out' test adopted by the European Court of Justice in *SAR Schotte GmbH* v *Parfums Rothschild SARL* [1992] BCLC 235, where it was held that third parties could rely on the appearance created that one company is the 'establishment' of another company even if in company law the two companies are technically independent of each other (see also *Imperial Chemical Industries Ltd* v *Commission of the European Communities* (case 48/69) [1972] ECR 619 and *Viho Europe BV* v *Commission of the European Communities* (case T–102/92) [1995] ECR II–17). This arose from the disputed interpretation of art. 5(5) of the Convention on Jurisdiction and the Enforcement of Judgments in Civil and Commercial Matters which states that:

> A person domiciled in a contracting State may, in another contracting State, be sued . . . as regards a dispute arising out of the operation of a branch, agency or other establishment, in the courts for the place in which the branch, agency or other establishment is situated.

The Convention itself is an illustration of the need for international legislative action to match the international operations of corporate groups which arrange their structures to their best advantage, as in *Adams* v *Cape Industries plc*.

Corporate Governance

In an assessment answer or project you should make some reference to the wider context, in particular through a reference to the current debate on corporate governance. This is dealt with in more detail in chapter 12, but there are some specific points that relate to the parent–subsidiary company relationship. In particular a current concern in the corporate governance debate is the accountability of senior managers to shareholders contrasted with their accountability to the legitimate wider company interest, partly as payment for the privilege of operating as a corporation, including limited liability. The situation is made even more complex where there is a parent–subsidiary relationship crossing national frontiers and cultures. The directors of subsidiary companies are in a totally different position to directors of stand-alone companies or the directors of holding companies.

Member States of the European Community will and are developing their own responses to the issue of corporate responsibility and will continue to do so if business itself does not respond in a responsible manner. This could lead to a wide range of measures in different Member States, as well as some European-wide initiatives particularly concerning the role of subsidiary companies and multinational enterprises. Subsidiaries are created for a variety of purposes: for example, to separate distinct business functions and provide the perception and sometimes reality of managerial autonomy; or for fiscal reasons, particularly in the European Union where companies operate across borders. Some subsidiaries are created as a mechanism for ensuring that risky elements of the business are channelled through a separate legal entity. To what extent will the agenda for corporate responsibility in the European Union incorporate the trend towards treating the 'group' as an 'ethical' entity? An example of where this occurred was the inability of the Union Carbide group to escape public and legal censure through negligence attributed to its Indian subsidiary (50.9 per cent) at its Bhopal plant in December 1984. This 'ethical entity' may also embrace dominant suppliers of such large groups. Regional groupings of governments as well as national governments in their own right may increase their challenges to these legal 'fictions' born of legal 'fictions'. The position faced by Union Carbide should encourage holding companies to monitor more closely the activities of subsidiaries, but ironically the threat of 'shadow director' status and possible liability for wrongful trading steers UK holding companies in the opposite direction. If this monitoring by a holding company is adjudged to be 'directions or instructions' which the subsidiary directors are accustomed to follow then the holding company will be a 'shadow director' and incur potential liability. The decision in *Dairy Containers Ltd v NZI Bank Ltd* (1995) 7 NZCLC 96–609 may deter holding companies from appointing their directors onto boards of subsidiaries leaving control to be exercised through other informal measures. The desire and ability to regulate multinational enterprises through growing and more authoritative multinational group-ings like the European Union is a distinct possibility.

There is a lot of material that could go into this answer. However, if the correct structure is adopted you can trim the material in each section to fit the time or word limit available. Do not be tempted to dwell on just one part of the answer. Try to maintain the framework you started off with, linking each section to previous ones if possible so as to create a structured answer and not one of numerous unconnected paragraphs.

FURTHER READING

Farrar, John, and Russell, Mark, 'The impact of institutional investment on company law' (1984) 5 Co Law 107.

Freeman, Judith, 'Small businesses and the corporate form: burden or privilege?' (1994) 57 MLR 555.

Gobert, James, 'Corporate criminality: four models of fault' (1994) 14 LS 393.

Hicks, Andrew, 'Reforming the law of private companies' (1995) 16 Co Law 171.

Jefferson, Michael, 'Recent developments in corporate criminal responsibil-ity' (1995) 16 Co Law 146.

Napier, Christopher, and Nokes, Christopher, 'Premiums and pre-acquisi-tion profits: the legal and accountancy professions and business combina-tions' (1991) 54 MLR 810.

Riley, Christopher A., Understanding and regulating the corporation' (1995) 58 MLR 595.

Sanders, Pieter, 'Implementing international codes of conduct for multina-tional enterprises' (1982) 30 Am J Comp Law 241.

Schmitthoff, Clive M., 'The wholly owned and the controlled subsidiary' [1978] JBL 218.

Wedderburn of Charlton, Lord, 'Companies and employees: common law or social dimension?' (1993) 109 LQR 220.

Wells, Celia, 'Corporate liability and consumer protection: *Tesco v Nattrass* revisited' (1994) 57 MLR 817.

4 CONTRACTUAL CAPACITY

INTRODUCTION

In 1985 the government appointed Dr Dan Prentice to examine the implications of abolishing the *ultra vires* rule. Dr Prentice published his report in 1986 in the form of a consultative paper. The Bill which was enacted as CA 1989 introduced provisions to abolish the *ultra vires* rule although the form was not exactly that recommended by Dr Prentice (see R. Pennington 'Reform of the *ultra vires* rule' (1987) 8 Co Law 103). These provisions are now law in the form of CA 1985, ss. 3A, 35 and 35A [CA 1989, ss. 108 and 110].

This change in the law represents a major shift of policy and the effects of the new provisions are still likely to engender a great deal of discussion and will possibly lead to litigation in the future. Because of this the topic is likely to be popular with examiners for some time to come.

MAIN ISSUES

(a)   Defining and drawing a distinction between corporate capacity and the capacity of directors and other corporate officers to transact. The pre-1989 law.

(b)   Corporate capacity and CA 1985 [CA 1989].

(c)   Capacity of directors, the rule in *Turquand's* case, agency and CA 1985, s. 35A.

Corporate Capacity and the Capacity of Directors and Other Officers to Act: the Pre–1989 Law

Following the decision in *Rolled Steel Products (Holdings) Ltd* v *British Steel Corporation* [1986] Ch 246, it was necessary to distinguish between situations where a company lacked capacity to do a particular thing and those where, although the company had capacity, the persons through whom it sought to act lacked capacity.

The former situation would arise where the transaction fell outside the scope of the company's objects and the resulting contract was void and incapable of ratification even by the unanimous consent of the company's shareholders (see *Ashbury Railway Carriage & Iron Co. Ltd* v *Riche* (1875) LR 7 HL 653).

In the latter situation the transaction would amount to a breach of directors' duties and was voidable. This meant it could be avoided at the company's option provided the outsider was not in a position to enforce it using either CA 1985, s. 35A as originally enacted, the rule in *Turquand's* case or the agency rules.

In order to establish whether a valid contract has been entered into by a company, it is necessary to ensure that *both* the company and the director or other officer acting for it have capacity.

One of the other effects of the decision in *Rolled Steel Products (Holdings) Ltd* v *British Steel Corporation* was to greatly reduce the practical importance of the *ultra vires* rule and thus lay the seeds of its ultimate abolition.

The main thrust of the provisions contained in CA 1989 is to regulate matters relating to the lack of corporate capacity. The law relating to the capacity of directors and other officers remains largely unchanged.

It is important to remember that issues arising out of questions of corporate capacity are quite different and quite separate from those arising out of questions over the capacity of directors and other officers. The rules and remedies applicable are also quite different and separate (see figures 4.1 and 4.2). It is important to bear this in mind when answering any examination or assessment question on this topic.

Corporate Capacity — the Companies Act 1985 (as Amended by the Companies Act 1989)

The effect of CA 1985, s. 35(1) [CA 1989, s. 108], is to cure any lack of capacity a company may experience by virtue of any provisions in its memorandum. As far as an outsider dealing with a company operating outside its memorandum is concerned, the validity of the act cannot be called into question. The outsider and the company have a right to enforce and the contract cannot be *ultra vires* the company. However, CA 1985 s. 35(1) [CA 1989, s. 108 must be read in the light of the effects of ratification under CA 1985, s. 35(3) and 35A [CA 1989, s. 108].

CA 1985, s. 35(3) [CA 1989, s. 108] allows the company's shareholders to ratify a contract which it lacks capacity to make by passing a special resolution. This resolution makes the contract good for all purposes. Four particular consequences can be identified:

(a)   Ratification will prevent a shareholder from exercising the right under CA 1985, s. 35(2) [CA 1989, s. 108] to obtain an injunction to prevent the transaction which lacks capacity being performed. This assumes that the ratification will not amount to a fraud on the minority by wrongdoers in control of the company. If it does, a minority shareholder may have a right of action under one of the exceptions to the rule in *Foss* v *Harbottle* (see chapter 10).

(b)   The outsider transacting with the company is relieved of the obligation of having to bring himself within the scope of CA 1985, s. 35A [CA 1989, s 108], as the contract is good for all purposes. However, if there is no ratification the outsider must be able to successfully plead CA 1985, s 35A [CA 1989, s. 108], to enforce the contract if the directors have acted in excess of their powers (see below and question 1 for a detailed discussion of this section).

(c)   However, ratification of the transaction under CA 1985, s. 35(3) [CA 1989, s. 108], will not relieve the directors from liability for breach of duty. This may only be achieved if a separate and additional special resolution is passed — see CA 1985, s. 35(3) [CA 1989, s. 108].

(d)   Unless s. 35(1) can be interpreted as equating *all* acts of the board of directors with acts of the company then ratification will be necessary before the company can avail itself of the protection of s. 35(1). The main problem here lies in the fact that in order to confer authority on an agent (the board) the principal (the company) must first have authority itself. How can the board be performing an act on behalf of the company which the company had no authority to authorise in the first place? Thus it would seem fair to assume that the board's act is not something the company can derive any contractual rights from unless it is first ratified by special resolution under s. 35(3) (see Ferran (1992) 13 Co Law 124 for a detailed discussion of this point).

This point links into the 'alter ego theory' which is discussed in chapter 3. It will be important to be able to distinguish between acts done on behalf of the company and acts carried out by directors which will not be classed as corporate acts but may be classed as acts for which they will be personally liable.

The amendments introduced by CA 1989 have hopefully removed some of the difficulties associated with the interpretation of what is now CA 1985, s. 35A (see, e.g. Collier and Sealy [1973] CLJ 1). To successfully plead the amended version of the section the outsider will have to prove five things:

(a)   He was an outsider (i.e. an unconnected person dealing with the company).

(b) He was acting in good faith.
(c) He was dealing with the company.
(d) He was dealing with the directors or others authorised by the board.
(e) The limitation was imposed by the company's constitution.

To assess how effective the amendments are likely to be, you will need to be familiar with the old and new versions of the section in some detail and be able to apply and discuss the points raised above to any question you are confronted with. There is a detailed discussion in question 1 at the end of this chapter.

Despite the fact that CA 1989 has supposedly abolished the *ultra vires* rule, the Act still provides for every company to include an objects clause in its memorandum.

CA 1989, s. 110, inserts a new s. 3A into CA 1985 which allows a company to state in its memorandum that the object of the company is to carry on business as a general commercial company. Where a company adopts this approach the following will appear in the memorandum:

(a) the object of the company is to carry on any trade or business whatsoever, and

(b) the company has power to do all such things as are incidental or conducive to the carrying on of any trade or business by it.

This means that lawyers can put away their word processors, and companies will no longer be registered with objects clauses that read like novels! Such hopes are, however, groundless. One of the issues that will have to be resolved by the courts is whether the powers in (b) above can only be validly exercised in pursuance of a business that the company *is actually* carrying on, or whether they can be validly exercised in pursuance of any business irrespective of whether the company is carrying it on at the time or proposes to do so at some time in the future.

To avoid difficulties like the one outlined above, the draftsman might have been better served by adopting an approach similar to the one adopted by the Isle of Man Companies Act 1986. This Act states that the company has the capacity to do anything it wishes unless the contrary is stated in its memorandum. Couple this with the abolition of constructive notice, and the *ultra vires* rule really is abolished as far as the outsider is concerned. Under the amendments introduced by CA 1989 it is still possible for the outsider to be a party to a contract which he cannot enforce for lack of capacity on the part of the company (see question 1).

Capacity of Directors — the Rule in Turquand's Case and Agency

Even in circumstances where the company has capacity to transact it remains necessary to establish two further things: that the director or other officer that the outsider is dealing with has:

(a)   been properly appointed to office; and
(b)   proper authority to transact.

Invalid appointments will be cured by either CA 1985, s. 285, or the rule in *Royal British Bank* v *Turquand* (1856) 6 E & B 327. In circumstances where there has been an attempt to appoint but that attempt is invalid due to a procedural defect, that defect will be cured by either of the rules mentioned above. Thus procedurally defective appointments will not present the outsider with any problems regarding enforceability. However, s. 285 will not apply in situations where there has been *no attempt to appoint* at all.

In circumstances where there has been no attempt to appoint but where a person has assumed the position of director or managing director, the outsider must rely on either the rule in *Turquand's* case or the agency principles established in *Freeman & Lockyer* v *Buckhurst Park Properties (Mangal) Ltd* [1964] 2 QB 480. To be in a position to plead this agency rule an outsider must satisfy the criteria set out by Diplock LJ in his judgment. You should note, however, that the criteria have been altered by changes introduced by the CA 1989, which are discussed below. You will need to familiarise yourself with these criteria as they represent an important rule which can be used by the outsider to enforce the contract (see question 2 at the end of this chapter).

If the defect or lack of appointment is cured by one of the rules mentioned above or if the director has been properly appointed to office you will still need to ensure that he has, in accordance with the company's constitution, proper authority to transact. In circumstances where a director has not got proper authority to transact you will need to consider whether that lack of authority can be cured by CA 1985, s. 35A [CA 1989, s. 108] (see above), the rule in *Turquand's* case or the agency rules. If any of these is successfully pleaded by the outsider then the company is prevented from avoiding the transaction.

The rule in *Turquand's* case, sometimes referred to as the indoor management rule, allows an outsider dealing with a company to assume that the company has complied with its own internal regulations. Thus if there is an internal procedural irregularity which may affect the validity of a contract entered into by a director or other officer of the company, the rule in *Turquand's* case will allow the outsider to enforce the contract. However,

Turquand's case cannot be successfully pleaded in some situations because there are a number of exceptions to the rule. You will need to know these in case one of them appears in an examination or assessment.

The agency rules. Directors of a company act as its agents when contracting on its behalf. When an agent acts on behalf of a principal he binds the principal only if he has the principal's authority or the principal ratifies the transaction later. However, it is possible for an outsider to deal with an agent (director) who has no actual authority to transact but who has *usual or ostensible* authority to act. For a discussion of how these agency principles apply to companies you will need to read Diplock LJ's judgment in *Freeman & Lockyer* v *Buckhurst Park Properties (Mangal) Ltd* [1964] 2 QB 480. You should note that the fourth of Diplock LJ's criteria regarding the fact that the company is not deprived of the capacity either to enter into the contract of the kind to be enforced or to delegate authority to enter into a contract of that kind to the agent can now be overcome by the outsider using ss. 35 and 35A. This is because limitations on the company's capacity to contract have been removed by s. 35 and limitations on the board's ability to delegate have been removed by s. 35A.

However, the position is complicated when considering the constructive notice rule. Although the CA 1989 abolishes constructive notice, ostensible authority still cannot arise where the outsider is aware of or put on inquiry about a limitation. To this extent some element of constructive notice may be preserved (see question 2 for a more detailed discussion).

Capacity of Directors — Companies Act 1985, Section 322A

In addition to the rules discussed above, s. 322A introduces a third category of contract which is classed as voidable. Under s. 322A a contract between the company and one of its directors, or a person connected with a director, in excess of the directors' powers under the company's constitution is voidable at the company's option. Irrespective of whether or not the contract is avoided the director concerned will be in breach of his fiduciary duty and accountable to the company for any profit made and liable to compensate the company for any loss suffered. The purpose of s. 322A is to prevent directors and other insiders availing themselves of the protection provided by ss. 35A and 35B. In many respects the section mirrors existing rules established in case law, e.g., *Hely-Hutchinson* v *Brayhead Ltd* [1968] 1 QB 549, but there is one notable point in s. 322A(7). This deals with transactions involving the company on the one hand and a mixture of insiders and outsiders on the other. The court has the power on the application of the outsider to either affirm, sever or set aside the transaction on such terms as appear just. Thus the outsider will still be protected by ss. 35A and 35B whilst the insider will not.

REVISION AND RESEARCH

It is easy to get tied up in knots when faced with the revision of this topic. Not only have you to cope with complex and largely untested legislation, you also have to get to grips with an abundance of case law. If you are an inspired and brilliant student you will be wondering what all the fuss is about; if you are not one of those lucky few you will be wondering where to start.

We suggest you concentrate on the following points:

(a) The distinction between the lack of corporate capacity and the lack of capacity on the part of the directors or other officers of the company.

(b) How the new statutory rules will effect a contract which lacks corporate capacity because it is outside the company's memorandum from:

(i) the outsider's point of view; and
(ii) the company's point of view.

(c) The effect of the rule in *Turquand's* case and the agency rules on contracts entered into by directors in excess of their powers.

The flow chart in figures 4. 1. and 4.2 takes you through a checklist signposting the important statutory provisions and cases at each stop along the way.

Figure 4.1

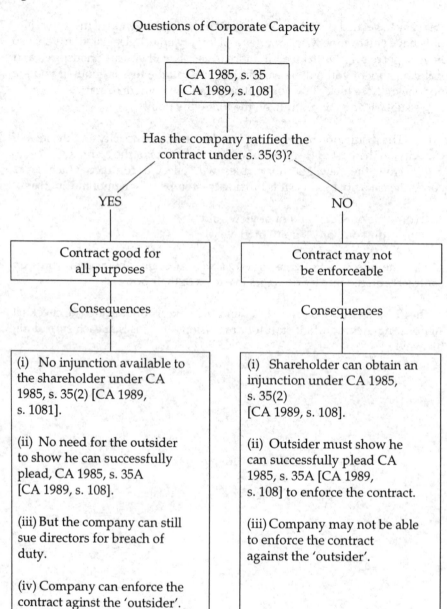

Questions of Corporate Capacity

CA 1985, s. 35
[CA 1989, s. 108]

Has the company ratified the
contract under s. 35(3)?

YES   NO

| Contract good for all purposes | Contract may not be enforceable |

Consequences   Consequences

(i) No injunction available to the shareholder under CA 1985, s. 35(2) [CA 1989, s. 1081].

(ii) No need for the outsider to show he can successfully plead, CA 1985, s. 35A [CA 1989, s. 108].

(iii) But the company can still sue directors for breach of duty.

(iv) Company can enforce the contract aginst the 'outsider'.

(i) Shareholder can obtain an injunction under CA 1985, s. 35(2) [CA 1989, s. 108].

(ii) Outsider must show he can successfully plead CA 1985, s. 35A [CA 1989, s. 108] to enforce the contract.

(iii) Company may not be able to enforce the contract against the 'outsider'.

Figure 4.2

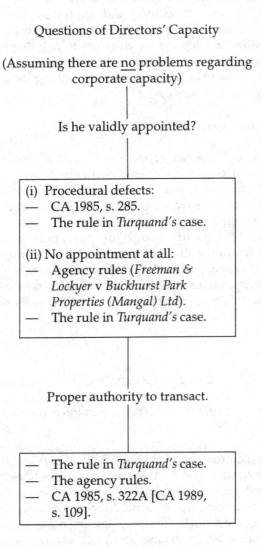

Questions of Directors' Capacity

(Assuming there are <u>no</u> problems regarding
corporate capacity)

Is he validly appointed?

(i) Procedural defects:
—   CA 1985, s. 285.
—   The rule in *Turquand's* case.

(ii) No appointment at all:
—   Agency rules (*Freeman &
     Lockyer* v *Buckhurst Park
     Properties (Mangal) Ltd*).
—   The rule in *Turquand's* case.

Proper authority to transact.

—   The rule in *Turquand's* case.
—   The agency rules.
—   CA 1985, s. 322A [CA 1989,
     s. 109].

In addition, you will need to bring some informed criticism to bear at
appropriate points in your answer. We suggest you look at some of the articles
listed at the end of this chapter. Remember that much of the law here is new
and untested so any point or criticism you make is likely to be reasonable so
long as it is supported by authority. What you do need to avoid doing is
merely churning out the statutory provisions parrot fashion without applying them to the question and commenting on their effectiveness.

The advantages of revising using the flow chart are that you can quickly get an overview of the whole topic and see the interrelationship of the different rules and cases. This may help you understand a particular rule or case more easily because you can see where it fits in. It should also assist you in a logical development of your answer in the examination because you know what options are available at any stage in the answer and the way in which the answer should move next.

IDENTIFYING THE QUESTION

Essay questions on corporate capacity are quite likely to be popular as examiners will want to know your views on the effectiveness of the legislation in abolishing the *ultra vires* rule. It is unlikely that there will be significant case-law developments so any problem questions will be focused on statutory interpretation and the agency rules.

Questions on the capacity of directors may take the form of mixed questions with breaches of directors' duties and minority protection included in them. These are more likely to be problem questions.

Most problem questions will ask you to advise on the validity of the transactions and this may be from either the company's or the outsider's point of view.

QUESTION 1

As a result of the passing of section 35 of the Companies Act 1985 as amended in CA 1989, a company has unlimited contractual capacity, consequently all contracts it makes are enforceable by it or against it. Discuss.

The question requires you to discuss the effect the CA 1989 has had on a company's contractual capacity. As with all essay questions it is important to plan. a structured answer or you may find yourself wandering off the point or, worse still, indulging in an 'aerial bombing attack' by writing down everything you know about the topic and leaving the examiner to answer the question from the material you have given him.

Pre–1989 Law

You could begin your answer by briefly explaining the limitations placed upon a company's contractual capacity under the pre–1989 law. This will involve an explanation of the *ultra vires* rule as it affected companies. You can illustrate this principle using the case of *Ashbury Railway Carriage & Iron Co. Ltd* v *Riche* (1875) LR 7 HL 653 and in particular explain that it was impossible to ratify an *ultra vires* act even if all the shareholders agreed the contract was still void. You should also mention the practice whereby companies adopted very long objects clauses listing every conceivable activity to prevent the *ultra vires* rule catching them out and the distinction drawn by the courts between clauses which were true objects and those which were merely powers (see *Re Introductions Ltd* [1969] 1 All ER 881).

Following the decision in *Rolled Steel Products (Holdings) Ltd* v *British Steel Corporation* [1986] Ch 246, it became necessary to draw a distinction between transactions that fell outside the scope of a company's objects which were *ultra vires* and void for lack of corporate capacity: and those which fell *within* the scope of its powers but the power was not being exercised to further a stated object as these were a breach of directors' duties and voidable for lack of capacity on the part of the director.

You should then explain that in order to ascertain the accuracy of the statement in the question it will be necessary to see whether either or both of the above consequences is possible in respect of transactions made post CA 1989.

Corporate Capacity

You should start your discussion of corporate capacity by examining the effect of CA 1985, s. 35(1) [CA 1989, s. 108]. It appears to cure any lack of capacity on the part of the company by virtue of any provisions in its memorandum. So the outsider and the company are given a prima facie right to enforce any contract. However, CA 1985, s. 35(3) [CA 1989, s. 108] gives the company the right to ratify a transaction which is outside its capacity by passing a special resolution. This subsection would appear to raise two issues which you need to explore further:

(a)   What is the effect of ratification?
(b)   What is the position of the company and the outsider if no ratification takes place?

Effect of Ratification

Ratification will make the contract good for all purposes. This means it is enforceable by or against the company. However, ratification of the transaction by the shareholders will not preclude the company from suing its directors for compensation for any loss or damage it sustains as a result of the contract being enforced. Such relief is available but must be approved separately by the shareholders again by special resolution.

No Ratification

If no ratification takes place then the company may find that a shareholder prevents it going ahead with the transaction by obtaining an injunction under CA 1985, s. 35(2) [CA 1989, s. 108]. This section preserves the old rule which allowed a shareholder to obtain an injunction to prevent a company acting outside its capacity. Thus in these circumstances, the company does not have unlimited contractual capacity.

From the outsider's viewpoint if no ratification takes place he has to be able to bring himself within the scope of CA 1985, s. 35A [CA 1989, s. 108] to enforce the contract. To do this he must establish the five points mentioned earlier in this chapter (see pp. 75–6). This section has been amended by CA 1989 to clear up some of the difficulties previously experienced by those seeking to use it. Some aspects of it require further discussion.

From the company's point of view, if no ratification takes place then the court may feel that the act done cannot be classed as an act of the company within the meaning of s. 35(1) which will mean that the company cannot enforce the contract.

Good faith — the section requires the outsider to be acting in good faith. CA 1985, s. 35A(2) [CA 1989, s. 108] states that a person shall be deemed to be acting in good faith unless the contrary is proved. In addition *actual* knowledge of lack of capacity alone is not sufficient to prove bad faith. It seems that an outsider will only be acting in bad faith if he has actual knowledge of the lack of capacity and he commits a fraud on the company. Fraud here would include both equitable and common law fraud (see chapter 10 for a definition of equitable and common law fraud).

Dealing — the outsider must be dealing with the company. CA 1985, s. 35A(2) [CA 1989, s. 108] states that an outsider will be dealing with the company if he is a party to any transaction or other act to which the company is a party. This definition is wider than the one placed upon the word by Lawson J in *International Sales & Agencies Ltd* v *Marcus* [1982] 3 All ER 551 where he limited dealing to legally binding transactions. This definition could include gratuitous dispositions of corporate assets.

Directors and others authorised by the board — the outsider must be dealing with the directors or other person authorised by the board. The last phrase is added by CA 1989 and resolves any difficulties that may have arisen where an outsider was not dealing with the board but was dealing with a managing director for example. This situation now clearly falls within the scope of the section.

In any circumstances where an outsider cannot satisfy the five points in s. 35A he cannot enforce the contract against the company.

Directors' Capacity

The bulk of your answer should concentrate on a discussion of CA 1989. However, it is worth mentioning that even where the company has capacity it is still possible for it to avoid a contract on the grounds that the director who entered into it exceeded his authority. In these circumstances the outsider would have to rely on either CA 1985, s. 285, the rule in *Turquand's* case or the agency rules to enforce the contract (see question 2). You should not go into any detail on this aspect of the law because the question quite clearly wants you to concentrate on corporate capacity and CA 1989.

Summary

Remember to finish you answer with a conclusion. You will need to make it clear to the examiner that you appreciate what effect CA 1989 has had on corporate capacity and that you understand its limitations. In conclusion the statement in the question is only accurate where the company has ratified the contract. This ratification makes the contract good for all purposes. Without ratification the enforceability of the transaction may be challenged by a shareholder under CA 1985, s. 35(2) [CA 1989, s. 108]. Alternatively, an outsider may be unable to enforce because he cannot bring himself within the scope of CA 1985, s. 35A [CA 1989, s. 108].

Consequently, it is not true to say that the CA 1989 gives a company unlimited contractual capacity. Indeed the wording of s. 35(1) recognises that lack of corporate capacity still exists in company law.

QUESTION 2

Century Ltd was established in 1989. Its memorandum states that it will 'carry on the business of a general commercial company'.

Bob, Jim and Sam are the company's directors. Sam has always acted as the company's managing director but has never been formally appointed to this office. At the general meeting that appointed Jim several shareholders failed to receive notice of the meeting due to a malfunction of the company's computer which sends out such notices.

The articles delegate the management of the company to the directors, but art. 10 states that for any borrowing over £500,000 approval of the shareholders must be first obtained. In addition art. 22 states that the board is quorate when three directors are present.

Sam arranges to borrow £1 million from Lend All Bank to develop a new wave pool. This loan agreement is concluded without shareholder approval. At a recent board meeting the directors agree to purchase from Dodgy Builders Ltd, for £150,000, a site on which to develop the wave pool.

The company fails to develop the wave pool and no longer requires the site. In addition it defaults on the loan repayments.

Advise Dodgy Builders Ltd and Lend All Bank on the validity of the contracts.

Identifying the Issues

This is a typical problem question dealing with company contracts. Your task is to determine the validity of the transactions described. Before dealing with each transaction you should start with an introductory paragraph distinguishing between lack of corporate capacity and situations where directors exceed their authority. The transactions outlined in this problem fall into the latter category so this part of the introduction should be highlighted. Whenever you are dealing with a question concerning excess of authority you will need to decide whether the directors have exceeded their authority because:

(a)   they have not been validly appointed to office, and therefore have no authority at all; or

(b)   they have been validly appointed to office but have exceeded the powers given to them by the company's constitution.

The Contract with Dodgy Builders Ltd

This contract was concluded at a recent board meeting by the directors. It would seem that provided the board meeting was quorate then the contract would be valid and enforceable by Dodgy Builders Ltd against Century Ltd. Article 22 of the company's articles requires all three directors to be present at a board meeting for it to be quorate. It would appear from the question that all three were physically present. However, there seems to be some problem with regard to the validity of Jim's appointment to the board. There was a procedural irregularity at the general meeting which appointed him as some shareholders failed to receive notice of the meeting. Unless Dodgy Builders Ltd can rely on a rule to cure this irregularity the contract will be voidable at the company's option.

Dodgy Builders Ltd should be able to rely on CA 1985, s. 285, to cure the defect in Jim's appointment; alternatively the rule in *Royal British Bank* v *Turquand* will allow Dodgy Builders Ltd to assume that all matters of internal management have been adhered to. In the circumstances the board meeting will be quorate and the company bound by its agreement with Dodgy Builders Ltd.

The Loan Agreement with Lend All Bank

This contract was concluded by Sam who acts as the company's managing director. There appear to be two difficulties facing Lend All Bank:

(a)   Sam has never been appointed managing director.
(b)   Shareholder approval for the loan has not been obtained in accordance with art. 10.

The first issue to deal with is the fact that Sam has never been appointed to office. CA 1985, s. 285 will be of no use here because it only cures procedural irregularities. It assumes that there has been an attempt to appoint. Where there has been no attempt to appoint the outsider will have to try to rely on the rule in *Freeman & Lockyer* v *Buckhurst Park Properties (Mangal) Ltd.* Remember to take account of the amendments as a result of the CA 1989. If Lend All Bank can show a holding out by Century Ltd of Sam as managing director then if they relied on that holding out this will make Sam an agent of Century Ltd with ostensible authority to contract. However, even with the problem regarding lack of appointment dealt with there is still the difficulty regarding the shareholders' approval for the loan. Lend All Bank may look toward the rule in *Turquand's* case and argue that they can assume that all matters of internal management have been properly conducted. If both rules can be relied on, Lend All Bank can sue to recover the loan.

Conclusion

To conclude, you need to sum up your advice to the respective parties by stating that both contracts are voidable but may be enforced against the company if the parties can rely on the rules outlined above.

An alternative version of this question could have contained a situation where a director entered into a contract with his company in excess of his authority. This situation is now governed by CA 1985, s. 322A [CA 1989, s. 109] discussed above. You need to be alert to its possible inclusion in a question of this type.

FURTHER READING

Ferran, Ellis, 'The reform of the law on corporate capacity and directors' and officers' authority' (1992) 13 Co Law 124 and 177.
Griffin, Stephen, 'Directors' authority: the Companies Act 1989' (1991) 12 Co Law 98.
Pennington, Robert, 'Reform of the *ultra vires* rule' (1987) 8 Co Law 103.
Poole, Jill, 'Abolition of the *ultra vires* doctrine and agency problems' (1991) 12 Co Law 43.

5 THE ARTICLES OF ASSOCIATION

INTRODUCTION

The articles of association are one of two constitutional documents governing the affairs of the company. The other document, the memorandum of association, publicly proclaims the name, capital and objects of the company, whereas the articles of association govern the internal affairs of the company. The articles provide the rules for such matters as the transfer, transmission or forfeiture of shares, the holding and conduct of general meetings, the powers and duties of directors and proceedings at board meetings, the rights attached to shares which may vary according to the different classes of share, such as votes, right to a dividend and the right to a return of capital on a winding up.

Table A provides a model set of articles as prescribed by regulations made by the Secretary of State under CA 1985, s. 8. Section 8 provides that companies can adopt all or part of Table A. Many companies will have articles of association that adopt Table A subject to a list of exclusions and alterations. For example, the requirement for directors to retire by rotation (Table A, arts 73–80) would normally be excluded in small private companies. The transfer of shares article (Table A, art. 24) could be changed giving the directors absolute discretion to refuse to register transfers, as could the ability of directors to vote and be counted in a quorum at a board meeting discussing any contract in which they have an interest (Table A, arts 94–7). The examination rubric or assessment question may well have a statement to the effect that:

> Articles are in the form of Table A, as prescribed by the Companies (Tables A to F) Regulations 1985, unless otherwise stated.

This allows you to assume that the companies involved have adopted Table A unless the problem tells you otherwise. If there is no such statement on the application of Table A it is permissible to comment, both in answers to essay and problem questions, on the hypothesis that the company's articles are in the form of Table A. Table A used to be a schedule to the CA 1948 but is now to be found in SI 1985, No. 805.

Because the articles cover a variety of different internal corporate affairs most questions will require some reference to particular provisions of Table A which can be cited and applied. The Table A introduced in 1985, alongside the consolidation of the Companies Acts in the CA 1985, introduced some substantial alterations to the 1948 version. The main changes are in the areas of directors' duties, the management of the company and alteration of class rights attached to shares. The provisions of Table A are put into the context of the various chapters of this book, but see in particular chapters 6 and 12, as well as the remaining part of this chapter.

MAIN ISSUES

This chapter concentrates on two specific problems concerning the articles that are common examination areas:

(a)   The status of the 's. 14 contract'.

(b)   The alteration of the articles by special resolution (under CA 1985, s. 9), and therefore the terms of this contract, with particular reference to the protection of class rights.

The s. 14 contract derives, as the title suggests, from s. 14 of the 1985 CA. The academic articles that you will be referred to prior to the CA 1985 will refer to the 's. 20 contract', because the relevant section prior to CA 1985, s. 14 used to be CA 1948, s. 20.

It is surprising how many times the actual wording of s. 14 is not looked at in any detail by candidates attempting answers in this area. The principle behind this statutory contract can cause great confusion. The articles, as we have seen, contain the rules that govern the internal affairs of the company. These rules, and the provisions of the memorandum, also form the terms of this statutory contract between the company and its members and the members *inter se*. The articles are the terms of the contract; the company and its members are the parties to the contract.

Although the principle is simplified by this application of standard contractual terminology, the issue is made more complex when another principle of company law is brought into the argument — the rule in *Foss* v *Harbottle* (1843) 2 Hare 461. Section 14 states that the contract applies to 'all the provisions of . . . the articles'. *Foss* v *Harbottle* provides that where a wrong is done to the company, the company is the proper plaintiff. Which prevails when the wrong done to the company is a breach of the articles? The issue is also confused when the courts start to question the type of articles, or terms of the contract, that a member can enforce under the s. 14 contract and the capacity (*qua* member or *qua* outsider) in which the member attempts to do so. This last point causes no end of confusion and the Latin terminology that is sometimes employed, although a good method of shorthand, sometimes adds to the confusion. Where you see '*qua*' read it as 'in his capacity as'. It is likely to arise in two areas that must be distinguished from each other:

(a)   It is often said that a member can only attempt to enforce the articles *qua* member and not *qua* outsider. This means that when he goes to court to enforce the articles he must sue as the member who is a party to the s. 14 contract. If, as in *Eley* v *Positive Government Security Life Assurance Co. Ltd* (1876) 1 ExD 88, he goes to the court and says that he is the solicitor mentioned in one of the articles and he wants to enforce that particular article, he is not saying to the court that he is suing *qua* member: he is saying that he is suing *qua* solicitor or *qua* outsider. In these capacities he is not privy to the s. 14 contract and the action will fail.

(b)   It is a different argument when the courts start to question the type of articles that can be enforced even when suing *qua* member. As will be seen when we get on to question 1, there are some articles that do not affect members *qua* members but which may affect them in an outside capacity (e.g., as managing director or solicitor). The question as to whether these 'outsider rights' can be enforced at all under the s. 14 contract has been the subject of apparently conflicting cases and a bone of contention for various academics.

Because of the difficulties facing shareholders regarding the enforcement of 'rights' under the articles, private shareholder agreements have become quite common. These agreements are enforceable in the same way as private contracts between the contracting shareholders and are purely personal to the shareholders who execute the agreement. They are valid as long as they do not purport to bind future shareholders. In *Russell* v *Northern Bank Development Corporation Ltd* [1992] BCLC 1016, the House of Lords held that a shareholder agreement as to how shareholders would exercise their voting rights on a resolution to alter the articles was not an unlawful and invalid fetter on the company's powers, although the company itself could not be a party to such an agreement to restrict the exercise of its powers.

Although the articles form part of the terms of a statutory contract the articles, and therefore the terms of the contract, can be altered by a special resolution of the company in general meeting. The articles can also be altered by informal consent of all the members of the company (*Cane* v *Jones* [1980] 1 WLR 1451 — see also CA 1985, s. 381A [CA 1989, s. 113] for the procedure for written resolutions of private companies). Because the articles are a special type of contract with statutory force and a statutory procedure for alteration the courts will not imply terms into the articles. This is where the contractual analogy stops as:

> ... the court has no jurisdiction to rectify the articles of association of a company, even if those articles do not accord with what is proved to have been the concurrent intention of the signatories of the memorandum at the moment of signature (per Dillon LJ in *Bratton Seymour Service Co. Ltd* v *Oxborough* [1992] BCLC 693 at p. 696).

There is special protection for members when alteration of the articles would involve a variation of any special rights they may have attached to their shares. This protection is to be found in various statutory and common law provisions, and also includes the general protection afforded to minority shareholders discussed more fully in chapter 10. In particular, that chapter looks at the details concerning the operation of the rule in *Foss v Harbottle*.

The articles of association are part of the 'web of contractual relationships' referred to in chapter 3 that comprise the 'contractarian model' of understanding and regulating the company. The decision in *Re Saul D. Harrison & Sons plc* [1995] 1 BCLC 14 is a good example of this model being used by the courts to assist in establishing whether or not a claim of unfairly prejudicial conduct against directors of a company was justified. In that case Hoffman LJ said (at p. 20) that:

> ... in the absence of 'something more', there is no basis for a legitimate expectation that the board and the company in general meeting will not exercise whatever powers they are given by the articles of association.

However, it can be seen from the *Bratton Seymour* case that the contractual analogy can be overridden by public policy regulatory considerations, the articles of association being public documents that are available for inspection by anyone and which therefore cannot be subject to alteration by the incorporation of implied terms. Such public policy considerations may lead to future developments whereby shareholders' agreements that affect the implementation of the articles as opposed to their content will also need public registration to be effective. At present they do not (*Russell v Northern Bank Development Corporation Ltd*).

It is important to note that, although this chapter concentrates on the enforcement of articles under the s. 14 contract, the contract also appears to confer a personal right on members to take action to prevent prospective corporate actions that are *ultra vires* because of a statutory provision (*Smith v Croft (No. 2)* [1988] Ch 114; *Precision Dippings Ltd* v *Precision Dippings*

Marketing Ltd [1986] Ch 447). Such *ultra vires* actions are not protected under the provisions of CA 1985, s. 35 [CA 1989, s. 108], as the lack of corporate capacity does not derive from deficiencies in the memorandum; it arises from statutory provisions, these being CA 1985, ss. 151–2 and 271, respectively, in the above cases.

REVISION AND RESEARCH

It is easy to get bogged down in case law surrounding the s. 14 contract. At the revision or research stage you will need to sort out the most important cases that can assist in a logical development of your s. 14 approach (see question 1).

This is also an area where you must refer to journal articles and authors who have attempted to unscrabble what is a maze of cases. In particular look at Gower's section on the s. 14 contract, Wedderburn [19571 CLJ 193 at pp. 210–15 (see also Gregory (1981) 44 MLR 526) and Goldberg (1977) 35 MLR 362 and (1985) 48 MLR 158.

Your argument around the s. 14 contract must be clearly established and this will involve an interpretation of the main authorities in the area using the cases and the articles cited above as both guides and authoritative interpretations of this difficult area of case law. Your focus of attention should always return to the content of s. 14 itself.

There is one method of revision in this area that involves using diagrams. The different arguments surrounding the s. 14 contract concern the parties to the contract and the terms of the contract. The circle in figure 5.1 encloses the terms of the contract. The parties to the contract are outside the circle. Apply the cases cited in question 1 to the diagram and the provisions of s. 14 itself. In each case:

(a)   Which party is trying to enforce the contract?
(b)   Which party is the contract being enforced against?
(c)   Which term of the contract is in dispute?

Figure 5.2 illustrates how you can use this technique to revise the enforcement of the statutory contract using *Wood* v *Odessa Waterworks Co.* (1889) 47 ChD 636, *Hickman* v *Kent or Romney Marsh Sheep-breeders' Association* [1915] 1 Ch 881 and *Rayfield* v *Hands* [1960] Ch 1. Using this technique try to revise the arguments surrounding the type of articles that a member can enforce: the 'outsider right' argument. To what extent is it necessary to study the terms of the contract (i.e., looking inside the circle) to assess whether or not the terms are enforceable and who can enforce them, or can this be established without looking at the particular terms?

Figure 5.1

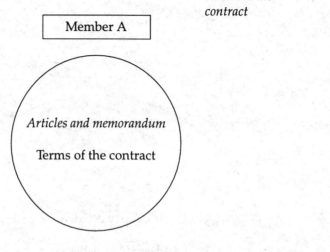

Parties to the contract

Member A

Articles and memorandum

Terms of the contract

The company

Member B

Figure 5.2

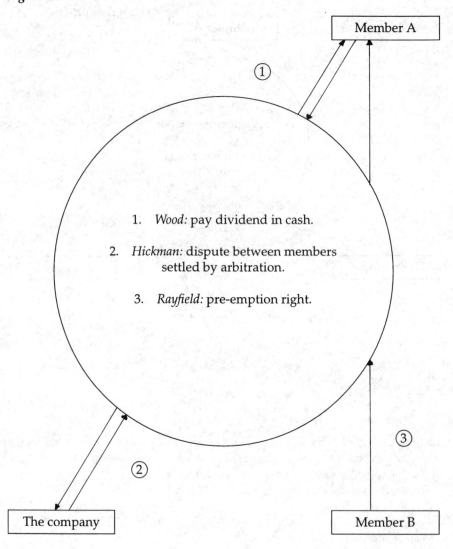

1. *Wood:* pay dividend in cash.

2. *Hickman:* dispute between members settled by arbitration.

3. *Rayfield:* pre-emption right.

Member A

The company

Member B

The alteration of articles involves both statutory and common law protection for the member and your research can be divided into analysing the various statutory provisions, their interpretation by the judiciary, and the specific common law protection afforded upon the alteration of articles. Any alteration of the rights attached to particular classes of shares, 'class rights', will require that some meetings are held, usually a class meeting and a general meeting. You will need to understand the procedures surrounding these meetings, including whether the correct number of meetings have taken place.

Another area that often occurs as an assessment question concerns contracts, such as directors' service contracts (see chapter 6), which incorporate part of the articles either expressly or impliedly, and the extent to which this affects the power to alter the articles. The cases you will need to look at include *Shuttleworth* v *Cox Bros & Co. (Maidenhead) Ltd* [1927] 2 KB 9, *Southern Foundries (1926) Ltd* v *Shirlaw* [1940] AC 701, *Read* v *Astoria Garage (Streatham) Ltd* [1952] Ch 637, and the section in Pennington on the limitations on the power of alteration of the articles.

IDENTIFYING THE QUESTION

The questions that follow include an essay question on the s. 14 contract and a problem question on the alteration of the articles. However, both these topics could appear in problem form and some assessments could even combine both these areas. How can you identify what the problem is about?

The 'Section 14 Contract'

The question will usually revolve around a director or other officer of the company, who is also a member, being given some special power or 'outsider right' which is then ignored. The answer will need to establish whether those rights can be enforced under the s. 14 contract.

These are two examples of extracts from such problems:

The articles of association of Floggit Ltd include a provision that Cautious, a shareholder and one of three directors, has a power of veto in board meetings over any contract to sell assets of the company valued over £100,000.

The articles of association of Construction Ltd are in the form of Table A except for a clause which provides that any dispute between the directors shall be referred to arbitration.

The problems would continue to establish that the veto in Floggit's case and the arbitration clause in Construction's case were ignored, and you would be asked to advise Cautious and one of the directors respectively whether they could enforce these special rights which, although they are members, are conferred on them as directors of the company (the 'outsider right' problem).

The 'Alteration of the Articles' Problem

These are less difficult to identify because the problem will have to state that the articles have been altered, although you should be alert to see if this occurs at a formal meeting or by informal agreement. Where the problem involves an alteration of class rights it will normally have to identify that there are at least two different classes of share in the company (as in the first paragraph of question 2). The problem will continue to establish the rights attached to the various classes of share and specify any alterations to those rights. The shares referred to need not be 'management' or 'ordinary' shares: they can be called 'A' shares, 'B' shares, 'preference' shares etc. Rights do not necessarily have to be attached to a particular class of shares to become class rights, but can be conferred on a person *qua* member or shareholder without the creation of a separate class of share. In *Cumbrian Newspapers Group Ltd* v *Cumberland & Westmorland Herald Newspaper & Printing Co. Ltd* [1987] Ch 1 the three rights in question were:

(a)   a pre-emption right over the defendant's ordinary shares,
(b)   rights over the allocation of the defendant's unissued shares, and
(c)   a right to appoint a director as long as the plaintiff held 10% of the defendant's ordinary shares.

Although these rights were not attached to any particular shares, it was held that they were conferred on the plaintiff as a shareholder in the defendant, the adoption of those rights in the articles being clearly linked to the plaintiff's acquisition of shares. As will be seen in question 2, there is statutory protection for class rights where those rights are 'attached to a class of shares' (CA 1985, ss. 125 and 127). Although the rights in *Cumbrian Newspapers* were not so attached, the court interpreted the phrase so as to include 'rights of any class member', another statutory phrase to be found in CA 1985, s. 17, and the plaintiff therefore fell within the statutory protection.

Once more than one class of share is identified, or where there is only one class of share but the rights are conferred on a member *qua* member as in *Cumbrian Newspapers*, look out for the alteration issue in the question. The question will also identify whether the class rights are contained in the articles (the normal practice), or in the memorandum. If the class rights are contained in the memorandum then you will need to apply CA 1985, ss. 17 and 125(5).

Problem questions in both of these areas can include other legal points, the most usual being: directors' duties and the allocation of shares for ulterior motives, restrictions on voting rights at class and general meetings, reduction of capital under CA 1985, ss. 159–81, removal of directors under CA 1985, s. 303, and the protection of minority shareholders, with particular reference to CA 1985, ss. 459–61.

QUESTION 1

'Section 14 of the Companies Act 1985 has been so overlaid with judicial interpretation that, on any count, it no longer means what it says'. Discuss.

The status of the s. 14 contract, like any other contract, needs consideration of the parties to the contract and the terms of the contract that the parties can enforce. The problems of judicial interpretation stem from these two issues and the difficulty of reconciling the statutory contract with the rule in *Foss* v *Harbottle* (1843) 2 Hare 461.

These three points, the parties to the contract, the terms of the contract and eventually the link to *Foss* v *Harbottle*, provide a plan for any answer to a s. 14 question. It will be necessary, in order to explain the judicial interpretations referred to, to illustrate how the parties and the terms have been linked together especially by Astbury J in *Hickman* v *Kent or Romney Marsh Sheep-breeders' Association* [1915] 1 Ch 881.

Any introduction should be a short paragraph which, as the answer progresses, can be broken down into its component parts. The only plan of your answer could be this first paragraph but if you feel that you need a more detailed plan to start off with you can expand on each of these three points. However, this does take up valuable time. It is important to let the examiner know at the beginning that you understand what the question is aiming at and that you are about to head off in the right direction.

How do you identify the three main points? During research or revision it is useful to break down fairly complex issues, like the s. 14 contract, into their component parts. You certainly do not have sufficient time to do this in the examination, and this sort of revision exercise can be useful.

Section 14 provides that the memorandum and articles shall 'bind the company and its members' as if they 'had been signed and sealed by each member'. The section does not state that the company will be treated as having signed and sealed the agreement. Prior to the Joint Stock Companies Act 1856 there was no need to state that the company should be treated as signing the deed of settlement that was registered instead of the modern memorandum and articles, because the deed was signed by the trustees for the company as well as by each member. Identification of the parties to the contract was therefore no problem. However, because s. 14 does not specifically identify the company as having signed the contract, there have been conflicting judicial attitudes to whether the company is a party to the statutory contract, although the Lords have always held that the company is a party as in *Quin & Axtens Ltd* v *Salmon* [1909] AC 442 (cf. dicta in *Eley* v *Positive Government Security Life Assurance Co. Ltd* (1876) 1 ExD 88).

The first point of dispute therefore revolves around whether the company is a party to the statutory contract. It is always useful to cite the relevant parts of the section in a question if at all possible; you do not need all of it, only the relevant part.

The statutory contract is therefore a contract which can be enforced between the member and the company (*Wood* v *Odessa Waterworks Co.* (1889) 42 ChD 636, *Hickman*), and between the individual members (*Rayfield* v *Hands* [1960] Ch 1). You can illustrate the parties to the contract and the terms of the contract by referring to these three authorities in a fairly concise manner. In an examination you do not have time to dwell on the facts of cases; even in an assessment answer you should try to extract the factor that is relevant to the issue being discussed, in this case the parties to the contract and the terms of the contract. The ability to select the relevant issue within a case illustrates a sufficient knowledge of the case as well as a good use of authorities.

The next step is to look at the terms of the contract (i.e., the articles themselves) that can be enforced. There are three stages involved:

(a)   What does s. 14 state?
(b)   The proposition that a member can only enforce those articles that affect his rights personally as a member.
(c)   The connection between s. 14 and the rule in *Foss* v *Harbottle*.

Section 14

Section 14 states that the statutory contract applies to 'all the provisions of the memorandum and of the articles'. The statement that the section 'no longer means what it says' stems from judicial interpretation that has turned 'all' into 'some of'.

In many answers on the s. 14 contract, s. 14 itself gets forgotten. The question makes specific reference to s. 14 and it is clearly necessary to refer to the actual provisions although this would apply to any discussion of the s. 14 contract whether or not the section is expressly mentioned in the question. This reference to the specific provisions of the section can then be contrasted with the judicial treatment of the statutory contract. This is where the problems start, because of the apparent inconsistencies between the cases and the difficulty of reconciling any interpretation of these cases with the provisions of s. 14 itself.

Which Articles Can a Member Enforce?

There are two main sides to this argument. Any discussion in this area must include *Eley* v *Positive Government Security Life Assurance Co. Ltd*. In *Eley*, Mr Eley, a member of the Positive Government Security Life Assurance Co. Ltd and, according to a clause in the articles, its solicitor for life, tried to enforce the clause and brought an action as the solicitor named in the clause, relying on the s. 14 contract. As the solicitor mentioned in the clause he was a stranger to the contract and was not suing as the member who was a party to the contract (*qua* member). Yet the case was apparently decided on the ground that the article concerned him as an outsider. i.e., as the solicitor mentioned in the article, and not as a member, and therefore could not be enforced. Astbury J appeared to confirm this in *Hickman* concerning a term that disputes between members shall be settled by arbitration, although Gregory has commented in his article (1981) 44 MLR 526 that Astbury J only reached his conclusion to avoid dicta in *Eley* that the company was not a party to the statutory contract.

Nevertheless, *Hickman* is a leading case supporting the argument that the statutory contract only applies in respect of the rights and duties of members, and that any other provisions do not fall with the terms of the s. 14 contract and are 'outsider rights'. As Astbury J commented in *Hickman* [1915] 1 Ch 881 at p. 900:

> ... no right merely purporting to be given by an article to a person, whether a member or not, in a capacity other than that of a member, as, for instance, as solicitor, promoter, director, can be enforced against the company.

These 'outsider rights' in the articles or memorandum cannot therefore be enforced under the s. 14 contract. The problem with these cases is that they confuse the parties to the contract and the terms of the contract: the term of the contract that affects X as a solicitor, director or promoter cannot be enforced by X, even though he is a member of the company, because in those capacities he is a stranger to the contract. Thus the parties to the contract have to be determined by looking at the content of the terms of the contract, the articles and memorandum, not 'all' of which can be enforced, although s. 14 provides otherwise.

There is a difference between the statement made by Astbury J and merely construing the articles. For example, if there was an article which provides that disputes between members shall be settled by arbitration (as in *Hickman*) and two members of the company crashed into each other in their cars, you could construe the term of the contract as not applying to that particular situation; but that does not affect their status as parties to the contract (see *Beattie* v *E. & F Beattie Ltd* [1938] Ch 708). If an article specifically states that X shall be solicitor for life why can't X sue as a member and a party to the contract to enforce that term of the contract? Section 14 applies to 'all' of the articles not 'some'.

The 'outsider right' argument can be supported by reference to just *Eley*, *Hickman* and a brief citation of *Beattie*. There are other authorities, but in this area in particular you must be careful not to let the authorities you know control you; you should control the authorities and use them to advance the arguments you want to make. It is very easy to get bogged down in a welter of case law on this issue and to forget about the legal points that these cases should be either supportive or destructive of. The other side to the argument will involve considering *Quin & Axtens Ltd* v *Salmon* and *Re Richmond Gate Property Co. Ltd* [1965] 1 WLR 335, contrasting them with the authorities already put forward. Again, you can get away with using only two cases to illustrate this argument.

In *Quin & Axtens* a clause in the articles gave the managing director a veto over certain board decisions. This is the term of the statutory contract that is in dispute in the case. The managing director sued successfully in his capacity as a member, and therefore a party to the statutory contract, to have the veto enforced under the statutory contract, even though the article affected him in his 'outsider capacity' as a managing director. Allied to this Lords' decision is *Re Richmond Gate Property Co. Ltd*. The term in the articles provided that the managing director should receive such remuneration as was to be determined by the board. The board did not make a determination and the managing director, also a member, was bound by the statutory contract: as no resolution had been passed he would get nothing. The article affected the managing director in his 'outsider capacity' yet it was enforced against him. In this case the events concerned an executive director. Under Table A, art. 84:

> Any such appointment . . . may be made upon such terms as the directors determine and they may remunerate any such director for his services as they think fit.

The same principle could also be applied to an ordinary director's remuneration, Table A, art. 82, providing that:

> The directors shall be entitled to such remuneration as the company may by ordinary resolution determine.

Presumably if the company does not pass an ordinary resolution then a director who is also a member cannot claim any fees for past services because he is bound by the statutory contract to get only what the company by ordinary resolution resolve, which is in this case nothing.

Wedderburn turns the case of *Re Richmond Gate Property Co. Ltd* around to argue that a member can enforce any article as long as he sues *qua* member (i.e., as the person who is party to the contract), whether the terms of the contract (the articles) affect him as a member or not. However, Gower feels that this ignores 'weighty dicta' and the 'leading cases' of *Eley* and *Beattie*. Goldberg uses a different argument. He argues that a member suing *qua* member has only got the right to have the affairs of the company conducted by the body stated in the Companies Acts, articles or memorandum, whether or not 'outsider rights' are affected. For example, in *Quin & Axtens* the appropriate body to exercise the affairs of the company was the managing director and therefore the article could be enforced as long as a member sued *qua* member. Gower suggests that Goldberg's analysis is nowhere near what s. 14 actually says and puts too much of a gloss on the section. Much of the academic argument concerns how far the exact wording of the section can be strayed from, not whether it should be. Gower calls for either a review of all the relevant authorities by the House of Lords or a statutory revision of s. 14, expressing a preference for the latter given that on the present wording it is difficult to see how any interpretation could cure all of the section's imperfections (Gower, *Principles of Modern Company Law*, 5th ed., p. 288).

Any answer should therefore refer back to the statement in the question after a tour of the academics' view of the various judicial interpretations of s. 14. If you read articles throughout your course then cite them in the assessment, ensuring that there is a balance between the cases cited and the academic opinion on them. But remember when reading articles or cases that any citation, particularly in an examination, is going to be, of necessity, brief. You need to be able to digest the main arguments and facts in a short précis form. When revising for an examination or writing an assessment paper with a word limit, this will probably be shortened even further and what you recall, or are able in to recall the time allowed, in an examination will be shorter still.

The Connection between Foss v Harbottle and the Section 14 Contract

The third point that remains to be discussed is the rule in *Foss* v *Harbottle* and its link to the s. 14 contract. As we have already seen s. 14 provides that 'all' the articles fall within the statutory contract. The rule in *Foss* v *Harbottle* provides that where a wrong is done to a company, the company is the proper plaintiff. Some breaches of the articles are wrongs which the company must put right either by ratification of the breach or litigation. The company, one party to the statutory contract, can thus enforce (or choose not to enforce) all the terms of the contract, but the other party may not be able to because of the rule in *Foss* v *Harbottle*. It is therefore necessary to establish which terms of the contract fall within the scope of *Foss* v *Harbottle* and which do not (i.e., which terms the member can enforce and which can only be enforced, or chosen not to be enforced, by the company). Breaches of the articles that are ratifiable by ordinary resolution of the company in general meeting are matters that the company can rectify and perhaps do not fall within the statutory contract although an assessment of which specific articles this applies to is not easy (see *Pender* v *Lushington* (1877) 6 ChD 70, cf. *MacDougall* v *Gardiner* (1876) 1 ChD 13 and chapter 10).

Summary

Any answer to a s. 14 question needs to confront the uncertainties head-on. The contractual argument, with reference to the terms of the statutory contract and the parties to the contract, provides a useful mechanism for both understanding what the s. 14 debate is all about, as well as providing a 'thread' that runs through your answer. You would boost your grade by making a link to the 'contractarian model' of understanding and regulating companies by referring to *Bratton Seymour Service Co. Ltd* v *Oxborough* [1992] BCLC 693 and *Re Saul D. Harrison & Sons plc* [1995] 1 BCLC 14 as well as the article by Riley (1995) 58 MLR 595 referred to in chapter 3. The question itself should not be forgotten and constant references to the specific provisions of s. 14 provide another 'thread' that can surface at various points in any answer.

The different judicial interpretations stem from the linking of the parties to the contract by reference to the actual terms of the contract, and the aligning of the scope of the statutory contract with the rule in *Foss* v *Harbottle*, which is discussed further in chapter 10. The wider interpretation of the contractual remedy certainly assists the protection of minorities, despite the increased protection given by CA 1985, s. 459. However, it might clarify matters if s. 14 was amended to fall clearly in line with one interpretation so as to sweep away any judicial and academic uncertainties. It would certainly assist those studying company law.

QUESTION 2

Alpha Ltd has a nominal capital of £300,000 of which the following has been issued: 150,000 ordinary shares and 30,000 preference shares. Each share has a nominal value of £1. The preference shareholders are entitled under the articles of the company to a cumulative dividend of 5 per cent, priority over the ordinary shareholders as to return of capital on a winding up and a right to participate in surplus assets on a winding up. Each ordinary and preference share has one vote.

A, B and C are directors of the company and between them hold 90 per cent of the ordinary shares. X and Y hold all of the preference shares. A, B and C are jealous of the preference shareholders' rights. They pay all dividends accruing to the preference shares and in a general meeting vote for the company to allot 100,000 bonus preference shares of the same class as the existing preference shares to the ordinary shareholders.

Several months later the company by special resolution decides to reduce capital and replace all preference shares with the same nominal amount of unsecured loan stock at 7 per cent redeemable 1996–2001. The company does not intend to compensate the preference shareholders for loss of their potential right of participation in surplus assets on a winding up. The company has reserves of £4 million.

At a separate class meeting of preference shareholders the change is approved by extraordinary resolution carried by the votes of A, B and C who vote in favour of the change because of its advantages to them as ordinary shareholders.

Advise X and Y who voted against the change.

This is a long question and you need to go through the individual paragraphs carefully. The main issue can be spotted in *the first paragraph*. There are two classes of shares. The 'special' rights attached to the preference shares are: dividend rights, return of capital, share in surplus assets and one vote per share (is the vote a 'special' right as it is the same as the ordinary shares?). These rights are contained in the articles not the memorandum — this is an important point to note as the location of class rights does affect their vulnerability to alteration.

On reading the first paragraph and establishing that it is laying down rights in the articles attached to classes of shares, it is highly probable that the main issue in the question is going to concern some alteration of those class rights.

The second paragraph gives the shareholding position before and after the bonus issue reducing X and Y's preference shareholding to less than 25 per cent of the total number of preference shares and diluting their overall voting rights. Has there been a 'variation' which would involve some statutory protection and class meetings? Have the directors broken their fiduciary duties?

The third and fourth paragraphs involve the reduction of share capital by the abolition of the preference shares. A general meeting and class meeting have approved the reduction. This again involves consideration of: (a) whether there has been a 'variation', (b) any statutory protection that might be available, and (c) any restrictions on voting rights that might be imposed when changing the articles.

Note carefully that it is X and Y you are asked to advise.

If you place these issues into some sort of order, you can develop a plan:

(a)   An introduction on the nature of class rights attached to shares and the main issues involved in the question.

(b)   Identification of the class rights and their alteration.

(c)   The bonus issue: has there been a 'variation'? Was there a breach of directors' duties (*Re Smith & Fawcett Ltd* [1942] Ch 304)? An application of CA 1985, s. 459.

(d)   The reduction of capital: has there been a 'variation'? Does CA 1985, s. 127 apply? Was the alteration of the articles made bona fide for the benefit of the company? Are there any restrictions on voting rights when altering the articles?

(e)   Conclusion.

The main part of the question is aimed at an application of material on the alteration of the articles and the protection of class rights. Other issues do arise, the most relevant to the question being the duties owed by the directors when they allotted the bonus shares, and CA 1985, s. 459. In the time allowed and under examination pressure you may be unable to identify all the issues; the important thing is to identify the main one and deal with that effectively, and preferably to make that identification known to the examiner in your first paragraph.

The Main Issues

A share gains its value from the rights that are attached to it. These rights are largely contractual and are to be found in the company's constitution, in practice, as in this problem, usually in the articles. These contractual rights are alterable by one of the parties, the company, either by special resolution under CA 1985, s. 9, or by the informal acquiescence of all the members (*Cane v Jones* [1980] 1 WLR 1451), subject to the restriction that any alteration must be made bona fide for the benefit of the company as a whole (*Allen v Gold Reefs of West Africa Ltd* [1900] 1 Ch 656). Class rights also have some statutory protection (CA 1985, ss. 125 and 127) as well as the general statutory protection offered to minorities in CA 1985, s. 459. Any introduction should indicate that these main issues have been identified and can act as a short plan for your answer.

The Class Rights in the Question

Table A, art. 2, provides that subject to the Companies Acts and 'without prejudice to any rights attached to any existing shares' that 'any share may be issued with such rights or restrictions as the company may by ordinary resolution determine'. This question does concern the possible prejudicing of existing shareholders' rights by the issue of new shares as well as the total abrogation of those rights by the abolition of the preference shares.

Somewhere in the answer the class rights and the possible 'variations' have got to be analysed. The 30,000 preference shares have class rights to a dividend, return of capital and a share in any surplus assets. They also have a class right to one vote which, although the same as the ordinary shares, is still a class right (*Re Stewart Precision Carburettor Co.* (1912) 28 TLR 335). CA 1985, ss. 125 and 127, refer to 'rights attached to a class of shares' and this undoubtedly applies to any rights which are conferred on one class of shares in contrast to the other classes or class of shares. In *Cumbrian Newspapers Group Ltd v Cumberland & Westmorland Herald Newspaper & Printing Co. Ltd* [1987] Ch 1 this phrase was interpreted as being synonymous with 'rights of any class of member'. It is submitted by both Gower and Boyle and Birds that the basic rights attached to shares, relating to dividends, voting and return of capital on a winding up, should also be seen as class rights even though they might not differ between the classes. In allotting bonus preference shares to the ordinary shareholders (see Table A, art. 110), X and Y might argue that their rights have been affected, their proportion of preference shares having fallen to less than 25 per cent, along with an overall decrease in their voting power, possible share of surplus assets and return of capital although, as will be seen *post*, this could be construed as an alteration of the enjoyment of their rights rather than as an alteration of the rights themselves. The later replacement of the preference shares with loan stock could also be seen to abrogate X and Y's class rights and give rise to some statutory or other legal redress.

You should identify these two separate events that have affected X and Y's preference shares. This then leaves the way clear to apply the substantive law to these events always ensuring that reference is made back to the issues and parties in the problem where it is appropriate; do not divorce the substantive discussion from the facts established in the question itself.

'Variation' of Class Rights

Prior to the Table A introduced in 1985, most articles that you would have come across in examination questions would have contained a modification-of-rights clause, because such a clause was included in the 1948 Table A (art. 4). Companies incorporated prior to 1985 may still have articles that contain such a clause, whereby rights attached to any class of shares can only be varied by an extraordinary resolution at a separate meeting of the holders of the class of shares. If the company's articles did not contain such a provision then CA 1985, s. 125, would operate to impose the same procedural requirement.

Table A no longer contains a modification-of-rights clause. Therefore any company with articles in the form of the 1985 version of Table A, and we can assume that Alpha Ltd is such a company, will be required to follow the procedure laid down in CA 1985, s. 125(2). Rights attached to shares, otherwise than by the memorandum, can only be varied if:

(a) the holders of three-quarters in nominal value of the issued shares of that class consent in writing to the variation; or

(b) an extraordinary resolution passed at a separate general meeting of the holders of that class sanctions the variation; and

(c) any requirement (howsoever imposed) in relation to the variation of those rights is complied with to the extent that it is not comprised in paragraphs (a) and (b) above. For example, the rights conferred on the class of shares under art. 2 of Table A could themselves include a provision as to the procedure to be followed on a variation of those rights.

However, these procedures only apply where there is a 'variation' of class rights and you need to establish whether or not a 'variation' has taken place. In the question the bonus issue reduced the surplus assets that the preference shareholders could participate in on a winding up, but this was held not to be a 'variation' in *Dimbula Valley (Ceylon) Tea Co. Ltd* v *Laurie* [1961] Ch 353. Although *Dimbula Valley* is directly on the point raised in the question, you might not know this case; this is not fatal to a successful answer. As long as you know the main authority in a given area and apply it to the question you will be awarded marks. The main authority in this area is *White* v *Bristol Aeroplane Co. Ltd* [1953] Ch 65, where a distinction was made between only altering the enjoyment of class rights by issuing new shares and thereby decreasing the effectiveness of the existing voting shares (not a 'variation'), and directly varying the rights by, for example, increasing the number of votes per share (a 'variation'). The *White* case involved, as in the problem, an issue of bonus preference shares to the ordinary shareholders although the same would apply if preference shares were issued so as to affect the ordinary shareholders (see *Re John Smith's Tadcaster Brewery Co. Ltd* [1953] Ch 308).

There are many cases on the interpretation of 'variation'. You need to cite and apply the authority that establishes the legal principle (*White*). Any others are a gloss on your answer, which could earn a higher grade but the omission of which is not fatal to a good answer. Of course, if there are authorities that seem to fit into the facts of the problem and you know of them, then it is appropriate that they be cited. In an assessment your research should have uncovered those authorities. There will often be some difference between the facts of the problem and the reported authorities in that area and if possible you should indicate that difference but establish nevertheless whether the general principles enunciated can be applied to the particular facts of the problem.

The issue of bonus shares in the question does not necessitate a class meeting as there has been no 'variation' of rights and CA 1985, s. 127, does not apply for the same reason. However, the bonus issue is made for reasons of jealousy, and the directors could have broken the fiduciary duty they owe to the company to act 'bona fide in what they consider — not what a court may consider — is in the interests of the company, and not for any collateral purpose' (per Lord Greene MR in *Re Smith & Fawcett Ltd* [1942] Ch 304 at p. 306). This is an objective review by the courts and it may be difficult to prove the primary purpose of the allotment, especially as the allotment of bonus shares is used for a legitimate purpose of capitalising reserves which were substantial in Alpha's case although a large amount remains outstanding. Despite this, the courts may intervene if there is clearly some ulterior primary purpose (see *Howard Smith Ltd* v *Ampol Petroleum Ltd* [1974] AC 821; see also *Brady* v *Brady* [1989] AC 755, discussed in chapter 8, for an analysis of the difficulties of implementing a 'purpose' test).

In Alpha's case there is clearly some personal interest with the shares being allotted to A, B and C. Where possible make references to the details of the problem and do not forget that you are advising X and Y; so advise as to the best possible options. For example, directors' duties are owed to the company which may pursue any remedy either directly or by a derivative action started by X and Y. However, it may be easier for X and Y to ask for the allotment of shares to be set aside under CA 1985, s. 459. This is a question on class rights and the protection available to X and Y, who are minority shareholders. Therefore, CA 1985, s. 459, needs to be included (see chapter 10).

Reduction of Capital

This section deals with the consequences of the reduction of capital. Just because you see a reduction of capital occurring in a question do not rush into all the provisions first introduced by the CA 1981 (see now CA 1985, ss. 159–81, dealt with in chapter 8); it is the consequences of the reduction, not the reduction itself, that is important in this question. Although time is scarce in an examination room, it does pay to read the question carefully to ensure that you are not side-tracked by taking out of context the appearance of a phrase in a question. Sometimes the examiner will include a clear indication that a certain area is not to be discussed. For example, a question could state that:

Bold Ltd wished to increase its share capital. It resolves, through regularly conducted meetings, to increase the share capital to £2.2 million, the whole of the increase to be issued as one million £1 ordinary shares. In order to preserve the voting strength of the 'management' shares, the articles were amended by special resolution to increase their weighting from eight to nine votes per share.

The reference to 'regularly conducted meetings' indicates that the examiner does not want you to look at the provisions relating to such meetings to, in this case, increase capital (see CA 1985, s. 121). Look out for the phrase in other areas as well; for example, in general meetings where directors are dismissed, as well as other phrases or statements that indicate that you are not expected to raise particular issues. In question 2 you should only briefly raise the procedures required for a proper reduction of capital, including confirmation by the court under CA 1985, ss. 135–41. In your assessment of whether any procedural points are raised in questions like this, it is important to remember that private companies can pass 'written resolutions' (CA 1985, s. 381A [CA 1989, s. 113]; see chapter 12).

The reduction of capital by repaying the preference shares (under either ss. 135–41 or 159–81 of CA 1985) could be regarded as a variation of rights, because not all of the rights that would be available on a winding up have been met (i.e., participation in surplus assets). You can therefore distinguish Alpha Ltd, from the situation in *Scottish Insurance Corporation Ltd* v *Wilsons & Clyde Coal Co. Ltd* [1949] AC 462. However, the abolition of preference shares with participating dividends was held not to be a 'variation' in *Re Saltdean Estate Co. Ltd* [1968] 1 WLR 1844, now approved by the House of Lords in *House of Fraser plc* v *ACGE Investments Ltd* [1987] AC 387 in the absence of any special provisions in the articles protecting preference shareholders as in *Re Northern Engineering Industries plc* [1994] BCLC 704. Participation in surplus assets could be treated in the same way, although Alpha Ltd has not risked this and has called a class meeting.

This is another example of where you need to distinguish authorities from the facts of the problem. It is a useful application of a common law technique because it forces you to analyse the facts in the problem and illustrates detailed knowledge of specific cases without having to write long segments setting out the detailed facts of those cases. A good application of this technique will raise the grade that you receive.

CA 1985, s. 127, allows holders of a class of shares to apply to the court to have any 'variation' of their rights set aside on the grounds that the 'variation' would 'unfairly prejudice' the shareholders of the class. However, for s. 127 to apply there are some conditions that must be satisfied, and this is best dealt with by splitting s. 127 into its component parts and applying X and Y's situation to each of these jurisdictional points. For revision purposes it is also easier to remember a section of a statute if you divide it up into separate parts, e.g.:

(a)   X and Y must constitute at least 15 per cent of the class and have dissented at the meeting (which they do and did).

(b)   They must apply within 21 days of the resolution being passed.

(c)   There must be a provision in the memorandum or articles authorising any variation of rights. If Alpha Ltd's articles are in the form of Table A, and do not contain a modification-of-rights clause then CA 1985, s. 125(2), will apply and also s. 127 (by virtue of CA 1985, s. 127(1)(b)).

(d) There must have been a 'variation' (which includes 'abrogation') of X and Y's class rights.

If these conditions are satisfied then the court will go on to assess in all the circumstances whether there has been unfair prejudice to X and Y, and the court has the power to disallow or confirm the variation.

This treatment of s. 127 has the added advantage of requiring you to bring in a discussion of CA 1985, s. 125. It also links into your previous discussion as to what constitutes a 'variation' of class rights.

The rights attached to the preference shares are in the articles, which have been altered under CA 1985, s. 9. Any alteration must be made bona fide for the benefit of the company (*Allen v Gold Reefs of West Africa Ltd* [1900] 1 Ch 656). In this question does the alteration benefit the company or A, B and C? There are two main tests which you will need to apply to the question. Looking at what the individual hypothetical member thinks, as suggested by Evershed MR in *Greenhalgh* v *Arderne Cinemas Ltd* [1951] Ch 286, is not of much use when there are two self-interested groups, although it was suggested that discrimination between the majority and minority might be grounds for intervention. The test in *Shuttleworth* v *Cox Bros & Co. (Maidenhead) Ltd* [1927] 2 KB 9 that the courts should not interfere if there are grounds on which a reasonable man would come to the same decision is perhaps illustrative of the judicial reluctance to intervene in the management decisions of companies as these have been delegated, through the contract in the articles, to the board of directors.

The judiciary have not been so reluctant to intervene to impose restraints on the voting rights of members, and an application of *Re Holders Investment Trust Ltd* [1971] 1 WLR 583 could help X and Y to get the resolution passed at the class meeting set aside. Similarly, if X and Y were able to establish a fiduciary relationship between themselves and the directors then *Clemens* v *Clemens Bros Ltd* [1976] 2 All ER 268 could be applied to the two votes at general meeting. Do not forget to include a brief reference to the possible protection afforded to minority shareholders by CA 1985, s. 459, which in practice could be more useful to X and Y because it does not require proof of a 'variation' as does CA 1985, s. 127, although the test of 'unfair prejudice' is the same in both sections.

Conclusion

Lawyers are prone to informing clients what they should have done to protect themselves after the event, and this mechanism is also a useful tool for winding up your answer to any problem in a concluding paragraph.

For example, although X and Y have some redress either by invoking CA 1985, ss. 127 or 459, or the common law protection afforded on the alteration of articles, you could make some comment in a conclusion to the effect that X and Y could have protected their rights by drafting them so that they are in proportion to the rights of the other shares or any new issues, and this should also include protection on a capital reduction. Rights expressed in this way and contained in the memorandum with no provision for alteration are virtually impregnable as they can only be varied if 'all the members of the company' agree (CA 1985, s. 125(5)). They could have also protected their position by entering into an appropriately worded shareholders' agreement with A, B and C which would prevent them from voting to take action that was detrimental to the preference shareholders.

Any answer to this sort of problem should include at least some of the ancillary issues involved (e.g. CA 1985, s. 459, directors' duties) while not forgetting that the main issue around which the others revolve is the alteration of articles and class rights. You can include other cases such as *Greenhalgh* v *Arderne Cinemas Ltd* and *Re Mackenzie & Co. Ltd* [1916] 2 Ch 450 to illustrate the very narrow interpretation of 'variation'. You can go into detail on the test of 'bona fide for the benefit of the company'. However, a decision has to be made somewhere whether to sacrifice detail and what can be seen as repetition through the citation of different authorities relating to marks that have already been awarded, for a more complete answer that never forgets the issues raised in the problem and relates to those issues throughout.

FURTHER READING

Drury, R. R., 'The relative nature of a shareholder's right to enforce the company contract' [1986] CLJ 219.

Goldberg, G. D., 'The enforcement of outsider rights under section 20(1) of the Companies Act 1948' (1972) 35 MLR 362.

Goldberg, G. D., 'The controversy on the section 20 contract revisited' (1985) 48 MLR 158.

Gregory, Roger, 'The section 20 contract' (1981) 44 MLR 526.

Wedderburn, K. W., 'Shareholders' rights and the rule in *Foss* v *Harbottle*' [1957] CLJ 194, [1958] CLJ 93.

6 DIRECTORS' DUTIES

INTRODUCTION

The law imposes various duties upon directors to ensure that they perform the functions of their office correctly. Most of the cases on this topic provide examples of situations where directors have failed to act in accordance with the duties imposed on them by law. But don't get the wrong impression; not all directors are rogues out to steal the company's assets, only some of them. It is important to understand the nature of these duties and the strictness with which the law ensures they are adhered to. It is equally important to appreciate some of the wider issues relating to the governance of corporations. The term 'corporate governance' was examined by the Cadbury Committee Report on Financial Aspects of Corporate Governance (May 1992), which has suggested reforms in the law relating to the way in which directors and managers are held accountable for their actions and, in particular, greater involvement by independent non-executive directors in the management of companies. Some of these suggestions and their implications are discussed further in chapter 12.

Nature of the Office of Director

In many ways a director is regarded as a trustee of the company and this is borne out by the fact that many of their duties have developed from the law of trusts. However, in reality you should only regard a director as a quasi-trustee because there are fundamental differences between the two functions. The director is obliged to speculate the company's property in order to make a profit for the company. The trustee on the other hand is severely restricted as to the type of investments he can make (see Trustee Investments Act 1961).

In some ways the director is regarded as an agent of the company because his function is to bring the company and third parties into contractual relationships. However, the extent to which directors are subject to 'control' by the company is part of the debate on corporate governance.

It will also be important to distinguish between executive and non-executive directors when examining the precise nature of the duty owed by a particular director to the company.

Executive Directors

Most modern sets of company articles provide that the formal decision-making role of directors will be performed only at board meetings. Because such boards, particularly in the case of large companies, meet infrequently, it is impossible for the day-to-day management of the company's affairs to be carried out by the board. Consequently most companies' articles provide that authority to conduct the business of the company is delegated to one or more managing or executive directors. The standard article appointing such a person to office is Table A, art. 84. Executive or managing directors are usually employed on separate contracts of employment.

In this respect they are to be regarded as employees and will have rights under the employment legislation if they are unfairly dealt with by the company (see *Trussed Steel Concrete Co. Ltd* v *Green* [1946] Ch 115 and cf. *Parsons* v *Albert J. Parsons & Sons Ltd* [1979] IRLR 117). You must distinguish between a contract of service and a contract for services. A contract of service is a contract whereby the director is employed by the company on a full-time basis. A contract for services is a contract whereby the director is employed to do a specific job or in a consultancy capacity and is not considered a full-time employee. It is sometimes difficult to distinguish clearly between a contract of service and a contract *for* services. Some important guidelines on this point were laid down by the Employment Appeal Tribunal in *Eaton* v *Robert Eaton Ltd* [1988] ICR 302 (discussed in (1988) 9 Co Law 187). Also note that copies of directors' service contracts have to be kept at the company's registered office or principal place of business (CA 1985, s. 318).

In addition remember that in small private companies the directors, employees and shareholders are usually the same people (as in *Lee* v *Lee's Air Farming Ltd* [1961] AC 12). The relevance of directors' fiduciary duties must be questioned in companies of this type. It is unlikely that shareholders are ever going to bring action against themselves for a breach of fiduciary duty.

Non-executive Directors

In recent years there has been a recognition of the need for boards which comprise a large number of executive directors to be counterbalanced by the appointment of experienced, knowledgeable yet independent individuals as non-executive directors.

The role of such non-executive directors varies. In quoted companies they act as an internal self-regulating mechanism providing the main and perhaps the sole membership of the board's audit committee and the remuneration committee. In small and medium-sized companies their role can vary considerably from the protection of a specific shareholder's or venture capitalist's interest to the injection of an external influence on executive directors stuck in the daily grind of running the business. They can also be valuable listeners to executive directors who have grievances about their boss, the managing director, who is also chairman and majority shareholder. Non-executive directors have less to lose where there is friction on the board and are more able to speak freely. In all cases non-executive directors are, like all other directors, involved in the strategic direction of the company.

The committee on the Financial Aspects of Corporate Governance under the chairmanship of Sir Adrian Cadbury made a number of recommendations on the appointment and role of non-executive directors in its final report in December 1992. In particular it recommended that:

(a)   The board should include non-executive directors of sufficient calibre and number for their views to carry significant weight in the board's decisions (para. 1.3).

(b)   Non-executive directors should bring an independent judgment to bear on issues of strategy, performance, resources, including key appointments, and standards of conduct (para. 2.1).

(c)   The majority should be independent of management and free from any business or other relationship which could materially interfere with the exercise of their independent judgment, apart from their fees and shareholding. Their fees should reflect the time which they commit to the company (para. 2.2).

(d)   Non-executive directors should be appointed for specified terms and reappointment should not be automatic (para. 2.3).

(e)   Non-executive directors should be selected through a formal process and both this process and their appointment should be a matter for the board as a whole (para. 2.4).

It is clear from what has been said above that the role of the non-executive director is envisaged to be a very different one from that of an executive director. It follows from this that his duties may be interpreted in a more restricted manner by the courts than those ascribed to executive directors. However, in *Daniels* v *Anderson* (1995) 13 ACLC 614, the New South Wales Court of Appeal considered that the first instance judge had been 'too soft' in stating that non-executive directors had a lower standard of duties compared to executive directors although, 'it would be unreasonable to expect every director to have equal knowledge and experience of every aspect of the company's activities' (per Clarke, Shelter JJA at pp. 662–3).

The Board of Directors

Chapter 12 illustrates that the board of directors is one of three organs that control the company. In fact most of the company's powers of management are vested in the board of directors. The board will either exercise these powers collectively or delegate some or all of them to a managing director appointed by them. The board of directors is theoretically the most powerful organ in the company's management structure. It is obviously important that the law ensures that these powers are exercised correctly and are not abused by the directors. This chapter examines the checks and balances that exist in the law to ensure that the company's powers are exercised competently, for its benefit and not for the personal benefit of its directors.

MAIN ISSUES

Directors owe their company two fundamental duties. These are:

(a)   A duty of care and skill.
(b)   Fiduciary duties.

Duties of Care and Skill

This aspect of the law relating to directors stands in complete contrast to the way in which fiduciary duties are imposed. The standard of care owed by a director to his company is a very low one and his duties in this respect are not onerous when compared with fiduciary duties. Essay questions will sometimes ask you to discuss the standard of care owed by a director to his company. Why is the duty so light? The reasons are historical. At one time a directorship was little more than a passive office, which at most required the director to attend occasional board meetings. Many of these directors were titled men who sat on a company's board in a figure-head capacity and for no better reason than to pass the time they had on their hands. Now they are MPs! In such circumstances they did not treat the office as full-time employment and the law did not see fit to impose duties of an onerous nature on them (see *Re Cardiff Savings Bank, Marquis of Bute's Case* [1892] 2 Ch 100).

A director of this type was only expected to display such skill as he happened to possess. So what happened if he was an 'amiable lunatic'? Basically the company just had to put up with him or dismiss him. They would find it difficult to bring a successful action for negligence. But times are changing, and in *Daniels* v *Anderson* the Chief Executive was held liable in negligence arising from a major loss incurred on a foreign exchange transaction. The non-executive directors escaped liablity.

Fortunately few 'amiable lunatics', ornaments or 'dummy directors' remain in the large public company. They have been replaced by a body of professional managers who are usually highly trained specialists, e.g., accountants, lawyers, economists, etc. What is the position of today's professional manager? The courts have in recent years displayed a different attitude to professional managers and expect them to display a standard of care and skill one would normally associate with a person with that particular qualification, although they were very slow to recognise that professional managers should display a higher duty of care (see *Harold Holdsworth & Co. (Wakefield) Ltd* v *Caddies* [1955] 1 WLR 352). Why were they reluctant to recognise this? It was probably due to the well-recognised judicial attitude of non-interference in matters requiring economic or business judgment (this is almost certain to have been one of the reasons behind the rule in *Foss* v *Harbottle* (1843) 2 Hare 461).

The law relating to duties of skill and care was discussed by Romer J in *Re City Equitable Fire Insurance Co. Ltd* [1925] Ch 407 who laid down three principles which are accepted as representing the law in this area. This is the most important case on this aspect of directors' duties and should be included in your revision programme. Also note the decision of the Court of Appeal in *Multinational Gas & Petrochemical Co.* v *Multinational Gas & Petrochemical Services Ltd* [1983] Ch 258, where the court held that although the directors had been negligent they had acted with the concurrence of the shareholders. Thus the shareholders could not afterwards seek to make them liable as they must be taken to have adopted the actions of the directors, but this is only possible provided there is no fraud on the minority (*Daniels* v *Daniels* [1978] Ch 406). The whole issue of the enforcement of duties of care and skill has been thoroughly reconsidered in an article by Finch (1992) 55 MLR 179. Finch argues that the law needs to be improved to check incompetent directors and calls for the use of s. 459 actions against negligent directors as well as a statute-based derivative action 'allowing public company shareholders to act in the company's name for breach of duties owed to the company'. Finch feels that the whole of the law on negligent directors needs to be reformulated on fiduciary duty principles which are owed to shareholders, allowing them to enforce the duty on suffering direct loss. In any discussions on the duties of care and skill you will need to consider these suggestions and assess their suitability and likely impact on the law in this area.

Fiduciary Duties

Duty to exercise powers bona fide in the best interests of the company

This forms the basis of the fiduciary duties imposed on the director. The classic statement on the nature of this duty is to be found in Lord Greene's statement in *Re Smith & Fawcett Ltd* [1942] Ch 304. The one thing that you must remember is that this duty is a *subjective* one. It is what the *directors*, not you or the courts, consider to be in the best interests of the company. Be careful not to substitute your objective viewpoint with the benefit of hindsight for the directors' subjective viewpoint at the time of the act.

The other aspect of this duty is that the directors must act in the interests of the company. What exactly does the 'interests of the company' mean? The company is in law a separate legal entity (see chapter 3) so does it mean that the directors must consider purely the economic interests of the separate entity and ignore the interests of the shareholders? The accepted view is that the interests of the shareholders as a body both present and future, are synonymous with the interests of the company. However, there is evidence in some Commonwealth and English authorities that the interests of the company are much wider than this (see *Teck Corporation Ltd v Millar* (1972) 33 DLR (3d) 288, Lord Diplock's comments in *Lonrho Ltd v Shell Petroleum Co. Ltd* [1980] 1 WLR 627 and Mayson, French and Ryan).

You should note that although the law talks about directors looking after the interests of shareholders present and future, directors do not owe duties to shareholders individually (see *Percival* v *Wright* [1902] 2 Ch 421 and *Dawson International plc* v *Coats Patons plc* [1989] BCLC 233). However, in some circumstances a relationship may arise between a shareholder and director but this is based on the ordinary principles of agency not company law (see *Allen* v *Hyatt* (1914) 30 TLR 444). Since 1980 directors also have to consider the interests of employees when exercising their powers (now see CA 1985, s. 309, discussed *post*). Furthermore, in a recent spate of cases the appellate courts have extended the duty for directors of insolvent companies and those whose financial position is precarious to cover the interests of the company's creditors, see *West Mercia Safetywear Ltd* v *Dodd* [1988] BCLC 250 and *Winkworth* v *Edward Baron Development Co. Ltd* [1986] 1 WLR 1512. It is clear that there has been a trend in recent years on the part of both Parliament and the courts to require directors to consider the interests of a greater range of persons adjusting the content of what is in the best interests of the company. This is inclusive with the wider view of the company's interests put forward by the *Tomorrow's Company Inquiry* as the 'inclusive approach'. You should consider whether the law now asks too much of directors.

The question as to who directors owe their duties to, and how they must exercise those powers is almost certain to crop up somewhere in the examination and should always be included in your revision programme.

Powers must be exercised for the proper purposes

If directors use their powers for some purpose other than those for which they were conferred they are in breach of their duty and will be liable to account to the company. Most of the 'proper purpose' cases, and consequently many questions, are concerned with the directors issuing shares to a friend or friendly company who they know will vote in accordance with their wishes and ensure control of the general meeting. The sort of issues likely to arise are directors issuing shares to ensure that they have control of the general meeting to allow them to ward off a take-over bid, or to alter the articles to suit their own ends.

For what purpose then can a director properly issue shares (see *Howard Smith Ltd* v *Ampol Petroleum Ltd* [1974] AC 821)? If the shares are found to be issued for an improper purpose what action can the company take (see *Punt* v *Symons & Co. Ltd* [1903] 2 Ch 506, cf. *Hogg* v *Cramphorn Ltd* [1967] Ch 254)? You should note that there are practical problems, namely the rule in *Foss* v *Harbottle*, associated with the enforcement of rights against directors. These problems will usually need to be discussed in a question on directors' duties. Which organ of the company can resolve to bring an action in the company's name to redress any wrong done to it? Problems can be encountered when the directors committing the wrong also control the board or the general meeting; although the law does sometimes give a minority shareholder a right to sue in these circumstances (for a more detailed discussion see chapters 10 and 12).

What is a proper purpose? A proper purpose is one where the action taken by the directors has been primarily motivated by desire to protect or further the company's interests even though it may also result in some benefit accruing to the directors personally. An improper purpose is where the directors are primarily motivated by their desire to further their own personal interests (see *Piercy* v *S. Mills & Co. Ltd* [1920] 1 Ch 77 and *Lee Panavision Ltd* v *Lee Lighting Ltd* [1991] BCC 620). However, as we will see in chapter 8, question 2, where a plurality of purposes exists this can cause substantial problems in ascertaining which purpose predominated.

Interests of employees

CA 1985, s. 309 requires directors to have regard to the interests of their company's employees when performing their functions as directors. However, s. 309(2) makes it quite clear that this duty is owed to the company and *not* to the employees individually and is enforceable in the same way as other fiduciary duties.

For example, it is not difficult to envisage a situation where the directors have to close down part of the company's operations to ensure the survival of the rest; the employees are to be made redundant. Although this course of action may be in the best interests of the company it can hardly be said to be in the best interests of those employees! Whose interests are to be regarded as paramount? The section says the interests are equal though logically it must be the company's that are paramount. In the above example if the company were to go into liquidation because part of it was not closed down then presumably all the employees would be made redundant and it is employees in general that must be considered not specific groups of employees. An interesting question, however, is what happens when the employee is also a shareholder. What difficulties would an employee shareholder face if he attempts to enforce the s. 309 duty via a derivative action (see chapter 10)? It is probable that s. 309 is not really meant to be enforced, but places in statutory form a provision for the creature that may come along one day in the distant future and appear on many company boards: the employee director. It would be too much for employees to be sitting on the board of directors and then not permit them to take into account the interests of their constituents, the employees. That is not to say that directors could never take employees' interests into account. Any director who ignores the interests of employees would create serious industrial relations problems for the company and the employees' interests and the company's often overlap. *Parke v Daily News Ltd* [1962] Ch 927 was based on rather special facts where the company was closing down and the payment to employees that was outlined in that case is now expressly provided for by CA 1985, s. 719. It is perhaps wrong to take *Parke* out of context and say that directors could not, under *Parke*, consider employees' interests. Section 309 gives statutory backing to what usually happens in practice in the well-run company as the broader interests of employees and of the company coincide.

Conflict of Duty and Interest

Secret profits

Like all trustees or agents a director must account to the company for any profit he makes from his office. The most likely situations that will appear in questions are those where directors come into possession of an opportunity or information which should be used for the company's benefit, but which they use for their own benefit and make a profit as a result. The law in England is applied very strictly and it does not matter that the company was not in a position to take up the opportunity itself (see *Regal (Hastings) Ltd v Gulliver* [1942] 1 All ER 378), or had decided to reject the contracts, although the attitude of the Commonwealth courts is far more relaxed (see *Peso Silver Mines Ltd v Cropper* (1966) 58 DLR (2d) 1). But note there must be a strong connection between the company and the opportunity to make it inequitable for a former director to pursue it (see *Island Export Finance Ltd v Umunna* [1986] BCLC 460).

This aspect of directors' duties is very popular for questions and is not difficult to learn. What you should always remember is that the rule is a very harsh one and it does not matter that the company is not in a position to take up the contract. In addition it is a *secret profit* rule. This means that it is possible for the directors to get authorisation from the general meeting to keep any profits they may have made. Thus the profit is no longer secret and therefore the shareholder cannot object to it. It is also important to remember that the fiduciary only has to make a profit, there is no requirement that the company must suffer any corresponding loss or damage.

Contracts with the company

Directors are in a position to influence contracts which their company may enter into. The rule is that a contract in which a director has an interest which has not been notified to the general meeting is voidable at the company's option (see *Aberdeen Railway Co.* v *Blaikie Bros* (1854) 1 Macq 461). However, if the company's articles are in the form of Table A, art. 85, then to prevent any biased judgment, any director who has a direct or indirect interest in a contract the company is contemplating must disclose it (CA 1985, s. 317). This includes situations where the director is the sole director of a company. In *Re Neptune (Vehicle Washing Equipment) Ltd* [1995] 3 WLR 108, the defendant was the sole director of the plaintiff company and as such passed resolutions purporting to terminate his contract of employment with the plaintiff company authorising a payment to himself of £100,892 which he claimed was due to him under his contract of employment. The court held that even though it may seem absurd a sole director is required to make a declaration in accordance with s. 317. Lightman J said, at p. 116:

> When holding the meeting on his own, he must still make the declaration to himself and have the statutory pause for thought, though it may be that the declaration does not have to be out loud, and he must record that he made the declaration in the minutes. The court may well find it difficult to accept that the declaration has been made if it is not so recorded. If the meeting is attended by anyone else, the declaration must be made out loud and in the hearing of those attending, and again should be recorded. In this case, if it is proved that the declaration was made, the fact that the minutes do not record the making of the declaration will not preclude proof of its making. In either situation the language of the section must be given full effect: there must be a declaration of the interest.

Disclosure must take place at the board meeting at which the contract is first discussed or, if the interest arises after that date, the next board meeting. Disclosure must be made to an independent board of directors (*Lee Panavision Ltd* v *Lee Lighting Ltd* [1991] BCC 620) and a company is not permitted to delegate the function of receiving disclosures to a committee of the board (see *Guinness plc* v *Saunders* [1988] 1 WLR 863). Failure to disclose will render the director liable to a fine (CA 1985, s. 317(7)), but will not render the contract voidable at common law merely for lack of disclosure (*Hely-Hutchinson* v *Brayhead Ltd* [1968] 1 QB 549), although the contract may be avoided in equity if there has been a breach of fiduciary duty. The House of Lords in another instalment of the Guinness litigation, *Guinness plc* v *Saunders* [1990] 2 AC 663, pointed out that since CA 1985, s. 317, will normally be read in conjunction with one of the company's articles which permits a director to have an interest in a contract with his company subject to disclosure (see, e.g., Table A, art. 85), thus negating the rule in *Aberdeen Railway Co.* v *Blaikie Bros*, a failure to disclose will normally amount to a breach of duty under the articles and render the contract voidable at the company's option. Under CA 1985, s. 317, not only must a director declare his interest but he must also state the nature of that interest (*Imperial Mercantile Credit Association* v *Coleman* (1873) LR 6 HL 189).

CA 1989, s. 109, inserts a new s. 322A into the CA 1985 to deal with situations where directors deal with their company in excess of their powers. The section sets out a statutory framework of rules identifying the circumstances in which the shareholders may avoid the contract and those where they may force the director to account to the company for any profit he has made or indemnify the company for any loss it has suffered.

In addition to these requirements certain types of contract are regulated by special statutory rules in the 1985 CA: service contracts (s. 319), substantial property transactions (s. 320) and loans (s. 330). You must look out for one of these issues as they appear in questions quite frequently.

A service contract is probably the most likely one a director is going to make with his company. CA 1985, s. 319, now requires that any service contract which runs for more than five years with no provision for termination or where termination can only take place in certain circumstances must first be approved by the shareholders in general meeting. In addition copies of all directors' service contracts must be made available for inspection to members (CA 1985, s. 318). Under CA 1985, s. 319(7), a contract for services is included. This is to ensure that the provisions of the section cannot be avoided by directors entering into long-term consultancy agreements rather than contracts of employment.

The provisions governing substantial property transactions reinforce the principles governing contracts discussed above. CA 1985, s. 320, seeks to regulate sales or purchases of non-cash assets between companies and directors. The assets that fall within the ambit of the section are those valued at over £100,000 or 10 per cent of the company's assets subject to a minimum of £2,000. The method of regulation is to require that the arrangement is first approved by a resolution in general meeting. Failure to gain such a resolution makes the transaction voidable at the option of the company. In addition the director concerned and any other director involved is liable to compensate the company for any loss it may have suffered.

CA 1985, s. 330 prevents a company making a loan in excess of £5,000 to a director or to a director of its holding company. This prohibition extends to entering into guarantees or providing security in connection with a loan made by any person to a director.

The provisions contained in these sections are extremely complex and the examiner will not expect you to know the detail of each section and subsection. What he will be looking for is your ability to identify one of these three types of contract, explain that they are regulated separately and briefly what that regulation consists of. For further detail on these provisions see Mayson, French and Ryan's chapter on directors' duties.

Dismissal of Directors

Provision for the dismissal of a director is made by CA 1985, s. 303. Under the section the company may remove a director by ordinary resolution even though he may be appointed for life by the articles! All the company has to do is to give special notice of the intention to pass such a resolution and give the director the opportunity to address the members in writing prior to the meeting. These representations can be read out at the meeting at the request of the director. If the company votes to dismiss the director he must vacate his office.

The only thing that may help him is a provision in the articles which has the effect of increasing the votes attached to his shares on a resolution to remove him or on any resolution to alter this article. This would normally raise the level of his votes to a level that ensures his continuance in office. This device was upheld as valid in *Bushell* v *Faith* [1970] AC 1099 despite the fact that it allows s. 303 to be undermined and may mean that the company is stuck with directors it can never get rid of, which of course is the desired result, especially in small private companies where participation in the management of the company wants to be ensured.

Relief from Liability for Breach of Duty

CA 1985, s. 310 makes void any attempt to exmpt a director from liability for breach of duty via a provision in the articles or elsewhere. Table A, arts 85 and 86, would appear to allow directors to be relieved of liability for certain breaches of duty if they have complied with the disclosure requirements in CA 1985, s. 317. Thus the exact scope of s. 310 is unclear. The apparent conflict was the source of much academic debate and was finally resolved by Vinelott J in *Movitex Ltd* v *Bulfield* (1986) 2 BCC 99, 403. It is now clear that arts 85 and 86 allow directors to put themselves in positions of potential conflict with the company; however, once in this position the director must deal honestly and fairly with the company. If he does not he is in breach of duty and may be liable to account to the company for any excessive profits made by him or loss suffered by the company (see Gregory (1982) 98 LQR 413 for an explanation of the principles involved). Additionally, note that it is possible for the court to grant relief to a director defending an action for negligence, default, breach of duty or breach of trust so long as the director can show that he acted honestly and reasonably and that having regard to all the circumstances he ought to be excused (CA 1985, s. 727).

One point of difficulty in this area is whether or not it is possible for a company to insure a director against liability he may incur toward the company for breach of duty as this may have infringed the provisions in CA 1985, s. 310. CA 1989, s. 137 inserts a new s. 310(3) into the CA 1985 which resolves the difficulty. It is now possible for a company to insure within the framework of CA 1985 s. 310. Directors' and officers' (D & O) liability insurance may be purchased out of the company's assets (CA 1985, s. 310(3) [CA 1989, s. 137(1)]) to cover losses resulting from a director's breach of duty. You should note that there are limits on cover in this area, e.g., it is not possible to insure against any *criminal activity* on the part of the director (see CA 1985, s. 310(1)).

If your course has dealt with the arguments surrounding the scope of CA 1985, s. 310, then there is a strong possibility that this will form part of a question.

REVISION AND RESEARCH

Questions on directors' duties can appear virtually anywhere in an examination paper and could be a component of an assessment question. If you look through the past examination papers, and indeed at the questions that are included in this book, you will see directors doing everything but running the company in a proper manner. Examiners spend hours trying to think of devious mechanisms by which a director could use the company's money or information for the director's own benefit. The examiners will spend even longer trying to think of appropriate names to call the fraudulent or negligent director he has characterised! Problems tend to attract some element of breach of directors' duties and will usually appear in the form of the dreaded 'mixed' question. In fact directors' duties could be mixed with almost any other aspect of your company law course. This should tell you two things about the topic:

(a)   It is almost certain to be on the examination paper and on your assessment.

(b)   It could, and probably will, crop up in more than one question.

Despite your undoubted hatred of 'mixed' questions it should be clear that you really ought to include it in your revision programme. If you don't you may find that another topic you have revised appears in a question with directors' duties and you won't be able to do that question at all.

Although directors' duties could crop up with almost any other topic, it does have some favourite bedfellows! The two most common partners are the rule in *Foss* v *Harbottle* and other aspects of minority protection (see chapter 10), and the relationship between the directors, the managing director and the general meeting (see chapter 12).

Other questions where directors' duties may play some part could be those involving company contracts (see chapter 4), an alteration of the articles (see chapter 5) or insider dealing (see chapter 7). Now that we have covered nearly every chapter in the book and said that directors' duties could occur in each of them, can you afford not to revise this topic? The best way to sort out the likely 'mixes' is to look at past examination papers and assessments to get an idea of the sort of question that has cropped up in the past.

Finally, mixed problem questions require practice. To get some practice find some mixed questions and try answering them as part of your revision programme. This will give you practice at splitting your time between different topics in the same question and linking the topics together. Essay questions are less popular. A typical essay question could ask you to 'Critically analyse the circumstances in which a director will be found to be negligent', or 'Compare the office of director to that of a trustee'.

Directors' duties is a heavy case law topic and it is important to sort out the major cases at the revision stage. Avoid learning more than one case to illustrate the same point as your time in examinations will be limited.

IDENTIFYING THE QUESTION

The word 'director' is likely to be mentioned in almost every question on an examination paper and most assessments but don't read too much into this — it doesn't necessarily mean that the question is concerned with directors' duties! The question is quite likely to be a 'mixed' one and this will make it one of the more difficult ones on the paper to identify.

There are three things you could look for to help you:

(a)   Improper purposes will usually involve an issue of shares by the directors to a friend or friendly company to secure voting control of the general meeting. There will also usually be some benefit involved for the director. It could also involve an alteration of the articles in the director's favour.

(b)   Secret profits — probably easiest to spot. A director will have used information or opportunity gained by virtue of his position to gain a contract or buy shares and have made a profit, not necessarily at the company's expense.

(c)   Contracts with the company-look out especially for service contracts, loans and substantial property transactions.

The rubric of the question will usually ask you to 'Advise the company' or 'Advise Fred, a minority shareholder'. Any attempt to enforce directors' duties by the company must take account of the rule in *Foss* v *Harbottle*, unless a minority shareholder can enforce rights in the articles via the s. 14 contract (see chapter 5), or use CA 1985, s. 459 (see chapter 10). Your main difficulty will be deciding the depth to which you are expected to go in discussing these other issues. The rubric may point you in the right direction, e.g., 'Discuss whether any directors have breached their duties to the company and the problems facing Fred, a minority shareholder, in suing the directors for any breach'. This rubric clearly requires you to divide your time equally between directors' duties and the rule in *Foss* v *Harbottle*. Some examiners will make it clear through the rubric of the question just what is expected of you so remember to read the rubric carefully before beginning your answer.

QUESTION 1

The issued share capital of Cosyhomes Ltd is divided into 40 ordinary shares held by Walter and 60 management shares held by Ronnie and Gary, the two directors of Cosyhomes Ltd.

Walter has expressed an interest in an offer for his shares from Shacks Ltd. To prevent Shacks Ltd obtaining a substantial holding in Cosyhomes Ltd, Ronnie and Gary issue 100 ordinary shares to Jess, a friend of the directors. Shacks Ltd immediately drops its negotiations with Walter.

Cosyhomes Ltd is offered a lucrative opportunity by Reegan Ltd to build nuclear shelters due to Ronnie's reputation as an applied nuclear physicist. The board defer a decision on the contract because they have insufficient finance to go ahead at present. However, Ronnie manages to secure the contract for himself personally. He establishes his own company to manufacture the shelters and makes a profit of £1 million.

Gary causes Cosyhomes Ltd to sign a five-year contract with Redbrick Ltd whereby Cosyhomes Ltd agrees to buy all its bricks from Redbrick Ltd. Gary is also a director of Redbrick Ltd. Gary also signs a service contract with Cosyhomes Ltd which lasts for six years and does not specify any grounds for termination of the contract.

Discuss any liability that may arise.

Several issues are raised by this problem and it is best to identify them before starting to plan the answer:

(a)   The issue of shares to Jess. Do the directors have the authority to issue the shares? Have the shares been issued for a proper purpose? If not what can be done about the issue?

(b)   The profit made by Ronnie. Has Ronnie made a secret profit in breach of his duty to the company? Can the company make him account for the £1 million he has made?

(c)   The contract between Cosyhomes Ltd and Redbrick Ltd. Is it a contract in which a director has an interest which should be disclosed?

(d)   The service contract. Has CA 1985, s. 319 been complied with?

The other thing that you must look at carefully before beginning your answer is the rubric. This particular one asks you to discuss any liability that may arise. You do not have to discuss in any detail the problems facing the company or minority shareholders in trying to sue the directors. However, the rubric could just as easily have asked you to discuss any liability that may arise and any problems that may face Walter (a minority shareholder) in trying to enforce these rights against the directors. This would have involved a more detailed discussion of the rule in *Foss v Harbottle* and CA 1985, s. 459 (see chapter 10), as well as the rules governing directors. You will need to let the examiner know that you are aware of the problems raised in this question by the rule in *Foss v Harbottle* and this will be looked at in question 2.

The Issue of Shares to Jess

The issue of shares to Jess may be challenged on two grounds. First of all, do the directors have authority to allot the shares in accordance with CA 1985, s. 80? If they have not been properly authorised the allotment will not be rendered void or voidable as far as the allottee (Jess) is concerned but the directors will have committed an offence which is triable either way (CA 1985, s. 80(9) and (10)) (see chapter 8, question 2). The second point the examiner wants you to consider is whether the allotment has taken place for a proper purpose. This begs the question, what purpose is a proper one where the allotment of shares is concerned? At one stage it was thought that any purpose other than the raising of new capital was an improper one (see *Piercy v S. Mills & Co. Ltd* [1920] 1 Ch 77). However, in a more recent Privy Council decision, *Howard Smith Ltd v Ampol Petroleum Ltd* [1974] AC 821, their lordships accepted that it might in some circumstances be proper to issue shares for purposes other than the raising of capital for the company, but it would be 'unconstitutional for directors to use their fiduciary powers over the shares in the company purely for the purpose of destroying an existing majority, or creating a new majority which did not previously exist' (at p. 837).

The question tells you that the reason that Ronnie and Gary have issued these shares to Jess is to prevent Shacks Ltd obtaining a substantial holding in Cosyhomes Ltd. This would seem to be in effect creating a majority that did not previously exist and is therefore open to question as an improper purpose. Have the directors sought to prevent Shacks Ltd obtaining a holding in the company because they don't think it would be good for the company or because they don't think it would be good for them personally? The question does not really give you any clues as to the true motives of the directors and you can only speculate. In *Hogg* v *Cramphorn Ltd* [1967] Ch 254 the directors honestly believed that by maintaining themselves in control they were acting in the best interests of the company. The court nevertheless held that the allotment was voidable and ruled that it could be rendered valid if approved by the shareholders in general meeting (the disputed shares not being voted). The principles enunciated in this case were approved and applied by the Court of Appeal in *Bamford* v *Bamford* [1970] Ch 212. This approach should be compared to that taken in some earlier cases where the court held the allotment to be void and offered no opportunity for the directors to seek forgiveness from the shareholders in general meeting (see *Punt* v *Symons & Co. Ltd* [1903] 2 Ch 506 and *Piercy* v *S. Mills & Co. Ltd*). It now seems following the *Hogg* and *Bamford* cases that acts done by directors honestly but for a collateral purpose can normally be ratified by the general meeting. You should refer to a case note by Wedderburn (1968) 31 MLR 688 for a discussion of the principles involved.

In this particular case, if the issues were referred to the general meeting the directors would be in a position to ratify their own breach. This could amount to a fraud on the minority (see *Cook* v *Deeks* [1916] 1 AC 554), and a better view is likely to be that, if challenged, the court will declare the allotment to Jess void. Walter may also be able to seek a remedy under CA 1985, s. 459 (see chapter 10), although this does not need to be discussed in detail in this question.

The Profit Made by Ronnie

It would seem that Ronnie has made the £1 million profit because of his position with the company. There is a wide principle which has developed from both trust and agency principles that any secret profit made by a director from his office with the company must be accounted for to the company (see *Reading* v *Attorney-General* [1951] AC 507, *Boardman* v *Phipps* [1967] 2 AC 46 and *Aberdeen Railway Co.* v *Blaikie Bros* (1854) 1 Macq 461).

In this problem it seems that the company was not in a position to take up the contract itself because of a lack of finance at the relevant time. In these circumstances is it possible for the director to take the benefit of an opportunity which the company cannot take up? The decision in *Regal (Hastings) Ltd* v *Gulliver* [1942] 1 All ER 378 establishes that it does not matter that the company cannot or will not take up the opportunity or that it has not suffered a loss as a result of the director's action. The director will still be liable to account for any profit he has made. This may result in some unmeritorious actions: *Regal (Hastings) Ltd* v *Gulliver* is itself an example. It is a good idea to discuss the attitude adopted in some Commonwealth jurisdictions to this problem. Both *Queensland Mines Ltd* v *Hudson* (1978) 52 ALJR 399 and *Peso Silver Mines Ltd* v *Cropper* (1966) 58 DLR (2d) 1 allow a director to take a contract personally if the board has decided to reject it, so long as he discloses the fact to the board. Although *Queensland Mines Ltd* v *Hudson* is a Privy Council decision, this approach has yet to find favour with the English courts and must be considered to be of persuasive authority only.

Ronnie seems to have been able to get the contract from Reegan Ltd because of his skill as an applied nuclear physicist. Could he argue that the profit was acquired because of his skill as well as his directorship? According to *Industrial Development Consultants Ltd* v *Cooley* [1972] 1 WLR 443, this is not a defence to an action by the company to recover profits. Therefore it seems probable that Ronnie will have to account to Cosyhomes Ltd for the £1 million profit he has made.

Contracts with the Company

The director like the trustee, cannot enter into contracts with his beneficiary (i.e., the company), or put himself in a position whereby his duty and interest come into conflict. As far as company directors are concerned there has been a relaxation of this rule by the statute. The Companies Act 1985 allows directors to make contracts of this nature so long as the conditions laid down by the statute are satisfied.

In this particular problem the examiner has included two different contracts that you need to consider. The first is the contract between Cosyhomes Ltd and Redbrick Ltd which Gary seems to have an interest in. This interest arises because he is in a position to influence Cosyhomes Ltd in its consideration of which supplier to choose. In these circumstances it is probable that he will want to 'sing the praises' of Redbrick Ltd to ensure that they get the contract to supply Cosyhomes Ltd. The interest in the contract is one which should be disclosed under CA 1985, s. 317 (*Costa Rica Railway Co. Ltd* v *Forwood* [1901] 1 Ch 746) and that disclosure needs to be made to an independent board of directors (*Guinness plc* v *Saunders* [1988] 1 WLR 863). If Gary fails to disclose his interest he will be liable to a fine under s. 317(7), but the contract will not be voidable at common law. However, if, as seems likely, Gary is in breach of his duty to Cosyhomes Ltd, the contract can be set aside in equity (*Guinness plc* v *Saunders* [1990] 2 AC 663).

The Service Contract

The other contract that needs to be considered is the service contract that Gary has entered into with Cosyhomes Ltd. This would seem to be a contract regulated by CA 1985, s. 319, as it is longer than five years and makes no provision for termination. The question here is whether this contract has been approved by the shareholders in general meeting. If it has not then the service contract between Gary and Cosyhomes Ltd can be terminated by the company upon it giving reasonable notice to Gary (see chapter 12).

Conclusion

This problem is quite long and involves the consideration of a number of issues. It is important to divide your time up properly between the various parts of the answer when you plan your answer. The question treats the three parts with roughly equal importance and your answer should reflect this. The other point to watch is the way you treat the case law you cite in the answer. It is easy to get bogged down in complicated facts and lose time and emphasis. Make sure you use the cases to illustrate the answer and don't use the answer as an excuse to write out a lot of cases! The liabilities considered in this answer do give rise to a discussion of the enforcement of those liabilities and the rule in *Foss* v *Harbottle*. This is now considered in question 2.

QUESTION 2

Travel Ltd is a private company which owns holiday homes in France which it lets each summer. Harry, Jerry and Stuart are the company's three directors and majority shareholders. Alan is the only other shareholder.

Lord Portly owns several country houses in France and wishes to let them to holiday-makers for the summer of 1985. He approaches Harry to discuss terms but refuses to let Travel Ltd handle the houses as he doubts the business sense of Jerry and Stuart. However, Lord Portly and Harry agree personal terms for the letting of these houses. Harry makes a profit of £5,000 during 1985 from the lettings.

Jerry buys a house from the company for £125,000. This is £5,000 below a recent valuation. Jerry says that the house is worth less because it has subsequently been damaged by holiday-makers. Harry and Stuart, the other directors, have approved this transaction.

Stuart has used some of the properties for the past five summers for his holidays but has never paid any rental. Neither the company in general meeting nor the board of directors have approved this arrangement. The normal cost of these lettings is £900 p.a.

None of the directors wish to bring an action against Harry because they fear that they will leave themselves open to an action by him. Alan, however, wishes to sue the three directors on behalf of the company to recover money which, he believes, belongs to it.

Advise Alan on the remedies that may be available and any problems he might encounter as a minority shareholder.

This question requires a discussion of directors' duties and the rule in *Foss* v *Harbottle* (1843) 2 Hare 461. It is a typical example of the sort of 'mixed' question that examiners often set on this area of law. The question can be divided into two parts.

(a)   Directors' duties consisting of the following issues:

(i)   The profit made by Harry from the letting of houses in France during 1985.
(ii)   The purchase by Jerry of a company asset valued at £125,000.
(iii)   The holidays taken by Stuart in the company houses without paying any rental.

(b)   The enforcement of the rights of the company against the directors:

(i)   A consideration of the rule in *Foss* v *Harbottle* and whether any exceptions apply.
(ii)   A consideration of whether Alan can seek a remedy using CA 1985, s. 459.

There is a lot to discuss in this question and it is important that you ensure that you divide your time up sensibly before you begin your answer. As we have stressed earlier, you must decide how much attention you are going to devote to each aspect of the answer and try to prevent your enthusiasm for one particular aspect of the problem preventing you from properly dealing with the remaining issues. There is nothing worse than running out of time near the end of a particular answer. It costs marks and is a result of bad examination technique.

The Profit Made by Harry from the Letting of Houses in France during 1985

Harry has gained the opportunity of handling these houses because of his connection with Travel Ltd. His fiduciary duty to the company requires him to secure the contract for the company. In this situation it seems that Lord Portly would not have given the contract to Travel Ltd because of his lack of confidence in Jerry and Stuart. However, if Harry had given an undertaking that he would handle the houses personally for the company on behalf of Lord Portly would the outcome have been different? It would seem that Harry is in breach of his fiduciary duty to the company (*Regal (Hastings) Ltd* v *Gulliver* [1942] 1 All ER 378). It is no defence to argue that the company was not in a position to take up the contract or would not have been awarded it at all (*Industrial Development Consultants Ltd* v *Cooley* [1972] 1 WLR 443). Therefore the company can force Harry to account for the £5,000 profit. The practical problems facing Alan in any attempts to enforce the company's rights are discussed below.

The Purchase by Jerry of a Company Asset Valued at £125,000

In this aspect of the question the examiner wants you to consider two things. First of all this is a contract between the company and a director involving the purchase of a company asset valued at over £100,000; therefore it is a substantial property transaction, which is regulated by CA 1985, s. 320. The contract between Jerry and the company is voidable at the option of the company unless the provisions of the section have been complied with, although not if restitution is impossible or a bona fide purchaser for value has acquired rights over the property. Before the transaction can be considered valid it has to be approved by the company in general meeting (CA 1985, s. 320).

Although the contract has been approved by the board of directors this is not sufficient to authorise a substantial property transaction. As the transaction has not been approved by the general meeting it is voidable at the option of the company. In addition, under the section failure to gain such a resolution will make the director, and any other director concerned, liable to account to the company for any loss it may have suffered. Consequently, Jerry, Harry and Stuart will all be liable to compensate the company for any loss it may have suffered as a consequence of the unauthorised contract.

Stuart's Use of the Company's Holiday Homes

Stuart owes a fiduciary duty to the company to act in its best interests. This duty prevents him from using the company's property for his personal benefit unless such an action has been authorised by the company in general meeting. The unauthorised use of the holiday homes by Stuart in these circumstances is a breach of fiduciary duty (see *Industrial Development Consultants Ltd* v *Cooley*). Consequently Stuart can be called to account to the company for the profit he has made.

Recovery by the Company

The second part of your answer should deal with the way in which the company can recover any money it is entitled to from the directors. This aspect of the question should make up half of your answer.

The normal rule is that if a wrong is done to the company the company is the only proper plaintiff entitled to redress that wrong (see *Foss* v *Harbottle*). This means that either the company in general meeting must resolve to bring an action in the company's name or if the power of management is delegated to the board of directors by Table A, art. 70, they must resolve to bring the action (discussed in depth in chapter 12). In this problem it will not make much difference where the power to start corporate litigation lies, because the directors control the votes in general meeting as well as in board meetings. In these circumstances Alan would appear to have very little prospect of persuading the directors to bring an action against themselves. However, there are exceptions to the rule in *Foss* v *Harbottle* one of which allows a minority shareholder to bring an action in the company's name when the wrongdoers are in control of corporate litigation. This would seem to be Alan's best course of action. You will need to discuss the application of this exception to *Foss* v *Harbottle* in your answer (see chapter 10 for a detailed discussion).

Will Alan be able to Obtain a Remedy under CA 1985, Section 459?

This is the other possibility you should consider in your answer. We only consider it briefly here. Remember that the remedy available under the section is a personal one. The section does not provide a procedure for the shareholder to recover on behalf of the company. Consequently, s. 459 requires the shareholder to show that *he* has been 'unfairly prejudiced' by the conduct of the company's affairs. In these circumstances Alan may find it difficult to prove he has suffered personally or that the value of his shares has been adversely affected (see chapter 10 for a detailed discussion of s. 459).

SUMMARY

We would again stress that it is important to remember that a question involving directors' duties is likely to be mixed with other topics. Be aware of this *before* you enter the examination room. Try to allocate your time adequately between the various issues raised by the question and more importantly do not treat issues in isolation. The way in which you link the issues will have considerable bearing on your final mark.

FURTHER READING

Dine, Janet, 'The Governance of governance' (1994) 15 Co Law 73.

Finch, Vanessa, 'Board performance and Cadbury on corporate governance' [1992] JBL 581.

Finch, Vanessa, 'Company directors: who cares about skill and care?' (1992) 55 MLR 179.

Finch, Vanessa, 'Personal accountability and corporate control: the role of directors' and officers' liability insurance' (1994) 57 MLR 880.

7 INSIDER DEALING

INTRODUCTION

The term 'insider dealing' conjures up ideas of directors dressed incognito buying and selling the shares of their companies on the Stock Exchange because they know something about the company that the general public do not know. They make huge profits and retire on them to the South of France. The reality of the situation as far as you are concerned is much less exciting but nevertheless very worrying from the perspective of effective legal regulation. Insider dealing is an extremely lucrative 'white collar' crime, and the enticement of such large rewards can only be deterred by effective sanctions. That insider dealing takes place can be clearly seen from the research published by *The Economist*, vol. 295 (15 June 1985), p. 79 and the *Sunday Times* (9 March 1986 and 14 January 1990). There are thus clear grounds for thinking that the present deterrents are not working. The 'big bang' on the London Stock Exchange gave rise to the creation of integrated financial services, and could provide a bonanza for insiders to make large profits with greater impunity if the new system of self-regulation within a statutory framework under the Financial Services Act 1986 turns out to be ineffective. The problem has been highlighted following disclosures on both sides of the Atlantic regarding the insiders Boesky and Collier and the massive profits they have made from insider dealing.

Since 1980 insider dealing has been a criminal offence. The provisions were originally contained in Part V of CA 1980, and then re-enacted with minor amendments in the Company Securities (Insider Dealing) Act 1985. Insider dealing is now regulated by Part V of the Criminal Justice Act 1993 which has implemented the EC Directive on the topic. The law governing insider dealing is complicated and in the main quite unexciting. This is due in no small part to the fact that statutory provisions dominate with very little case law to illuminate the topic.

In addition to the statutory rules you will usually need to consider the regulations made and policed by the Stock Exchange and the City Panel on Take-overs and Mergers. Coupled with these aspects of the topic are the rules governing a fiduciary's accountability to the company for any profits he may make by virtue of his office, and some adventurous courses will also deal with the legislation of the USA on insider dealing.

It is easy to get weighed down by such a welter of rules and statutory provisions. This chapter will try to take some of that weight off your shoulders and develop a plan of attack for your revision and examination answer.

MAIN ISSUES

Criminal Justice Act 1993

The provisions contained in this Act form the basis of the government's response to insider dealing implementing the recent EC Directive (89/592 EEC). It will be necessary to be fully conversant with the provisions of the Act and in particular changes from the previous legislation. The provisions can be broadly divided into two categories:

(a)   The definitions of 'insider', and 'inside information'.
(b)   The offences, defences and criminal sanctions.

The Act has made insider dealing a criminal offence, but there is no attempt to provide any civil remedies to compensate shareholders who have dealt with the insider and lost money as a result. The reason the Act does not attempt to impose any civil liability stems from the difficulties faced in matching up 'buyers and sellers' on the Stock Exchange, due to the way in which bargains are concluded. (See Pennington for a discussion of how the 'TALISMAN' system operates. This is still the way bargains are conducted following the 'big bang', although the system has been amended to cope with the larger number of market makers dealing in any one security — see Jones (1986) 7 Co Law 99.)

Despite the TALISMAN system remaining essentially the same, other changes may mean that it will become easier to detect insiders in the market and also restrict the amount of information available to them by ensuring speedier publication. Three changes are important for you to note:

(a)   The introduction of last-trade tapes (tapes produced by TALISMAN recording last dealings and prices in a particular share) and the obligation that market makers have to report all deals within five minutes, enables the Stock Exchange to computerise its scrutiny of share price movements and allows irregular and unexplained price movements to be spotted rapidly.

(b)   The material available to the Surveillance Department giving information on the history of companies and company directors is also computerised so that identification of insiders is easier.

(c)   Company announcements to the market-place are made by using the quick Company News Service, which can capture information electronically transmitted by listed companies and retransmit it on terminals.

Furthermore, changes are to be introduced in the latter half of 1996 in the form of CREST. This system will complement TALISMAN inasmuch as when a bargain in a fully paid listed security is struck, transfer of share ownership would be completed by a computer program without the need for certificates and transfer forms. Thus the transfer will no longer depend on entry or removal from an individual company's share register and share certificates would become a thing of the past. Shareholders will instead have their holdings recorded electronically in an account with CREST rather like a bank account. The introduction of CREST will not really aid the matching of buyers and sellers. However, it should allow easier detection of unusual dealings in a particular company's securities at an earlier stage. Even with all these changes the only identifiable parties to the transaction are TALISMAN and SEPON.

There are few reported decisions under the legislation to date, although there are a few unreported decisions which you will find it useful to look up. You will find these cases discussed in journals like the *Company Lawyer* or the *Journal of Business Law.*

The other factor that has contributed to the paucity of prosecutions brought under the Act is that the prosecuting authorities have to prove that a criminal offence has been committed with all the consequent problems of proving *mens rea* and satisfying the criminal standard of proof. A proportion of the small number of prosecutions brought have collapsed because of these difficulties — see *Guardian,* 24 January 1990 and *Daily Telegraph,* 26 January 1990 for examples of such cases.

However, you should note the changes introduced by the Financial Services Act 1986. Following the 'big bang' a number of opportunities for abusing unpublished price sensitive information arose which previously did not exist. When the amount of information which is transmitted via the computer network which the Stock Exchange now uses and the dismantling of job demarcation barriers are taken into account it is clear that it is more likely that more individuals are going to come into possession of more unpublished price sensitive information than was previously the case.

To provide an effective counter to these new opportunities the FSA 1986 has provided increased powers of investigation into suspected cases of insider dealing — see FSA 1986, s. 177. Anyone failing to cooperate with an investigation being carried out under s. 177 will be subject to one of the penalties laid down in s. 178. The section was tested in *Re an Inquiry under the Company Securities (Insider Dealing) Act 1985* [1988] AC 660, where a financial journalist of a national newspaper was held by the House of Lords to have no reasonable excuse for refusing to answer questions put to him by inspectors under s. 177 to investigate suspected insider dealing using unpublished price sensitive information obtained from civil servants. A £20,000 fine was imposed. It was hoped that these increased powers would improve the rates of detection and prosecution of insiders.

Unfortunately this has not proved to be the case. Figures to 1994 show just 18 convictions from 44 prosecutions (see (1995) 16 Co Law 164). The significance of these figures is really brought home if they are compared to the US figures for 1987 alone when the American authorities handled 36 prosecutions.

It is very likely that discussion of the provisions and changes introduced by the 1993 legislation will form the main part of any assessed work in this area. At the very least you will be expected to:

(a)   Identify any people in the question who might be insiders. It will be important not only to explain the definition but also to identify differences between the old and new law. The main changes are:

(i)   specific inclusion of a shareholder as an insider, and
(ii)   the introduction in s. 57(2)(a)(ii) of the term 'access' means that there need be no obvious connection between the insider and the securities about which he obtains the information.

It appears that all that is required is 'access to the information by virtue of his employment, office or profession'.

(b)   Explain what constitutes inside information. Section 56 sets out the characteristics the information must have and is more detailed than its predecessor. Of particular importance here will be your ability to explain the boundaries of the s. 56 definition. We would suggest the two most interesting aspects are:

(i)   The use of the term 'specific and precise' in s. 56(1)(b). This is wider than the requirement set out in the Directive which simply requires that the information be precise. The addition of the term 'specific' will have the following effect. Specific information regarding a takeover bid would be the fact that a bid is to be made. Precise information would be the price at which a bid will be made. Both would fall within the definition in the Act.

(ii)   The fact that the information has not yet been made public (s. 56(1)(c)). The meaning of this aspect of the section is explained and amplified in s. 58, in particular s. 58(2) and (3). It is likely that the application of these rules to practical situations may prove difficult, e.g., s. 58(3)(e) states that the information will still be deemed published even though it is published outside the UK. Taken literally, information published in the *Falklands Daily News* will be treated as made public. It will be interesting to see how these provisions are interpreted by the courts.

(c)   Examine the activities proscribed by the new Act. Section 52 sets out one offence of insider dealing which can be committed in three ways. You will need to be familiar with all three.

The main changes involve the types of securities and dealings covered by the Act. Schedule 2 to the Act adds public-sector debt instruments and associated derivatives to the more traditional securities covered by the 1985 legislation. Additionally the dealings caught by the Act extend to those carried out on regulated markets or by relying on a professional intermediary (ss. 52(3), 59 and 60). Furthermore the new territorial limits of the offence are set out in s. 62.

The defences set out in the Act are of increased importance due to the increased scope of the offences. The potential these defences enjoy to 'drive a coach and horses' through the Act is well articulated by Alcock in (1994) 15 Co Law 67, and we would refer you to that article for a discussion of the problems. The Act does not change any of the sanctions or enforcement procedures. The difficulties experienced under the old law with regard to enforcement are likely to remain. In addition to these changes you should also consider how more use may be made of Chinese Walls (see below) by financial institutions to prevent insider dealing occurring, particularly in light of the fact that there will be no demarcation of function in the future.

The examiner may also expect you to comment on the effectiveness of the Act. Your ability to bring some informed comment to bear on the operation of the provisions will earn you extra marks. To do this you will find it useful to look at the views of some academics. We suggest you look at the articles listed at the end of this chapter.

Companies Act 1985, Sections 323 to 329

This Act also contains provisions which have an effect on insider dealing. The sections make it a criminal offence for a director to deal in 'put and call' options in the securities of his company or its subsidiary. These sections also require the company to keep a register of directors' shareholdings and any dealings that occur in these shares. This should at least ensure that it will be possible to determine whether or not a director has dealt at a particular time. The extension of the requirements to a director's spouse and children will also prevent a director instructing his spouse or child to deal in order to hide the fact that he has dealt. For a more detailed discussion of this see the chapter in Mayson, French and Ryan on insider dealing.

These sections are not likely to be the subject of a separate examination question although they do illustrate one method of tackling insider dealing by requiring disclosure of deals by those most likely to be in a position to profit by using inside information. If your course has dealt with these provisions you should certainly include them in your revision programme, and any treatment of insider dealing without mentioning disclosure as one method of dealing with the problem would be incomplete.

Self-regulation

Prior to 1980 the only real checks on insider dealing were contained in the regulations of the Stock Exchange and the City Panel on Takeovers and Mergers. While these provisions were very useful when they alone regulated insider dealing, they must now be viewed as supplementing the law contained in the 1993 Act.

One of the important features of the Stock Exchange regulations is contained in the Stock Exchange Model Code for Securities Transactions by Directors of Listed Companies, which was introduced in 1981. The current version is printed as an appendix to ch. 16 of the Listing Rules. The code lays down a procedure whereby a director's intention to deal in the securities of his company or a subsidiary company is notified to an officer of the company who keeps a register of all such dealings. If it is not safe for the director to deal, because something has happened or is going to happen which when it is made public will affect the price of the securities, the officer charged with keeping the register must inform the director that it is not safe to deal. The rationale of the code is to provide an atmosphere in which company directors can deal in the securities of their company without contravening the provisions of the Act. The amendments have extended the range of transactions to which the restrictions on directors' dealings apply. The aim is to make the code more effective. The main features of this code can be found in the insider dealing section of Mayson, French and Ryan.

The City Code on Takeovers and Mergers contains several provisions aimed at insider dealing. General principle 5 of the code emphasises the desire of the panel to avoid the creation of a false market in the relevant securities. This principle is then amplified by several rules, namely rules 4, 5 and 8 of the code which stress the importance of early announcements to avoid rumour or speculation in the shares and the early issue of copies of the offer document so that the terms of the offer are made public. Rule 4 prohibits dealings in shares by anyone privy to the takeover negotiations, and stresses the confidentiality of information connected with an offer or contemplated offer and that it must not be passed on to any other person.

The self-regulatory provisions are limited in their effectiveness for two main reasons:

(a) Lack of an effective system of investigation and the inability to subpoena witnesses to make a full finding of fact.

(b) Lack of effective sanctions. The sanctions available to the City institutions are public censure, exclusion from the facilities of the Stock Exchange, suspension of the company's listing, or reporting the offenders to the Department of Trade and Industry to prevent them obtaining a licence to deal in securities at a future date. From the list of sanctions you will probably think they are most effective. However, they are effective only against those sensitive to public censure or those whose livelihood depends on their ability to use the facilities of the Exchange. A retired ex-company director, for example, would probably not be affected by either type of sanction if he picked up a bit of information on returning to visit his old colleagues.

Criminal Sanctions and Civil Remedies

Contravention of the provisions of the 1993 Act makes the individual guilty of a criminal offence (s. 61). Furthermore, by s. 63(2), no transaction is void or voidable by reason only that it was entered into in contravention of the act. This provision is to prevent the disruption of completed Stock Exchange bargains. However, you should look at the interesting decision in *Chase Manhattan Equities Ltd* v *Goodman* [1991] BCC 308, where the court applied the *ex turpi causa* doctrine and held such a sale agreement was unenforceable because it was tainted in its creation by illegality. As has been pointed out the Act does not attempt to provide a civil remedy for the shareholder who may have suffered loss as a result of the insider's activities. This factor was criticised when the Act was passing through Parliament but no attempt to introduce civil liability was made, although it is possible that compensation may be awarded under the Powers of Criminal Courts Act 1973, ss. 35 and 39. In addition FSA 1986, s. 62 also provides the possibility that, because the Stock Exchange is a self-regulating organisation recognised under the Act, a breach of the Stock Exchange's own rules forbidding insider dealing could give rise to a civil remedy for breach of statutory duty. This remedy would be available to anyone who can show that they have suffered because of the breach.

However, if the insider is in a fiduciary relationship with the company, dealing will amount to a breach of duty to the company and the company will be in a position to recover the secret profit made by the fiduciary. Directors are the most obvious fiduciaries who may contravene the law and be called to account for their profits by the company to whom they owe their duty. The case law in this area is well-established. Authorities such as *Regal (Hastings) Ltd* v *Gulliver* [1942] 1 All ER 378, and *Industrial Development Consultants Ltd* v *Cooley* [1972] 1 WLR 443 suggest that the company will not find it difficult to force directors to disgorge the fruits of their activities.

Other persons involved with the company may occupy a fiduciary position is still possible for the company to recover a secret profit from these people on agency principles (e.g., *Reading* v *Attorney-General* [1951] AC 507). However, the likelihood of success here is less certain than with directors as can be seen by comparing the decisions in *Brown* v *IRC* [1965] AC 244 and *Regal (Hastings) Ltd* v *Gulliver*, especially the constrasting fortunes of the solicitors involved.

Conflicts of Interest: the Chinese Wall

Some questions may contain situations where the 'insider' is a financial adviser acting for more than one client. This person may find himself in a difficult position when he gains price sensitive information performing his obligations to one person which may affect the fortunes of another for whom he is also acting. The law provides no guidance as to the adviser's best course of action, but see the similar situation in *North & South Trust Co.* v *Berkeley* [1971] 1 WLR 470. If he spreads the information around he will be guilty of counselling or procuring another to deal. If he does nothing then his client may wonder why he has employed such an adviser who cannot give him the advice he has paid for because it falls within the definition of inside information. The client in these circumstances is as well off without an adviser.

The answer for institutions engaged in multiple functions which produce these difficulties has been to erect a 'Chinese Wall' or 'bamboo curtain' between the various functions. The result is to isolate information in particular departments of an institution with members of other departments gaining no knowledge of it, hence removing the conflict of interest. However, the erection of a 'Chinese Wall' will not provide a watertight system. It is inevitable that the 'top flight' management of this type of finance house must have knowledge of all its activities. In these circumstances reliance can only be placed on the integrity of the person not to deal supplemented by sufficient enforceable sanctions to deter dealing. Self-regulation by the City institutions has always played a large role in the deterrent structure, although its effectiveness has already been questioned. The basis of the regulation of financial services contained in the Financial Services Act 1986 is self-regulation within a statutory framework, 'up-dating' regulatory procedures in line with changes in the market-place following the 'big bang' on the Stock Exchange in October 1986. 'Dual capacity', the merging of the functions of stockbrokers and jobbers, brings with it the danger of abuse as highlighted in the insurance world in *North & South Trust Co.* v *Berkeley*. The Financial Services Act 1986 lays down investment principles as a basis for the self-regulatory organisations to make rules, breach of which could give rise to disciplinary and civil action. These principles are subject to the same criticism that has been made of Chinese Walls in that 'they restrict flows of information and not the conflicts of interest themselves' *(Financial Services in the UK* (Cmnd 9432, 1985); see also (1985) 6 Co Law 137; Rider, 'The fiduciary and the frying pan' [1978] Conv 114; and Rider, 'Down with the Chinese Wall' (1984) 5 Co Law 106).

REVISION AND RESEARCH

The topic of insider dealing consists of a number of component parts that must be considered in any revision programme. They are:

(a)   The UK legislation.
(b)   The self-regulatory provisions.
(c)   The civil remedies.

It is unlikely that any question will require an answer based on just one of these areas. You are more likely to be confronted by a combination of at least two. Consequently it would be unwise to revise just one of the above aspects of insider dealing. The best course of action would be to revise them all. What can be said with some degree of certainty is that the UK legislation will usually form a major part of the answer and should not be excluded from your revision.

The possible effect of the dramatic changes that have taken place in the securities markets, including the introduction of dual capacity and computerised share dealings through the Stock Exchange Automated Quotations system (SEAQ), on the ability to deter and catch those taking part in insider dealing should not be overlooked. Some knowledge of the new regulatory procedures would therefore be of considerable value in this area.

Revising the 1993 Act

First of all make sure the Act applies to the company. Is it a listed company or a company whose shares are traded through an off-market dealer? If so then the Act applies. If not then you are left to apply the common law remedies that may be available. It is obvious that you must be able to ascertain when to apply the provisions of the 1985 Act to any question and that this will involve a certain amount of learning. Be careful not to fall into the trap of merely reciting the statutory provisions without making any attempt to apply them to the question. It is the salient points of the statute that you need to learn. The examiner will not expect, or want you to quote, the provisions verbatim. What he will be looking for is your ability to recognise a situation where an 'insider' has committed an offence of 'Insider dealing'. To be in a position to do this you will have to know the following things:

(a)   The categories of people who are considered to be insiders (s. 57).

(b)   The type of information considered to be inside information (ss. 56 and 58).

(c)   The circumstances which may amount to an offence (s. 52) and any defences that might be available (s. 53; FSA 1986, ss. 173 and 174). The Court of Appeal in *R* v *Cross* [1990] BCC 237 has made it clear that the evidential burden of proof in respect of a defence under s. 53 falls on the defendant. Thus the defence must bring forward evidence to establish their defence.

If you know how to identify these aspects you will be able to prove that the '*actus reus*' of the offence has been committed. Once you have shown that 'prima facie' an offence has been committed you will have to discuss the task upon the prosecution to prove that the accused had the necessary '*mens rea*' to commit the offence and also be able to point out any defences that the accused may be in a position to plead. Having reached this stage in your revision programme you should also revise the civil remedies that might be available to the company to allow it to recover any profit made by the insider. Whether you revise the provisions of the self-regulatory bodies will depend to a large extent on whether they have been included in your course and what emphasis has been placed upon them.

As a revision exercise using a copy of the statutory provisions go through the three problems below and apply the flow chart to each of the individuals involved in the problems. You will notice that this sort of exercise is mainly one of statutory interpretation and is probably best attempted after looking at the treatment of question 1 in this chapter.

Revision Exercises

Assume that the shares of all the companies mentioned are listed on the Stock Exchange.

1   Sheila is the secretary to Mr Shaw, director of High Hills Merchant Bank plc. During the course of her work she reads a report drawn up by Mr Shaw recommending that Alpha plc make a take-over bid for Delta plc. Sheila's husband Mike is a shareholder in Delta plc and on the basis of the information passed on to him by Sheila he buys another 1,000 shares in Delta plc.

Mike, who is having an affair with his secretary Nora, advises her to buy some shares in Delta plc as he believes they are a good investment. She buys 200.

Sheila also buys 500 shares for herself.

Alpha plc makes an offer of £1.55 (per share) for Delta plc's shares currently valued at 90p each. The shareholders accept the offer and the bid succeeds.

Discuss whether any offences have been committed under the Criminal Justice Act 1993, Part V.

2   Charles is a director of Panarama Developments plc and has just received a letter from Prestown Council informing him that the company has been awarded a contract worth £2 million to build the new Prestown University.

He carelessly leaves this letter on his desk. Florence, the office cleaner, reads the letter when she is cleaning the office that night. Later that evening she tells her friend Jackie of the contents of the letter at the weekly bingo session. Jackie wins £500 at bingo and decides to invest it in some shares in Panarama Developments plc.

When the news of the contract is announced the company's share value increases by 50p.

Discuss whether any offences have been committed under the Criminal Justice Act 1993, Part V.

3   Mark is the accountant of Fiddles plc and James is the company secretary. While preparing the company's accounts Mark realises that the company is going to declare a big loss when it makes its annual report. He also realises that the value of the company's shares will drop when this announcement is made.

Mark sells all the shares he owns in the company the next day.

James, who also owns shares in the company, has decided to sell them because his wife has to go into hospital and he needs the money to pay the bill. When Mark tells him of the loss that will be declared James says that it will make no difference to him because he was going to sell them anyway.

Have any offences been committed under the Criminal Justice Act 1993, Part V?

IDENTIFYING THE QUESTION

Questions on this topic are just as likely to take the form of essays as problems. In an essay it is likely that you will be required to discuss how effective the statutory provisions have been in combating insider dealing. Alternatively you may be asked to contrast the effectiveness of the statutory provisions with those of the self-regulatory bodies in combating insider dealing. As ever, it is important to read the question carefully. It is common to receive an answer from a candidate which discusses every statutory and self-regulatory provision in existence when the question asks only for a discussion of the statutory provisions. You will not be awarded marks for telling the examiner things he does not want to know!

Application and understanding are as important as a good knowledge of the available material in an essay question of this type. It can be very tempting to resort to writing down everything you can remember about this topic ('aerial bombing' again!) with very little attempt to use the relevant provisions to answer the question. This approach will mean that you will need to know a great deal about the topic to obtain a good pass mark.

Questions on insider dealing may also appear in problem form. This will usually require the application of the statutory or self-regulatory provisions, or both, to a given set of facts in order to determine whether or not a person is guilty of insider dealing or has broken one of the codes. In these circumstances it will be important to note whether or not the person or persons accused is a director or not. If a director is accused it will also be necessary for you to consider whether the company will have any remedies against him for breach of fiduciary duty (see chapter 6), and therefore be able to recover any profit made. You will also need to assess whether any other individuals in the question can be classed as fiduciaries and accountable on this basis. These points should be borne in mind when revising the material for this topic.

QUESTION 1

Martin and Tom are directors of Construction plc, a listed company. They also own a substantial number of shares in the company. They are aware of a possible takeover bid for the company by Build-It plc, also a listed company. If the bid took place it would mean that the shares in Construction plc would rise in value and the shares in Built-It plc would marginally fall in value.

Tom discussed the bid with Alex, a friend, at a dinner party. Later that week Alex buys 100 shares in Construction plc.

Martin instructs his wife Joan to sell her shares in Build-It plc and to buy shares in Construction plc but does not tell her why she should do this.

Martin buys another 500 shares in Construction plc.

After the bid is announced Construction plc's shares rise substantially in price and Build-It plc's fall in value.

Discuss any legal liability that may arise.

The rubric of the question asks you to discuss any *legal* liability that may arise. This should immediately tell you that the examiner only wants a discussion of the *legal* controls over insider dealing in the UK. This would exclude any substantive discussion of the Stock Exchange rules and the USA legislation although these may be mentioned briefly in passing. The main part of your answer should consist of a discussion of the 1993 Act (as you are told in the question that both companies are listed on the Stock Exchange), the way it regulates insider dealing and a discussion of any civil remedies that may be available to the company.

Before starting your answer you will find it useful to make a few notes on the following aspects of the problem:

(a)   Who are the possible insiders?
(b)   Is the information they have dealt with unpublished price sensitive information?
(c)   Have any offences been committed?
(d)   What penalties (if any) will be imposed for each insider?

At this stage these points represent questions you should consider when dealing with each character in the problem. They will all be looked at in more detail below.

Introduction

In this question you could usefully explain what insider dealing is, how it occurs and that it is regulated in this country by statute and common law. Then go on to state that the statutory and common law rules need to be examined to determine liability.

Who Are the Insiders? The Provisions of the Criminal Justice Act 1993

The first thing to do in any question involving this Act is to make sure it applies. The insider dealing provisions only apply to share dealings on regulated markets or those relying on a professional intermediary. Therefore, the companies regulated by the provisions must be public companies whose shares are dealt with by either of the above methods.

Construction plc and Build-It plc are public companies whose shares are quoted on the Stock Exchange and both are therefore subject to the provisions of the Act.

The next step is to identify the insiders in the problem. Section 57 of the Act defines an insider as an individual who has information as an insider if and only if:

(a)   it is, and he knows that it is, inside information, and
(b)   he has it, and knows that he has it, from an inside source.

The section goes on to point out that a person has inside information from an inside source if and only if:

(a)   he has it through:

(i)   being a director, employee or shareholder of an issuer of securities; or

(i)   having access to the information by virtue of his employment, office or profession; or

(b)   the direct or indirect source of his information is a person within paragraph (a).

The definition is wide particularly when s. 57(2)(a)(ii) and the way it will apply to tippees is considered. It is probably easiest to decide who are insiders first as this will allow you to exclude anyone who is not an insider from further consideration.

Martin is a director of the company and would clearly be an insider for the purposes of the Act.

Tom is in an identical position to Martin and would also be classed as an insider.

Alex is not directly connected with the company so at first sight you may not consider him to be an insider. However, s. 57(2)(b) will make him a 'tippee'. Consequently, we must consider whether Alex has *obtained the* information from an insider — Tom. Consequently he may still be guilty of an offence.

Joan would not fall within the definition of a 'primary' insider but has clearly obtained the information from someone connected with the company and like Alex maybe a 'tippee' within s. 57(2)(b) and there fore capable of committing an offence.

Is the Information 'Price Sensitive'?

An application of s. 56 is required here. The information on which the insider bases his decision to deal has got to relate to a *specific or precise matter* of importance and it must be the case that if the information were generally known it would have a significant effect on the value of that company's securities. Remember that the effect may be likely to result in either an *increase* or a *decrease* in the value of the shares. A possible take-over bid would seem to fall within the definition of price sensitive information. Be careful not to judge the effect of the information with hindsight because you have been told of the result of its publication. You must judge it at the time the dealing took place (i.e., before publication of the information).

Have Any of the 'Insiders' or 'Tippees' Committed an Offence?

At this stage in your answer it is best to deal with each person in turn and arrive at a final conclusion in respect of each individual. One offence is identifiable within s. 52 of the Act, although it may be committed in three different ways. It is obviously important that you are familiar with all three. They are:

(a)   dealing in securities where the price will be affected by the inside information (s. 52(1)).
(b)   encouraging another person to deal (s. 52(2)(a)); and
(c)   disclosing the inside information to another person (s. 52(2)(b)).

The major difference between this and the old law is that for procuring or disclosing the prosecution no longer need to show that the insider knew or ought to have realised that someone would deal. This will obviously improve the chances of successful prosecutions and give the legislation some teeth.

Tom

You should have decided that Tom is an insider in possession of unpublished price sensitive information. He has not dealt personally but has passed on information to another person. Is he, therefore, guilty of an offence under either s. 52(2)(a) or s. 52(2)(b)? The question gives no indication as to whether or not it was likely that Alex would buy the shares and under the old law that would have made the prosecution's task difficult. Under the 1993 Act this factor is no longer an issue for the prosecution and will make the offence easier to prove to a jury.

Alex

It would seem that Alex purchased the 100 shares as a direct result of information being passed on to him by Tom and therefore could be guilty as a 'tippee' dealing on the basis of inside information under s. 52(1).

The prosecution will need to prove that Alex *knew* that Tom was an insider and that Alex *knew* the information that he received was inside information. The new law no longer uses the term 'knowingly obtained' and as a consequence the decision in *Attorney-General's Reference (No. 1 of 1988)* [1989] AC 971 is no longer relevant. The fact that Alex has acted promptly in response to the information suggests that he has understood its significance.

Martin

Martin provides you with the classic case of insider dealing. He is an 'Insider' in possession of unpublished price sensitive information, he has bought shares and made a profit. It is fairly certain that he has committed an offence under s. 52(1). This aspect of the problem is similar to the facts of the Scottish case *Lord Advocate* v *Bryce* (unreported 21 August 198 1), where the defendant Bryce bought 3,900 shares knowing that information was going to be released the following day which would force the share value up. In this case the court rather surprisingly agreed to give Bryce an absolute discharge when Bryce agreed to compensate the jobber he had bought the shares from for the loss he had suffered!

In addition Martin has told his wife Joan to sell shares which he *knows* are likely to fall in value and to buy shares that he knows are likely to increase in value. Therefore, it is probable that he is guilty of an offence under either s. 52(a) or (b). You can compare this situation with the one that occurred in the case *R* v *Titheridge* (unreported 17 December 1982). In that case the insider (Mrs Titheridge) passed on information to her husband who bought shares on the basis of the information and made a profit in excess of £6,000. The interesting point to note is that the insider was charged with 'counselling and procuring' another to deal under s. 52(a) (then CA 1980, s. 68(6)) rather than 'tipping' under s. 52(b) (then CA 1980, s. 68(7)) when on the facts of the case a charge of 'tipping' could have succeeded. Consequently it seems likely that a charge of counselling or procuring will be successful in this situation.

Joan

Joan has clearly bought and sold shares as a direct result of Martin's instructions. The real question here is does she have the necessary *'mens rea'* to be guilty of an offence under s. 52(1)? The question tells you that Martin does not reveal his reasons for asking her to carry out these transactions. If, as seems likely, she does not deal on the basis of inside information then she will not be guilty. However, remember that this will make no difference to Martin's guilt on the issue of encouraging another to deal.

Civil Remedies

Those insiders found to be guilty under the 1993 Act may also find that they are forced to disgorge the fruits of their activities to their company. To be able to force the insider to hand over his profits you will first have to establish that he stands in a fiduciary relationship with the company.

In this particular question there are two obvious fiduciaries — Tom and Martin the two directors of Construction plc. Of the two directors only Martin has made a profit as a result of his activities. On the basis that the law will not allow a fiduciary to derive any advantage from his position Martin will have to disgorge his profits to the company. The authority for this principle is well-established (see *Regal (Hastings) Ltd* v *Gulliver* [1942] 1 All ER 378 and *Industrial Development Consultants Ltd* v *Cooley* [1972] 1 WLR 443). The fact that the company has not suffered any direct loss is not important. The deciding factor is whether the fiduciary has made a profit. Therefore, Martin will have to hand over the money he has made to Construction plc. You must also consider whether a civil liability could be imposed under FSA 1986, s. 62. This may be possible if it is shown that the insider is in breach of statutory duty and the person bringing the action has as a consequence suffered loss.

This might now be a good opportunity to return to the revision exercises given earlier and to apply the same sort of treatment given to question 1 to those exercises. You will need a copy of the statutory provisions to hand while you are doing this because the exercises do highlight some of the problems surrounding the interpretation of the 1993 provisions.

QUESTION 2

More than a decade after it was declared illegal, insider dealing in the UK remains rife. Despite all the efforts of the Fraud Squad and the International Stock Exchange there have been few successful prosecutions.

Critically analyse this statement.

Identifying the Main Issues

As with all essay questions it is easy to launch into an answer without any real idea of what you are going to write or the order in which you are going to write it. The question asks you to critically analyse the statement. This should tell you that the examiner wants an analysis of the insider dealing legislation and what is more, a critical analysis of the legislation's effectiveness.

The easiest way to structure your answer is on the following lines:

(a)   The main thrust of the provisions of Criminal Justice Act 1993.

(b)   Problems of enforcement, particularly problems relating to detection of insiders, overseas nominee companies, proving the criminal offence.

(c)   Are the present remedies and sanctions effective? Should we consider the introduction of civil remedies?

(d)   Conclusion.

Main Issues

The Criminal Justice Act 1993

The provisions regulating insider dealing were originally contained in the CA 1980, so they have been in force for more than a decade. The provisions make it a criminal offence for an insider (defined by s. 57 of the 1993 Act) to deal in one of the ways prohibited by the Act (see s. 52) in the shares of a public limited company on a regulated market on the basis of unpublished price sensitive information. The Act makes no attempt to provide civil remedies for any person who has dealt with the insider. Having set the scene by outlining the way in which the legislation operates, you now need to address the specific issues raised by the question.

Prior to the passing of the legislation it was thought that insider dealing was rife on the Stock Exchange. However, since the legislation came into force only 33 prosecutions have been brought resulting in just 18 convictions. The figures would seem to indicate one of two things — either:

(a)   insider dealing is not as widespread as was originally thought (but as the question tells you it is, consider the second); or
(b)   the legislation is not doing the job in catching and convicting insiders.

In this question the examiner clearly wants you to concentrate on the second possibility. Therefore we need to examine the problems that have been apparent in the legislation and which limit its effectiveness.

Problems of enforcement
The Criminal Justice Act 1993 does not establish a body comparable to the Securities Exchange Commission (SEC) in the USA to police the Act. Instead the task is entrusted to the Stock Exchange Surveillance Department in conjunction with the Department of Trade and Industry. When compared to SEC the powers and forces of their UK counterparts are extremely limited (see 'The 50 year-old Wall Street Cop still on the beat' *The Economist,* vol. 291 (30 June 1984), p. 67) despite the attempts to increase powers of investigation (see FSA 1986, ss. 177 and 178), detection is still a problem. In addition the over-the-counter market in the UK is virtually non-existent when compared to the USA. Thus in the USA it is easier to pinpoint insiders dealing on the over-the-counter market.

An additional problem for the enforcement agencies is the use by insiders of nominee companies located overseas to deal in shares. It is usually the case that the national laws of the countries in which the nominee companies are located prohibit the release of information which might identify the beneficial owner of the shares. The introduction of the EEC Directive on insider dealing will improve this situation as between member States (see *Law Society's Gazette,* vol. 86, No. 22 (7 June 1989), and a recent agreement between the UK and USA will resolve difficulties between these countries. However, it is likely that insiders will simply move elsewhere.

The final problem lies in proving the criminal offence once a prosecution has been brought. The prosecution have to prove that the accused had the necessary *mens rea* and prove it beyond a reasonable doubt. Coupled with these factors is the fact that insider dealing is a white-collar crime. Acquittal rates in jury trials are very high.

Having identified the major drawbacks with regard to enforcement you need to examine whether the sanctions provided act as a deterrent or not.

Sanctions and remedies
The Criminal Justice Act 1993 provides no civil remedy, only criminal sanctions. The criminal sanctions have been strengthened following the passing of the Criminal Justice Act 1988. However, to date no one in the UK has been imprisoned for the crime of insider dealing. This is in stark contrast to the USA, for example, where insiders are regularly imprisoned.

Additionally, the greatest deterrent in the USA seems to be the potential civil liability for insiders. Anyone who can show that he dealt simultaneously in the same securities as the insider can recover losses from him. There is no need to show that you actually dealt with the insider. This has led to insiders being sued for more than the net worth of the company. The introduction of such a remedy would undoubtedly act as a deterrent to potential insider dealers.

Conclusion

Remember to finish your answer with a conclusion drawing together all the problems you have identified in your answer to show why the legislation is not working.

It is too early to judge how effective the changes introduced by the 1993 legislation will be. A number of academics have expressed opinions on the likely effect of the changes and we would advise you to consider these views in an answer of this type. We list the main articles below.

FURTHER READING

Alcock, Alistair, 'Insider dealing — How did we get here?' (1994) 15 Co Law 67.
Dine, J., 'Implementation of the EC insider trading Directive in the UK' (1993) 14 Co Law 61.
White, Matthew, 'The implications for securities regulation of new insider dealing provisions in the Criminal Justice Act 1993' (1995) 16 Co Law 163.

8 SHARE CAPITAL AND THE MAINTENANCE OF CAPITAL

INTRODUCTION

This is not exactly one of the most riveting areas of company law that you will ever encounter. Since the passing of the 1980 and 1981 Companies Acts, now consolidated into the CA 1985, it is mainly concerned with complex statutory provisions which lay down strict, boring-to-learn procedures relating to the payment for, and maintenance of, share capital. This topic also involves the use of terms and phrases, the meaning of which you may have been able to get away with not fully understanding up until now: nominal or par value, redeemable shares, share premiums, capital redemption reserve, to mention a few. The spaghetti bowl of statutory provisions is thus liberally topped with a thick sauce of jargonese.

The share capital of a company is only one source of external funding that a company uses to finance its activities. It is not a major source; of far greater importance are retained earnings, a form of internal funding comprising profits that a company does not distribute to its shareholders in the form of dividends. Indeed, Galbraith (*The New Industrial State*, 2nd ed., p. 95) has commented that,

> It is hard to overestimate the importance of the shift in power that is associated with availability of such a source of capital. Few other developments can have more fundamentally altered the character of capitalism. It is hardly surprising that retained earnings of corporations have become such an overwhelmingly important source of capital.

However, managers of companies have to remember that one of the proper and legitimate expectations of members is the distribution of profits via dividends, and that it could amount to unfairly prejudical conduct under CA 1985, s. 459:

> . . . to retain in the company for the greater growth and glory of the company profits which could with entire propriety and commercial ease be paid out to members in dividends for the benefit of members (*Re a Company, ex parte Glossop* [1988] 1 WLR 1068 per Harman J at p. 1075).

Funds are also raised through loans to the company which are dealt with in the next chapter.

To raise a significant amount of 'equity finance', public companies need to offer investors the facilities of trading shares on the Stock Exchange. A company's shares may be 'officially listed' on the Exchange's main market, or traded on the Alternative Investment Market (AIM) established in June 1995 to give new and growing companies a cheaper mechanism for raising equity capital on the London Stock Exchange. Private limited companies cannot offer their shares or debentures to the public (CA 1985, s. 81; FSA 1986, s. 170).

What is 'equity finance'? We have already seen that the share capital of a company can be divided into different classes of shares (see chapter 5). A company's 'equity share capital' excludes shares which do not have a right to participate, either in dividend or capital distribution, beyond a specified amount. This normally excludes preference shares which will usually only have a limited right to a set dividend (e.g., 7 per cent) and no right to participate in surplus assets on a winding up. A slightly different form of wording is used with regard to the pre-emption rights conferred on existing shareholders when 'equity securities' are allotted (see CA 1985, ss. 89 and 94, in relation to 'equity securities' and CA 1985, s. 744, for 'equity share capital').

Prior to the CA 1980 the courts had developed complex rules in what was often an unsuccessful attempt to ensure that the company's capital remained intact as a fund which creditors could look to as security for their debts. These rules were partially consolidated, and considerably strengthened, in the CA 1980 which, together with the CA 1981, provided the statutory framework relating to the maintenance of capital now found in Parts IV and V of CA 1985. These rules are tighter for public companies which have a minimum capital requirement. The statutory reforms were prompted by the Second EEC Council Directive on Company Law (OJ 1977 No. L26/1). You therefore have the ingredients for the examiner's delight: common law rules partially codified and strengthened by statutory provisions prompted by an EEC Directive. If you ally this to the remaining common law rules which could impose a trust or constructive trust in respect of the misuse of corporate funds in relation to the payment for shares, then any examiner can go into ecstasies developing a problem to test the confused and unsuspecting student.

Share capital is not just a way of raising funds, as is loan capital. The company is not the shareholder's debtor as it is the debenture holder's. Pennington refers to shares as 'simply bundles of contractual and statutory rights' conferred on the holders of the shares. The right to a dividend and a return of capital on a winding up are the two rights which really give the share a value. There are other rights which will usually include the right to vote and have the company managed according to its constitution (see CA 1985, s. 14, and chapter 5). Share capital therefore occupies a special place in the funding and management of the company's activities.

MAIN ISSUES

Minimum Capital Requirement

The CA 1980 introduced substantial changes regarding the law on the maintenance of share capital, including a provision that public companies required a minimum paid-up capital of £50,000 (now see CA 1985, s. 11). It has been suggested that there should be a minimum capital requirement for all companies so as to discourage the under-capitalised business and thus give some protection to creditors. This links up to some of the problems associated with the abuse of the corporate form seen in chapter 3, a minimum capital requirement being another method of tackling some aspects of these abuses.

A minimum capital requirement was required by the aborted Companies Bill 1973, and was also looked at in the Green Paper, *A New Form of Incorporation for Small Firms* (Cmnd 8171, 1981). It was anticipated in the Green Paper that such a requirement could lead to businesses looking for an alternative constitution to trade under, including the limited partnership or the suggested 'incorporated firm' proposed by Professor Gower in the Green Paper. These proposals, which included provisions for a form of articles for a partnership company (CA 1989, s. 128), have been overtaken by the Department of Trade and Industry review of company law which included a feasibility study into the reform of company law as it affects small private companies. Any question that asks for a discussion of the relative merits of the various forms of business organisation should include some reference to the proposals put forward in this Green Paper and the current review (see chapter 2).

Maintenance of Capital

The original common law rules relating to the maintenance of capital were designed to ensure:

(a) that the money or other consideration that the company actually receives from, or is promised by, the shareholders for their shares, is equivalent to the nominal value and any premium payable for the shares, and

(b) that the moneys received by the company are maintained as a capital fund to which the creditors of the company can look as security for their debts.

However, these rules must be put into the context of the overall financial position of a company. In practice the moneys received from shareholders are used to purchase corporate assets: land, buildings, plant, stock etc. Many creditors take charges over these and other assets of the company. The rules relating to the maintenance of share capital do not prevent companies obtaining loan capital or incurring debts that exceed the amount of share capital that has been raised. Indeed, this is often the case, although companies must be wary of the ratio of equity to loan capital getting too unbalanced. This is called the gearing ratio. Heavy reliance on loan capital, a high gearing ratio, where interest must be paid whether or not a profit has been made, can cause problems in lean years. If a company cannot pay its interest charge in a year it will be in serious financial difficulties which could lead to liquidation. A low gearing ratio, where the company is not guaranteeing its shareholders a return each year, puts a company at less risk when there are interruptions in production and sales.

The trade creditor has difficulties in obtaining security for his debt and is often the first to discover that, on a corporate liquidation, the company does not have sufficient capital to repay all or even any of its unsecured creditors, let alone thinking of returning capital to its shareholders. Such trade creditors have tried to resort to reservation of property clauses to protect their interests with limited success (see *Aluminium Industrie Vaassen BV v Romalpa Aluminium Ltd* [1976] 1 WLR 676 and chapter 9).

The main statutory rules ensure that the shares are paid for in money or money's worth to the extent of the nominal value of the share and any premium, and that these moneys do not disappear. They involve consideration of the following points:

(a) What restrictions are there on the consideration that must be offered in return for shares?

(b) When can a company purchase its own shares?

(c) When can a company provide financial assistance for the purchase of its own shares?

(d) Can capital be returned to the shareholders in the form of dividends?

(e) When can a company reduce its capital?

These main areas are considered further in questions 1 and 2 along with a brief consideration of what authority is required to issue shares and the statutory pre-emption right on allotment of shares.

REVISION AND RESEARCH

Because the law on the issue and maintenance of share capital is governed largely by statutory provisions, it is easy to fall into the trap of simply stating these provisions in any answer without really applying them to the facts in a given problem. For some reason, the technique of applying and distinguishing any decided cases from the facts of a problem seems to evaporate when it comes to the application of statutory materials. But, just as you need to know the salient points of cases, so you also need to know the important parts of the relevant statutes, particularly in company law which is dominated by statutory provisions. Even if you are provided with statutory materials in examinations you still need to know which section to look at and which part of that section is at issue; this is a research and revision exercise.

The detailed provisions of some of the procedures involved are less likely to be needed to answer an essay question (see question 1); you need to know the general content of the provisions rather than the specific details. In problem questions the details may need to surface to a far greater extent: the definition of 'financial assistance' (CA 1985, s. 152(1)(a)) or the method of payment for shares are examples. If the proper procedures have not been complied with in that either shares have been issued at a discount or have been paid for incorrectly, you will need to be aware of any liabilities that may ensue, both civil and criminal (see the provisions for civil liability in CA 1985, ss. 99–102, and criminal liability in s. 114).

The statutory provisions replaced a substantial body of case law. How far do you need to delve into the old common law provisions? In assessment and examination essay questions in particular it is desirable to make some historical statement as to how the present situation has been arrived at: question 1 falls into this category. However, the statutory provisions are numerous and complex, and a balance must be achieved, preferably with a bias in favour of the current situation. Refer to the old common law to illustrate where it was inadequate and to show off your knowledge, but beware of spending too much time on it. A sprinkling of applied references to the contents of the Second EEC Directive will boost your grade.

If you are preparing an assessment question and time is not so pressing, then these are two areas where you might want to expand the content of your answer. Assessment answers can also be a useful way of illustrating to the examiner your breadth of reading. Such reading could include the Wilson Committee's Report (Committee to Review the Functioning of Financial Institutions, *Report* (Cmnnd 7937, 1980)), and the sections on equity finance in Samuels and Wilkes, *Management of Company Finance*. References to these sources can put any answer on share capital into the context of the overall funding requirements of the company. They also help to expand a bibliography.

Any question that is specifically aimed at the development of the company's ability to purchase its own shares should also include some references to the common law situation and the Second EEC Directive, as well as an appraisal of the Department of Trade's consultative document (*The Purchase by a Company of Its Own Shares, A Consultative Document*, Cmnd 7944, 1980).

The terminology that is used in this area of company law needs to be understood. We have already looked at the definition of 'equity capital', and a revision programme could include ensuring that you are clear in your mind as to the meaning of certain words and phrases. As a revision exercise it may be useful to run through the terms in italics in the following paragraph and, where relevant, recall the statutory provisions, procedures, and articles of Table A that are applicable to each.

The *nominal value* of the share is stated in the memorandum of association and is the value of the share as printed on the share certificate. The memorandum also states the total number of shares that can be issued, the *authorised capital* of the company. If there is a market in the shares then the *market value* will rarely be the same as the nominal value which is also sometimes referred to as the *par value* of the share. It has been suggested that shares should not carry a par value as this can lead some people to buy a £1 par value share on the Stock Exchange for 50 pence thinking that they have got a bargain! Shares can be issued at a *premium,* the proceeds of any such sale being transferred into a protected capital account called the *share premium account*. If a company issues shares with a nominal value of £1 with a 20p premium, £1 goes into the share capital account and 20p into the share premium account. If a company has been doing well it may wish to *capitalise its undistributed profits;* that is, convert its profits which have not been distributed as dividends, or which are disallowed from being so distributed under Part VIII of the CA 1985 (as they are not *distributable profits* within the meaning of the Act), into *bonus shares* which are allocated to existing shareholders. The contents of the share premium account, which also cannot be distributed as dividend, can be similarly capitalised, because the company is simply replacing its share premium account by an equivalent increased amount in the share capital account. *Redeemable shares* are issued shares which, at the option of the company or the shareholder, can be repurchased by the company. Such a repurchase must be funded from the proceeds of a new issue of shares or from distributable profits, and in the latter case a sum equivalent to the repaid capital must be transferred to a capital account called the *capital redemption reserve*, which can also be used to finance an issue of bonus shares.

IDENTIFYING THE QUESTION

Essay questions in this area should really pose no great difficulties of identification. They are usually concerned with the rules on maintenance of capital (see question 1) or the development of the power of a company to purchase its own shares.

Problem questions can cause difficulties. Any problem which involves an issue of shares may require a consideration of the authority for that issue and possible pre-emption rights (see question 2). However, look out for whether the question states that the issue was 'regularly made' or 'properly approved' because this would then indicate that the examiner does not want you to consider the 'issue' question, but is using the share issue in the problem to open up other areas of law (e.g., alteration of class rights: see question 2 in chapter 5; or a breach of directors' duties in respect of the issue).

Where shares are paid for in a problem, it is important to identify the method of payment. For example, part of a problem involving a public company could state either:

(a)   B was allotted 600 shares in return for a painting commissioned by the company, but which he has not yet finished; B has now given 300 of the shares to his brother, and sold the rest to D; or

(b)   E was allotted 2,000 shares in return for a car number-plate for the managing director's car (IX). E has now sold 1,000 of these shares to F who has sold them to G, the managing director's wife.

You would need to establish what sort of consideration has been supplied for the shares and whether the correct statutory procedure had been followed. In B's case, for example, is the consideration a future non-cash consideration under CA 1985, s. 102, or a prohibited form of non-cash consideration, that is, an undertaking to do work or provide services (see CA 1985, s. 99(2))? Note that insertions into problems as illustrated above are also raising the issue of liability to pay for the shares.

We now turn to identifying the issues raised in two questions which are mainly concerned with the maintenance of capital.

QUESTION 1

'The company has only its capital to back its credit, and this being so it is essential that capital should be more carefully defined and inviolable' (Gower, 1979).

Critically analyse the extent to which the statutory rules relating to the raising and maintenance of capital achieve these aims.

The rules relating to the raising and maintenance of capital are full of procedural requirements and, in respect of dividend payments, complex accounting requirements. The theme of this question concerns to what extent those rules are sufficient in safeguarding the company's capital. You should also note that the question asks about the 'statutory rules', and any reference to common law provisions needs to be linked to the statutory measures. Given that Gower's statement was made prior to the Companies Acts 1980 and 1981, some reference to the previous common law situation will be necessary in order to compare the effectiveness of the statutory provisions in safeguarding the company's capital. But, be careful with your timing. The answer to this question requires that you 'critically analyse' the statutory rules, and any overindulgence or 'overkill' in the treatment of the previous common law provisions could jeopardise this requirement. However, any introduction could refer to the development of the statutory provisions from the basic principles outlined in the common law, supplemented by the requirements of the Second EEC Directive on Company Law, noting that public and private companies are now treated differently. The main part of the answer would then look at:

(a)   A minimum capital requirement.
(b)   The issue of shares for proper consideration.
(c)   The company's ability to buy its own shares.
(d)   The provision of funds by a company to enable third parties to buy the company's shares.
(e)   A dividend can only be paid out of distributable profits.
(f)   The statutory restrictions on any formal reductions of capital.

As you can see, the answer to this question could be extremely long if you went into great detail on all of these points; you have to be selective in your answer directing your attention as much as possible towards the principles outlined in the question, that is, a critical analysis of the definition and inviolability of capital.

The first two categories concern whether the company actually puts into its coffers a sum which is equivalent to the nominal value and any premium of the shares allocated. The remaining categories concern the maintenance of that capital fund to which the creditors look as security for their debts.

A Minimum Capital Requirement

Public companies require a minimum allotted share capital, and one-quarter of the nominal value and all of any premium must be paid on allotment (CA 1985, s. 11). There are exceptions to the one-quarter requirement for shares allotted in pursuance of any employees' share scheme or as bonus shares, but otherwise the allottee is liable to pay the minimum amount if a contravention occurs.

Prior to the CA 1980 there was no minimum capital requirement for any company. Now, in respect of public companies, the appearance of 'plc' after a company's name informs the unsuspecting creditor that this company should have received the grand sum of at least one-quarter of £50,000 from its shareholders and can call on the remaining three-quarters. Whether that capital fund is still there, and represented by assets that are at least equivalent to the capital moneys received, is another question. Also, as we have seen earlier in this chapter, the total volume of debts could exceed the total amount of capital. However, before we move on to consider the rules relating to the maintenance of the capital fund we still need to ensure that the correct amount is actually received into that fund.

Proper Consideration

It is impossible to maintain the company's capital if, at the outset, shares are issued for less than their nominal value and any share premium. The common law rule which prevented the issue of shares at a discount (*Ooregum Gold Mining Co. of India Ltd* v *Roper* [1892] AC 125) is now expressly stated in CA 1985, s. 100. If a share has a nominal value of £1 it must be issued for at least £1, and not for 50p (but see the exception in CA 1985, s. 97). A loophole existed where shares were issued for a consideration other than cash, the courts adopting the typical contractual stance and being reluctant to intervene with the nature of the consideration, at least in the absence of fraud, patent inadequacy or unless the company had never assessed the value of the consideration (see *Re Wragg Ltd* [1897] 1 Ch 796; *Tintin Exploration Syndicate Ltd* v *Sandys* (1947) 177 LT 412). Although there will be insufficient time to go into great detail about the common law situation you need to mention it, because this loophole still exists for private companies. You also need to contrast it with the extensive valuation provisions for non-cash assets accepted by public companies as payment for shares (see CA 1985, ss. 103 and 108–1 1). The statutory rules also prevent shares in public companies being paid for by an undertaking to do work or provide services, and any future non-cash considerations must be contracted to be transferred within at least five years (CA 1985, ss. 99 and 102). The sanctions that apply if the valuation provisions are breached are severe. A good illustration is *Re Bradford Investments plc (No. 2)* [1991] BCLC 688, where an existing partnership was sold by Hall to the plc in exchange for £1 million of shares in the plc. No independent valuation of the partnership took place (CA 1985, s. 103). The judge concluded that the partnership had no net value at the time of the sale and Hall was liable to pay the company the nominal value of the shares with interest (CA 1985, s. 103(6)). Hall had not discharged the burden of proving that the company received value for its shares (CA 1985, s. 113). Liability also extends to the subsequent holders of shares unless they are purchasers for value and did not have notice of contravention of the valuation provisions (CA 1985, s. 112; see also *System Control plc v Munro Corporate plc* [1990] BCLC 659). You can therefore use this section of your answer to illustrate how provisions first introduced in the CA 1980 have generally tightened up the law relating to the moneys that must actually flow into the capital account. These provisions concentrate on the public company to ensure that the minimum authorised capital that is required, and which 'plc' indicates a company has got, at least starts off in the company's coffers, even if it disappears thereafter. That is the next part of the answer: the maintenance of the capital funds.

Corporate Purchase of Own Shares

Throughout the provisions that relate to the maintenance of capital you will come across various statutory procedures. In an essay question of this sort it is unnecessary, and indeed impossible in the time allowed, to go into great detail about these procedures; the basic provisions will usually suffice so as to convey the theme of the legislation. That is, to erect as many procedural barriers and safeguards for the protection of creditors and shareholders as are commensurate with the fairly recent desire to allow companies to develop by allowing them to purchase their own shares, issue redeemable shares and, in the case of private companies, provide finance for the purchase of their own shares.

If a company buys back its own shares, and Table A, art. 35 does confer that power, it is reducing its capital. Until the CA 1981 this was expressly prohibited, CA 1980, s. 35, recognising the previous common law rule in *Trevor v Whitworth* (1888) 12 App Cas 409, and making such purchases a criminal offence with a maximum criminal liability of two years' imprisonment plus a fine for breaches of the prohibition. However, two reports had suggested that in some cases, especially for private companies, it could be advantageous for companies to be able to buy their own shares (Committee to Review the Financing of Financial Institutions, *The Financing of Small Firms* (Cmnd 7503, 1979); *The Purchase by a Company of Its Own Shares, A Consultative Document* (Cmnd 7944, 1980)). The CA 1981 therefore allowed for such purchases subject to a number of severe restrictions (now found in CA 1985, ss. 159–81). The question is aimed at whether the capital of the company is inviolable. Statutory permission for companies to purchase their own shares could lead to the capital being lost and therefore more vulnerable than under the previous common law rules. You therefore need to assess whether the greater freedom given to companies is counterbalanced by procedures which ensure that the capital fund remains intact.

With regard to the corporate purchase of its own shares the CA 1985 provides a general rule against a company acquiring its own shares (CA 1985, s. 143). This is subject to statutory authority to do so in three main areas where creditors of the company are safeguarded from the possibility of a company using its assets to finance the purchase to the detriment of security for creditors. The three main provisions are:

(a)   A general power to issue redeemable shares (CA 1985, s. 159). Table A, art. 3, provides that, subject to the Companies Acts, 'shares may be issued which are to be redeemed or are to be liable to be redeemed at the option of the company or the holder on such terms and in such manner as may be provided by the articles'. This contrasts with the pre–1981 situation where only redeemable preference shares could be issued. However, the capital fund is still maintained by the company because the company must either finance any repayment of the redeemable shares by the issue of new shares (figure 8.1) or by transferring distributable profits into a capital fund called the capital redemption reserve (figure 8.2 — see CA 1985, s. 170). Prior to the CA 1981 any premium paid on a redemption of shares could be paid out of the share premium account. This would amount to a loss of capital. Under the CA 1981 such redemption premium must also be paid out of a new issue of shares or distributable profits. However, it could be that the premium was actually contributed when the shares were issued and paid into the share premium account. In that case the redemption premium is in effect a repayment of capital and the share premium account can be written off as long as it is replaced by the proceeds of a new issue of shares (CA 1985, s. 160(2)). Therefore, overall in respect of replacing the premium paid on redemption, it could be argued that the provisions first introduced in the CA 1981 are tighter in maintaining the capital fund.

Figure 8.1

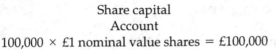

Share capital
Account
100,000 × £1 nominal value shares = £100,000

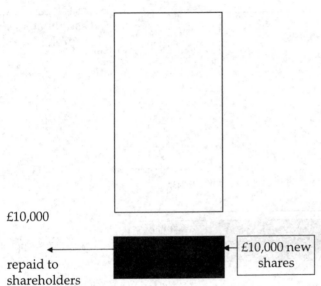

£10,000

repaid to
shareholders

£10,000 new
shares

(b) All companies are given the power to purchase their own shares whether issued as redeemable or not (CA 1985, s. 162; Table A, art. 35). This new provision could obviously lead to companies reducing the capital fund that Gower suggests should be 'inviolable'. But if the procedures require that equivalent sums to those which are repaid must be found and transferred to the protected capital accounts then the capital fund remains the same. These equivalent sums must be obtained either by issuing new shares and therefore replenishing the share capital account or by putting distributable profits into a protected account, the capital redemption reserve. This is required, as it was for the redemption of shares (see Figures 8.1 and 8.2 and CA 1985, ss. 160, 168 and 170–2).

Figure 8.2

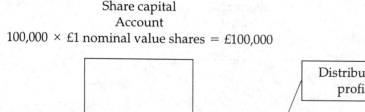

Share capital
Account
100,000 × £1 nominal value shares = £100,000

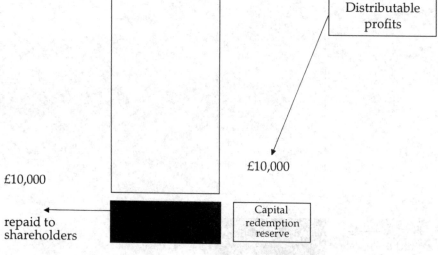

Distributable
profits

£10,000

£10,000
repaid to
shareholders

Capital
redemption
reserve

(c) Private companies can redeem or purchase shares out of capital and this is a situation where capital funds are lost (CA 1985, s. 171). There are strict procedures which must be followed, including a special resolution, a statutory declaration of solvency and strict time-limits. Also, the courts have wide powers on application by a shareholder or creditor, including the cancellation of the special resolution (CA 1985, ss. 173–7). After conferring the power in the articles for a company to purchase its own shares, Table A, art. 35, continues to provide that a private company can 'make a payment in respect of the redemption or purchase of its own shares otherwise than out of distributable profits of the company or the proceeds of a fresh issue of shares'. Although this power is subject to the restrictions in the Companies Acts, you need to make the point that despite these protections, and they are considerable, this is one area where capital can be effectively reduced that Gower had not envisaged in 1979 (see also CA 1985, ss. 135–41, for the statutory procedures for a formal reduction of capital for all companies).

Any answer on this topic would need to mention the odd decision in *Acatos & Hutcheson plc* v *Watson* [1995] 1 BCLC 218. This decision permits a holding company to purchase the shares of a company, turning it into its wholly owned subsidiary, even though the wholly owned subsidiary owns 29 per cent of the shares of the holding company. This is a judicially authorised 'sidestepping' of the principle in CA 1985, s. 143, the court acknowledging that the capital of the plaintiff was 'expended in buying (in effect) its own shares' (per Lightman J at p. 221). This seems to conflict with the requirement in s. 143 that a company should not acquire its own shares by purchase, subscription 'or otherwise'. The only way in which this case could be seen to be an isolated exception is that the court placed reliance upon the application of CA 1985, s. 23(4), which allows the wholly owned subsidiary to continue to hold the shares but not vote where the acquisition of the shares took place prior to November 1990. Otherwise subsidiaries could be used to avoid s. 143 with no protection for creditors.

Financial Assistance for the Purchase of the Company's Own Shares

Instead of a company buying its own shares, it could provide finance for a person to buy its own shares. This is tantamount to a company buying its own shares and was often used as a means by which speculators could buy a substantial amount of a company's shares and arrange matters so that the purchase money was provided by the company whose shares they had acquired (see *Selangor United Rubber Estates Ltd* v *Cradock (No. 3)* [1968] 1 WLR 1555). If there arc insufficient legal safeguards against this sort of practice then a gap exists whereby the capital of the company can be lost. In 1948 such conduct attracted a £100 fine. From 1981 the criminal sanction was increased to a maximum of two years' imprisonment and a fine, although there are some specific exceptions to the general principle that a company cannot provide funds for the purchase of its own shares (CA 1985, s. 151).

As we saw with the company purchasing its shares directly, the question is really asking in which areas will capital not be maintained? Are the penalties against reduction severe enough to deter it? Are the exceptions constrained sufficiently so as not to allow for easy avoidance of the general principle? A restatement of the various statutory provisions will reap greater rewards if you look at and make specific comments on the statutory requirements that can provide some of these answers.

The offence under CA 1985, s. 151, is for the company whose shares are to be acquired, or any of its subsidiaries which are English companies (*Arab Bank plc* v *Merchantile Holdings Ltd* [1994] 1 BCLC 330), to provide direct or indirect financial assistance either before or at the same time as the acquisition, or to reduce a liability incurred as a result of an acquisition. The exceptions are contained in CA 1985, s. 153, with extra restrictions on public companies in some cases if to give the assistance would involve a reduction of net assets. You would need to outline these exceptions which include where the principal purpose of the transaction is not for the assistance of the acquisition. This is one of the exceptions that could cause problems, as question 2 illustrates. There are concerns that the decision in the *Arab Bank* case appears to follow the same path as the decision in *Acatos & Hutcheson*, allowing the use of subsidiaries to avoid the statutory provisions.

The general prohibition in s. 151 is relaxed for private companies but again there are several procedural restrictions. There has to be a special resolution, no reduction in the company's net assets (or if there is, it has to be made up out of distributable profits) and another statutory declaration. There is also a strict time-scale as to when the assistance can be given, although in this case only dissentient shareholders, not creditors, can apply to the court to cancel the special resolution (CA 1985, ss. 155–8).

Therefore, you can see that the procedural requirements for a company purchasing its shares and providing financial assistance for the purchase of its own shares are exacting and similar in both cases. 'Inviolability' is protected by imposing legal penalties and procedures which you will need to analyse briefly to examine their effectiveness. The other requirement that can be seen from Gower's statement was that capital should also be 'more carefully defined'. We have already seen that the capital accounts, including the capital redemption reserve and share premium account, have been protected in greater detail and therefore more carefully defined. We now turn to another area where the definition of capital that is protected is important, it concerns the restriction on distributing dividends from capital.

Dividends Are Only Payable out of Distributable Profits

Dividends are only payable out of profits calculated by reference to the last properly prepared accounts and the rules laid down in Part VIII of CA 1985. A rule that applies to all companies requires the auditors, when giving a qualified report on a company's accounts, to state whether or not the matter in respect of which the report is qualified is material to a lawful distribution of profits. This statement must be laid before the general meeting (CA 1985, s. 271). This is a mandatory requirement and a 'major protection for creditors' according to Dillon LJ in *Precision Dippings Ltd* v *Precision Dippings Marketing Ltd* [1986] Ch 447 at p. 457. Any payment of dividend in breach of this provision is *ultra vires* the company as is any payment of dividend except out of profits available for that purpose as defined in Part VIII of CA 1985. This *ultra vires* action does not fall within the protection offered by CA 1985, s. 35 [CA 1989, s. 108] as the lack of capacity does not arise from the company's memorandum. Generally, the rules vary in their strictness according to the status of the company: public, private or investment. There are now restrictions on the distribution of profits that are unrealised (i.e. capitalised profits). For a clear description of the effect this has on different companies with respect to the amount they could distribute both before and after the CA 1980, which first introduced these provisions, you should look at Renshall's article at (1980) 1 Co Law 194. Generally, less can be distributed after the restrictions in the CA 1980 came into operation than before, and capitalised profits in particular are protected. This has led to some criticism that the provisions are too harsh. Mayson, French and Ryan, in their section on distributions, argue that the new principles:

> ignore the fact that the contributed capital of a company is not simply kept intact waiting for winding up: it is used to buy a continually changing set of assets whose value may go up and down but rarely stays the same. In addition, retained profits, whether capitalised or not, are also spent on assets which change in value over time.

Indeed, a company can lose 'capital' simply through bad investment or depreciation of assets. There is little that can be done about this, the £1 nominal value of shares that have been issued not being matched in value by an equivalent amount of corporate assets. However, there is provision for an extraordinary general meeting where there is such a loss of net assets, although there is no indication as to what steps might be taken at that meeting (CA 1985, s. 142).

The Statutory Restrictions on Formal Reductions of Capital

These restrictions have already been briefly referred to and can be cited to illustrate, yet again, the restrictions on such reductions and the protection offered to shareholders and creditors (see CA 1985, ss. 135–41). Given Gower's statement, it is interesting to note that the statutory procedure for a formal reduction of capital has been said to demonstrate that 'there is no status of inviolability ataching to a company's capital' (*Re Grosvenor Press plc* [1985] 1 WLR 980 at p. 985 per Nourse J). As a consequence of the strict rules that have been placed on the profits available for dividend distribution, many companies applied for a formal reduction of capital in order to dispose of any deficit on their profit and loss account, and so enable dividends to be paid. Normally such formal reductions require a special resolution of the company in general meeting as well as the sanction of the court (CA 1985, s. 135; but see *Re Barry Artist Ltd* [1985] 1 WLR 1305). An undertaking to protect existing creditors will also be required as in *Re Grosvenor Press plc*. As we saw with the provisions relating to the purchase by a company of its own shares, there is a general flexibility supplemented by various procedural mechanisms to protect members and creditors.

Conclusion

Any conclusion on this type of question will require a gathering together of the direction you have taken when analysing the statutory provisions into a final crescendo. It is also permissible to question the validity of the statement you are presented with. The examiner can set up statements an answer to which will demand a criticism of the statement itself. In this case to what extent does the requirement of personal guarantees from directors, especially in private companies, or the holding company's backing of a subsidiary's credit through 'letters of comfort' to the subsidiary's auditors (see chapter 3, question 2) or mere presence in the background, decrease the reliance placed by creditors on the company maintaining its capital. The creditors who suffer most on liquidation are the unsecured trade creditors, and their concern must be not just the maintenance of a company's capital, because even if it is maintained the debts owed could exceed that capital; the main problem is that they don't get a look in upon a liquidation because the creditors with security, normally the banks, and the preferential creditors, usually the government as tax-collector, swallow up what assets remain. Protection of creditors can therefore concentrate on areas other than the maintenance of capital (*see Insolvency Law and Practice: Report of the Review Committee* [Chairman: Sir Kenneth Cork] (Cmnd 8558, 1982), chs 35 and 36, and the provisions relating to a temporary stay of the enforcement of any security in the IA 1986). It could involve the reduction of limited liability, a minimum capital requirement for all companies or widening the scope of fraudulent trading to cover wrongful trading (see chapter 3).

In this way you can link up various areas of company law and turn what could be a turgid description of the statutory provisions into a more comprehensive answer. This illustrates an awareness of areas of company law other than those immediately identifiable in the question. These comments could be interspersed throughout your answer but should be drawn together in a conclusion. However, don't let your enthusiasm for bringing in these other issues distract you so much that you fail to deal with the substantive content of the answer. This relates to the statutory procedures and how they allow companies to adapt their capital structure according to the needs of the individual company, but nevertheless contain this 'freedom' with strict procedural requirements.

QUESTION 2

Glasshouses plc is a company that specialises in property development and it needs to acquire new land. It is also the subject of a take-over bid by Conglomerates plc which is opposed by all the directors of Glasshouses except Gerry, the managing director. Fanny plc wants to acquire a shareholding interest in Glasshouses but lacks sufficient liquid funds to do so.

An agreement is reached whereby Glasshouses is to purchase land owned by Fanny for £1 million, and the directors of Glasshouses are to allocate to Fanny 1 million shares with a nominal value of £1 each. Fanny pays for these shares from the proceeds of the sale of its land. All the cheques for the transactions pass through Barcland Bank plc, the manager of which is assured that Glasshouses' funds are not being misapplied.

Gerry resigns and is paid £25,000 compensation. Conglomerate discovers that the land acquired by Glasshouses is really only valued at £$\frac{1}{4}$ million.

Discuss the lawfulness of these actions.

This problem doesn't just involve issues concerning the share capital of the company. That does comprise the main part of the problem, but the facts surrounding Gerry's resignation require an application of CA 1985, s. 312 (see *Re Duomatic Ltd* [1969] 2 Ch 365 and *Taupo Totara Timber Co. Ltd v Rowe* [1978] AC 537). The question illustrates how 'mixed' questions can be strung together. You need to identify the problem as being predominantly concerned with share capital, its issue and the source of the payment received for it, and allocate your time accordingly. However, in any problem concerning the issue of shares by directors you will undoubtedly have to consider the purposes behind the allocation and assess whether or not there has been any breach of directors' duties (see *Howard Smith Ltd v Ampol Petroleum Ltd* [1974] AC 821, *Hogg v Cramphorn Ltd* [1967] Ch 254 and chapter 7). You will have to do that to answer this question adequately.

The facts of the problem bear some resemblance to the two main cases in this area: *Belmont Finance Corporation Ltd v Williams Furniture Ltd (No. 2)* [1980] 1 All ER 393 and *Selangor United Rubber Estates Ltd v Cradock (No. 3)* [1968] 1 WLR 1555. Glasshouses is involved in providing finance for the purchase of its own shares by Fanny via a circular transaction which involved the Barcland Bank. Note that all the companies, and Glasshouses in particular, are public companies. Any answer can be split up into the following main areas:

(a)   Is there a power to issue the shares and has the statutory preemption right been ignored (CA 1985, ss. 80 and 89)?

(b)   The application of CA 1985, ss. 151–4, as regards Glasshouses providing finance for the purchase of its own shares.

(c)   Possible breaches of trust by all those involved in the transaction which involves a possible misuse and loss of Glasshouses' funds. This could also include a consideration of whether the tort of conspiracy applies as suggested in *Belmont Finance Corporation Ltd v Williams Furniture Ltd.*

You would also need to insert into that structure the other issues which have been identified but which do not fall within the remit of this chapter: the treatment of CA 1985, s. 312, and the aspect of directors' duties relating to the exercise of their powers for proper purposes.

As an introduction to the answer you could outline these points that you intend to discuss later in detail. A higher grade could be achieved by mentioning the predecessor to the provisions regulating the giving of finance by a company to purchase its own shares. This was CA 1948, s. 54, which was fairly uncertain in its scope and offered only a limited sanction (see *Armour Hick Northern Ltd* v *Whitehouse* [1980] 1 WLR 1520 and the Report of the Company Law Committee [Chairman: Lord Jenkins] (Cmnd 1749, 1962), paras 170–6).

Authority to Issue Shares and Pre-emption Rights

This requires a straightforward application of ss. 80 and 89 of the CA 1985, and easy marks can be picked up speculating as to whether Glasshouses went through the correct procedure. You are not told that the issue was approved by a 'regularly conducted general meeting of the shareholders', and therefore you need to state what the correct procedures are for the authority to issue shares and to override the statutory pre-emption right. If Glasshouses had been a private company you would have needed to refer to the different procedures introduced by the CA 1989 regarding authority for allotments and the disapplication of pre-emption rights (CA 1985, s. 80A [CA 1989, ss. 113 and 114]. Although criminal penalties are provided for directors who knowingly and wilfully issue shares without the requisite authority, the validity of the allotment is not affected (CA 1985, s. 80(10)). A contravention of the pre-emption right gives rise to a civil sanction against the company and its officers to compensate for any loss suffered as a result of the contravention, but again does not appear to invalidate the allotment itself (CA 1985, s. 92). You need to make clear the effect of the possible breaches of ss. 80 and 89 on the facts presented in the Glasshouses problem.

CA 1985, Sections 151–4

You need to establish that, under ss. 151 and 153, the purpose of the financial assistance is of crucial importance to the lawfulness of the transaction. There appear to be two transactions in the question: the contract to buy the land and the contract to buy the shares. The sums of money changing hands in each transaction are conveniently matched. A careful look at these statutory provisions reveals uncertainties which the examiner is attempting to exploit in the question, and which you need to identify and discuss. The issue is largely one of statutory interpretation and you must analyse the detail of the statutory provisions to achieve a good grade.

The basic prohibition in s. 151 makes it unlawful for a company to provide 'financial assistance' (see s. 152(1)(a)) directly or indirectly for the purchase of that company's own shares. This basic prohibition has several exceptions contained in s. 153. The exceptions that this question is probing concern the purpose of the assistance. Glasshouses did not need land, and can it therefore be said that their purchase of Fanny's land was carried out for an ulterior motive, that of providing finance to purchase Glasshouses' own shares so as to frustrate the take-over bid? Can there be a plurality of purposes and, if so, which one counts: the lawful or unlawful? To answer some of these questions it is necessary to look at the 'purpose' exceptions in s. 153 and the interpretation placed upon them by the House of Lords in *Brady* v *Brady* [1989] AC 755. The exceptions apply where:

(a)   the principal purpose of the assistance is not for the acquisition of the company's own shares, or
(b)   the assistance is an incidental part of a larger purpose of the company, and
(c)   in respect of both (a) and (b), the assistance is given in good faith in the interests of the company.

You will need to apply these tests to the facts in the problem. It is not easy. In *Brady* v *Brady*, Lord Oliver commented, at p. 778, that:

The ambit of the operation of the section is . . . far from easy to discern, for the word 'purpose' is capable of several different shades of meaning.

It was clear in *Brady* v *Brady* that the provision of assistance by one company (Brady) was intended to reduce the liability incurred in the course of the acquisition of Brady shares by another company (Motoreal). This fell within CA 1985, s. 151(2). The transaction was part of a reconstruction by two brothers, the sole directors of a family business, in order to get the business out of a management deadlock. It was argued that this was the 'purpose' of the transaction. The difficulty in interpreting s. 153 was illustrated in that the trial judge and the Court of Appeal judges thought that the arrangement failed the 'good faith' test but passed the 'purpose' tests, whereas the House of Lords arrived at exactly the opposite conclusion. You will need to apply the reasoning in *Brady* v *Brady* to each part of s. 153:

(a)   What was the 'principal purpose' of the assistance? The facts seem similar to *Belmont Finance Corporation Ltd* v *Williams Furniture Ltd (No. 2)* [1980] 1 All ER 393, and the problem suggests that the whole arrangement, including the undervaluation of the land, was concocted so as to financially assist the purchase and defeat the take-over bid. But was the principal purpose to frustrate the take-over bid or assist the purchase? In *Brady* v *Brady* the House of Lords held that the principal purpose of the transaction was solely to reduce Motoreal's indebtedness. The provision would cover a

SHARE CAPITAL AND THE MAINTENANCE OF CAPITAL

situation where a company purchased an asset for its business and, incidental to that purchase, the consideration is used to acquire that company's shares or to reduce a liability already incurred by such an acquisition.

(b) The second test seems similar to the first, but worded slightly differently referring to 'some larger purpose' of the company, the assistance being only an 'incidental part' of that larger purpose. Presumably, 'larger purpose' in this second test means bigger than the otherwise unlawful purpose which is the subject of the basic prohibition in s. 151. In the problem, if 60 per cent of the company's purpose is to buy the land and 40 per cent is to provide the financial assistance, the exception could apply if it could be shown that the assistance was an 'incidental part' of this legitimate larger purpose and made in good faith (remember it cost them £¾ million more than the true value of the land). Putting the purpose of a company's actions on a scale from 1 to 100 is not a practical test, but it does illustrate the problems that occur when draftsmen start getting involved with plurality of purposes. In *Brady* v *Brady*, Lord Oliver considered that the purpose which had to be identified was that 'of the company'. Did the company have a purpose for the transaction which exceeded that of providing financial assistance for the purchase of the shares? He commented, at p. 779, that: 'I have not found the concept of a 'larger purpose' easy to grasp'. Lord Oliver rationalised the provision by drawing a distinction between a purpose and the reason why a purpose is formed. This distinction may seem as vague as the statutory provision itself, but it is important that you grasp the purported logic involved because problem questions could test you upon it. In *Brady* v *Brady* Lord Oliver stated, at p. 780:

> The purpose and the only purpose of the financial assistance is and remains that of enabling the shares to be acquired and the financial and commercial advantages flowing from the acquisition, whilst they may form the reason for forming the purpose of providing assistance, are a by-product of it rather than an independent purpose of which the assistance can properly be considered to be an incident.

Lord Oliver's reasoning does not allow a retracing of the chain of reasoning that led to the financial assistance in order to arrive at what constitutes 'larger purpose'. To this extent 'purpose' is being interpreted as 'immediate purpose', and it is now difficult to envisage a situation where this proviso to the general prohibition on financial assistance would apply.

It should be noted that the House of Lords was fairly indulgent in *Brady* v *Brady* in that they allowed arguments to be heard which were not raised in the courts below. This enabled the prohibition in s. 151 to be overcome by the application of CA 1985, ss. 155–8, because both companies were private companies.

In this problem you have the added difficulty of looking at improper purposes in the different context of directors' duties where common law rules prevail.

(c) The good faith test was interpreted in *Brady* v *Brady* as a 'single composite expression' to be assessed by analysing the motives of 'those responsible for procuring the company to provide the assistance'. It required them to 'act in the genuine belief that it is being done in the company's interest' (per Lord Oliver at p. 777).

You can use these confusions to your own advantage in, first of all, not giving a definite answer and secondly, showing your knowledge about the difficulties in analysing and applying particular statutory provision.

If s. 151 has not been, complied with then you need to look at any liabilities that are imposed, both criminal (see CA 1985, ss. 151(3) and 730(5)), and as regards the enforceability of the transaction (void and unenforceable, *see Selangor United Rubber Estates Ltd* v *Cradock (No. 3)* [1968] 1 WLR 1555). Also, with respect to public companies only, the shares must be disposed of within one year or cancelled and the amount of share capital reduced by the nominal value of the shares. Conglomerates plc might also be interested to learn that there will be no voting rights for such shares if it can be shown that Glasshouses plc has a beneficial interest in the shares as this will affect their ability to secure control of Glasshouses (CA 1985, s. 146(1)(d)).

The problem concerns two public companies, but you need to be careful in identifying whether the companies involved in possible s. 151 situations are public or private, because s. 151 is relaxed for private companies if they follow a special procedure (as occurred in *Brady* v *Brady*; see CA 1985, ss. 155–8; see also CA 1985, s. 146). The instruction at the end of the problem could have read: 'Discuss any possible liability for these actions and comment on any procedures that could have been adopted had Glasshouses been a private company'.

The Glasshouses problem has enough in it already without the insertion of this sort of additional instruction. But be on the look-out for it.

Breach of Trust

Glasshouses has suffered loss; the price that has been paid to frustrate the take-over bid was £¾ million. The directors can be made responsible as trustees to look after the company's money, as can any third parties who can be deemed to be constructive trustees. This involves a move away from dealing with the interpretation of statutes to the treatment and application of case law, and in particular the main authorities of *Selangor United Rubber Estates Ltd* v *Cradock* and *Belmont Finance Corporation Ltd* v *Williams Furniture*

Ltd. You would also need to mention that there is possible liability for the tort of conspiracy and the question as to whether a co-conspirator (Glasshouses) can sue the other conspirers (the directors of Fanny and Glasshouses, and Fanny itself). Such an action was allowed to proceed in *Belmont Finance Corporation Ltd* v *Williams Furniture Ltd* where the actions of the directors were not imputed to the company whose assets were the subject of the conspiracy. This is an interesting application of the alter ego theory discussed in chapter 3, a brief reference to which illustrates an ability to draw on areas of company law other than those immediately in point and can secure extra marks as well as giving the answer more vitality. Presumably because Fanny's assets are not the subject of the conspiracy the knowledge of the directors of Fanny can be imputed to Fanny plc. But can the knowledge of Glasshouses' directors be imputed to Glasshouses plc? Is this distinction as to which company's assets are being misapplied a logical one to make when, even under CA 1985, s. 151, the company which provides the finance for the acquisition of its own shares can be made criminally liable?

The main difficulty in this area concerns the test that has to be applied to establish whether or not an involved party is liable as a constructive trustee. In *Selangor United Rubber Estates Ltd* v *Cradock* the bank was held liable as a constructive trustee as a reasonable bank should have concluded that the moneys passing through its accounts were for the unlawful purchase of shares. It is always useful to have a bank liable as a constructive trustee, because they may be the only ones made liable that can pay up at the end of the day. However, in *Belmont Finance Corporation Ltd* v *Williams Furniture Ltd* the imposition of liability as a constructive trustee was held to require actual knowledge of the 'fraudulent' or 'dishonest' breach of trust, a stricter test than that required in *Selangor United Rubber Estates Ltd* v *Cradock*. So which test do you apply? A useful review of the authorities was made by Lawson J in *International Sales & Agencies Ltd* v *Marcus* [1982] 3 All ER 551 at p. 558, a case that has already been looked at in respect of contractual capacity (see chapter 4). Lawson J declared that a knowing recipient of trust property will be a constructive trustee:

> ... if either he was in fact aware at the time that his receipt was affected by a breach of trust, or if he deliberately shut his eyes to the real nature of the transfer to him (this could be called 'imputed notice'), or if an ordinary reasonable man in his position and with his attributes ought to have known of the relevant breach. This I equate with constructive notice.

He went on to make a distinction between those who knowingly are in receipt of the trust monies for their own use (where dishonesty is not required), and those who knowingly assist in the breach of trust (where dishonesty is required).

Apply these tests to the facts of the problem. Fanny has used the trust funds. The directors of both companies and Glasshouses itself know of the arrangement and assist in it. The bank manager of Barcland is obviously suspicious, but is that enough? An 'assist' appears to require a dishonest intention (*Belmont Finance Corporation; International Sales & Agencies*; cf. *Selangor United Rubber Estates* and *Baden* v *Société Générale pour Favoriser le Développement du Commerce et de l'Industrie en France SA* [1983] BCLC 325).

The concluding paragraphs in problems usually involve a summary of the points raised and a commentary on the possible liabilities of the parties involved. However, it is useful if a short sharp retort on some aspect of the problem can be included illustrating that you have thought about the issue and have some thoughts to contribute. Apart from arousing the examiner from a lethargy caused by marking hundreds of very similar answers, it is a useful method of completing a structured answer. In your research and revision you should develop some ideas about the various aspects of company law, preferably based upon some authority and, in a couple of short sentences, sum those ideas up ready for inclusion in an answer if the right question comes along.

What could you say in a conclusion to this question? In this case, it is not a complex analysis of the law; indeed it rarely will be. Instead, simply ask why Glasshouses didn't accept the land as a non-cash consideration for the shares, instead of splitting the transaction into two parts? Is this an attempt to avoid the valuation provisions in CA 1985, ss. 108–11? Are there examples you can think of where a similar set of two transactions could avoid those valuation provisions and not be caught by CA 1985, s. 151? If so, is this a loophole in those valuation provisions?

FURTHER READING

Committee to Review the Functioning of Financial Institutions, *The Financing of Small Firms* (Interim Report, Cmnd 7503) (London: HMSO, 1979).

Committee to Review the Functioning of Financial Institutions, *Report* (Cmnd 7937) (London: HMSO, 1980).

Department of Trade, *The Purchase by a Company of its Own Shares: A Consultative Document* (Cmnd 7944) (London: HMSO, 1980).

9 LOAN CAPITAL

INTRODUCTION

Companies obtain funds externally through the raising of equity and loan finance on the financial markets, and through the provision of loans normally from banks but sometimes from governmental sources. This chapter is concerned with the raising of loan capital. Loans to a company are usually evidenced by a document called a debenture. This is simply an acknowledgement of indebtedness by the company. Some loans are raised on the financial markets and are marketable in the same way as shares in a company. These marketable loans are often called corporate bonds and, with the increasing internationalisation of the financial markets, are raised and traded on the international (Eurobond) market. Although the raising of loan capital through bank loans is still very popular there is a move towards the financial markets or 'securitisation', particularly through equity finance in the United Kingdom and Germany and bonds in the United States, as the method for raising money (see *The Economist*, vol. 299 (7 June 1986), p. 56 et seq. and vol. 336 (30 September 1995), p. 107 for an analysis of the reasons why companies are changing the way that they raise money). As with any loan, the lender will usually require some security or charge to back his investment. There has been a growth in loans that have no security attached to them to support takeover bids. Because of the high risk associated with these loans they are often referred to as 'junk bonds'. Charges can take the form of:

(a) Fixed charges, taken over a specific asset (e.g., a factory or land, and often called a mortgage) or group of assets of the company which usually cannot be sold or altered without the permission of the holder of the charge (the chargee).

(b)   Floating charges, which hover over a group of assets of the company that are constantly changing in the ordinary course of business. The charge descends on whatever assets are present that fall within its scope upon some act of 'crystallisation' (e.g., the appointment of an administrative receiver). Banks frequently hold floating charges over all the assets of the company both present and future as security for loans to companies.

The need for security for loans was well summarised by Nourse LJ in *Re New Bullas Trading Ltd* [1994] 1 BCLC 485, where he commented (at p. 487):

> He who lends money to a trading company neither wishes nor expects it to become insolvent. Its prosperous trading is the best assurance of the return of his money with interest. But against an evil day he wants the best security the company can give him consistently with its ability to trade meanwhile. Hence the modern form of debenture, which, broadly speaking, gives the lender a fixed charge over assets that the company does not need to deal with in the ordinary course of its business and a floating charge over those that it does.

Trade creditors are often at a disadvantage if a company goes into receivership or liquidation because they will not normally have any security for the debts owed to them and, as unsecured creditors, will be at the bottom of the list of those to be repaid out of the remaining assets that the company may have. This list of priorities, and the various attempts by all parties to try to jump as far up the list as possible (priority gaining), provides the focal point of the topic of this chapter. Trade creditors have attempted to gain priority through the development of reservation of property clauses, also referred to as retention of title clauses or '*Romalpa*' clauses (named after the decision that brought such clauses into prominence in the United Kingdom, *Aluminium Industrie Vaassen BV* v *Romalpa Aluminium Ltd* [1976] 2 All ER 552). The banks have attempted to gain priority through a variety of techniques, but in particular by trying to draw in assets under fixed charges that would normally be seen to be only capable of being subject to a floating charge (i.e., book debts, see *Re New Bullas Trading Ltd* and *Siebe Gorman & Co. Ltd* v *Barclays Bank Ltd* [1979] 2 Lloyd's Rep 142, discussed in question 1).

MAIN ISSUES

Most of the discussion in this chapter will revolve around the question of how creditors of companies can protect their investment, loan or supply of goods on credit terms so as to ensure the best possible chance of repayment should the company get into financial difficulties. This question can be looked at from several different angles.

Priorities

Given that in a receivership or liquidation the creditors of a company will usually be owed more than the total amount of the assets of the company, as in question 1, who gets paid first? A table of priorities can be seen in table 9.1, although for charges to obtain priority they have to be registered with the registrar of companies.

Floating Charges and Fixed Charges

The distinction between a floating charge and fixed charge is important given their relative positions in the table of priorities, but this distinction is less easy to make following the decision in *Siebe Gorman & Co. Ltd* v *Barclays Bank Ltd* [1979] 2 Lloyd's Rep 142. A straightforward application of the table of priorities could be made more complicated by the creation of more than one fixed or floating charge over the same group of corporate assets. Some of the consequences of 'double-charging' assets are identified in question 2.

Statutory Registration of Charges

The registration of charges with the registrar of companies is required by CA 1985, s. 395, if the chargee is to keep his place in the order of priorities. Registration creates commercial certainty for those lending to companies in that they can identify from the public register maintained by the registrar which assets of a company are already subject to charges. A duty is placed on companies to register charges over their assets, the sanction for contravention being a default fine (CA 1985, s. 399). A failure to register makes the charge void and the money secured by it becomes payable immediately (CA 1985, s. 395(2)). The charges that need to be registered are listed in CA 1985, s. 396, and include a charge on land, book debts of the company or the company's undertaking. The CA 1989, part IV, contained provisions that would have fundamentally altered the law relating to the registration of charges. The provisions were never brought into effect because the demise of the current system whereby a conclusive certificate of registration is issued by the Registrar of companies was not welcomed by users of the charges register or those who take charges. There was also a problem concerning the interaction with the Land Registry. The certificate from the Registrar of Companies assures the Land Registry that a charge is not void under the Companies Act. A certificate under the CA 1989 would not have given that assurance and would have provided the Land Registry with a difficulty as they indemnify searchers against loss from reliance on registered particulars. Some 70 per cent of charges that are currently registered by the Registrar of Companies are, or include, charges over land. The Department of Trade, as part of its Company Law Review, has put forward proposals for revising the law on the registration of charges in a consultative document issued in November 1994 (*Company Law Review: Proposals for Reform of Part XII of the Companies Act 1985*). You will need to be able to refer to this document in any answer on the registration of charges even if the context of the question requires only a fleeting reference.

The Department accepts the need for publicly available information on the extent to which corporate assets are subject to security interests:

> This information is needed by those proposing to do busines with the company. It is also of value to analysts and providers of commercial information in compiling a financial profile of a company. In addition, since failure to register registrable charges results in their avoidance, the system provides a mechanism for confirming the validity in that respect of company charges as against certain third parties, such as a liquidator and creditors in a winding up. (Consultative document, para. 1.)

The two main areas of concern about the current system are reflected in questions 1 and 2. They are:

(a)   There are 21 days to register a charge from its creation. A valid charge is thus invisible to inspectors of the register for this period and the further period it takes from delivery of the particulars to appearance of the charge on the register. This may delay funding for business as potential lenders wait for 21 days or more to ensure that there are no prior charges. This is discussed in question 2.

(b)   The list of registrable charges is out of date.

Although the aim of disclosure through registration is to inform creditors and potential creditors of the amount of assets of the company that are charged or are freely available as security for any loan, developments in business finance have not been matched by similar advances in the requirements relating to disclosure. A simple glance at the charges register could be misleading given the growth of hire-purchase, leasing, and refinancing (sale and leaseback), whereby the company may appear to have a lot of assets but they do not belong to the company and are not available to the general creditors on a receivership or winding up. Property held under a *Romalpa* clause does not have to be registered either. Trade creditors were aware that the banks, as holders of floating charges over all a company's assets, normally take a large proportion of what remaining assets insolvent companies may have. This left the trade creditors with very little and often nothing. Therefore, they inserted reservation of property clauses (known as *Romalpa* clauses) into contracts of supply in order to retain title to the goods supplied until paid in full. The effectiveness of such clauses depends on the drafting and whether they need registration as will be discussed in question 1.

The Department of Trade has put forward three options for consultation: retain the existing system; retain the core of the current system with some alterations to improve the process such as updating the list of registrable charges; or replace the current system whereby the charge is registered after it is created with a 'notice filing' system where a 'financing statement' is filed before or after a charge is created. The first two proposals will be dealt with in the context of questions 1 and 2.

'Notice filing' differs from the existing system in two fundamental ways:

(a) a notice can be filed before a charge to which it applies is created;
(b) a single notice can cover several transactions between the chargor and the chargee, each of which would require separate registration under a transaction filing system (para. 67).

The main disadvantage of this system is the loss of publicly available information as the register will only inform that a charge may have been created, not that it has been. Failure to file a financing statement would not render a charge void against a creditor, liquidator or administrator as it does now, but it would affect priority as against other filers of financing statements. The other problem with this option is that it would take several years to develop and progress the necessary legislation. Its implementation is unlikely.

Administrative Receivers and Administrators

A creditor with a floating charge over the assets of a company enforces that charge by appointing an administrative receiver to take control of the assets charged and to realise them in payment for the amount owed. Normally this power to appoint a receiver will be contained in the charge agreement as will the circumstances under which such an appointment can be made and the receiver's powers, although the IA 1986 confers a standard array of powers (IA 1986, s. 42(1) and sch. 1).

The IA 1986 (ss. 8–27) introduces a procedure whereby a company that is, or is likely to become, unable to pay its debts can obtain a moratorium of three months on actions by creditors so that a precipitate receivership will not prevent the company from surviving if only in part. An insolvency practitioner, called an 'administrator', can be appointed by the court under an 'administration order'. The court must be satisfied that one of the purposes of the order as specified in IA 1986, s. 8(2), will be met. These range from securing the survival of the company or part of it to a more advantageous realisation of the company's assets than on a winding up. However, the usefulness of the procedure could be frustrated in that the court cannot make an order if an administrative receiver has been appointed and does not consent to the order. This gives the holders of floating charges a practical veto over the making of an order because even if an administrative receiver has not been appointed before the order is applied for, one could be appointed before the court decides on the petition.

Increasing the Assets Available for Distribution and Avoiding Charges

In any question relating to loan capital you will need to be aware of one or more of the methods by which either a liquidator, administrative receiver or administrator can take steps to increase the assets of a company or invalidate certain charges over a company's assets:

(a) The assets can be increased by applying the statutory provisions relating to:

(i) transactions at an undervalue — application by the administrator or liquidator under IA 1986, ss. 238 and 423,

(ii) wrongful trading — application by the liquidator under IA 1986, s. 214,

(iii) fraudulent trading — application by the liquidator under IA 1986, s. 213,

(iv) misfeasance proceedings — application by, amongst others, the liquidator or any creditor of the company under IA 1986, s. 212.

(b) Charges can be invalidated and set aside by applying the statutory provisions relating to:

(i) floating charges securing debt incurred before the charge was created — application by the liquidator or administrator under IA 1986, s. 245,

(i) preferences — application by the liquidator or administrator under IA 1986, s. 239.

These procedures are looked at in questions 1 and 2.

REVISION AND RESEARCH

As you work through questions 1 and 2 it will become apparent that there are certain procedures that must be revised to have any hope of answering questions in this area successfully. In particular, we urge a revision of the list of priorities in table 9.1 as this provides the main basis on which problems will be set. Question 1 provides a practical exercise whereby this table of priorities can be applied to establish what amounts each creditor should be repaid. Revision exercises are also included in question 2 relating to the crystallisation of floating charges and the effect on priorities of a rectification of the register of charges under CA 1985, s. 404. Professor Diamond has suggested that a statutory list of priorities should be introduced to replace the current mixture of common law, equitable and statutory provisions which table 9.1 is based upon. However, the Department of Trade and Industry consultative document indicates that it is unlikely that this will occur (para. 64).

Table 9.1 Order of priority for creditors and members

1   The owners of goods which although in the possession of the company are subject to valid reservation of property clauses or hire-purchase agreements etc.

2   The holders of fixed charges (if the asset charged turns out to be worth less than the debt for which it was taken, the chargee has to queue up as an unsecured creditor for the balance).

3   The liquidation costs.

4   The holders of preferential debts as stated in IA 1986, sch. 6, including income tax and national insurance deductions due for the previous 12 months, value added tax due from the previous six months, and arrears of wages for employees for four months preceding the winding up (to a maximum amount of £800), and all accrued holiday pay. It is more usual that banks have advanced money for wages as they know that they can claim as preferential creditors for these sums under a form of statutory subrogation (sch. 6, para. 11). Employees also get protection under the Employment Protection (Consolidation) Act 1978 whereby debts owed to employees can be claimed from the Redundancy Fund (s. 122, see also ss. 40–2, 106–8 and 125; Wedderburn, *The Worker and the Law,* 3rd ed., ch. 5).

5   The holders of floating charges. On a winding up or where an administrative receiver is appointed any moneys realised from the assets charged must be applied to the preferential debts first (IA 1986, ss. 175(2)(b) and 387(4); see also ss. 40 and 59).

6   The unsecured creditors.

7   Persons made liable to contribute to the company's assets following court orders under IA 1986, ss. 213–4 and 'Bathampton' orders (*Re Bathampton Properties Ltd* [1976] 1 WLR 168 — costs incurred by the company in unjustifiably opposing a winding-up petition).

8   Return of capital to the members in accordance with any priority that may be laid down in the articles, together with any arrears of dividend declared but not paid.

9   Any surplus is distributed to the members.

The statutory provisions are now largely contained in the Insolvency Act 1986 which adopted many of the recommendations contained in the Cork Report (*Insolvency Law and Practice. Report of the Review Committee*, Cmnd 8558, 1982). Some of the Cork Report's suggestions were also followed up by Professor Diamond's Report on Security Interests in Property, which have now been enacted but not brought into force through the CA 1989. We suggest that, as part of your research and revision, you read the relevant parts of the reports. At the appropriate place in essays and problems you can cite these proposals very briefly and link them into the provisions of the IA 1986 and CA 1989 that eventually followed. The examiner will take this as evidence of wide reading and you will gain valuable marks for this sprinkling of the reports' recommendations. However, you must be careful to relate such inclusions in any answer to the question that is being asked and the actual provisions contained in the Acts. To assist you in this revision exercise, we have included below a list of some issues covered by the Cork Report and the relevant chapter in the report. As you work through questions 1 and 2 you may find it useful to identify the places where brief details of the report could be inserted.

Cork Report

Fixed charges (ch. 35):

(a) preference rule should not apply to fixed charges,
(b) administrator's powers,
(c) expansion of registrable charges.

Floating charges (ch. 36):

(a) 10 per cent fund for the unsecured creditors to be taken from the assets subject to a floating charge,
(b) preferences,
(c) crystallisation of charges to be restricted by statute,
(d) definition of a floating charge, with a criticism of *Siebe Gorman & Co. Ltd* v *Barclays Bank Ltd* [1979] 2 Lloyd's Rep 142.

'*Romalpa*' clauses (ch. 37):

(a) disclosure and registration (para. 1639),
(b) extended clauses to be limited (paras 1644–5),
(c) powers of administrative receivers or administrators (paras 1647–50).

Fraudulent/wrongful trading (ch. 44)

Preferential creditors (ch. 32):

(a) the Crown as preferential creditor (paras 1413 and 1423),
(b) preference for rates (para. 1427),
(c) preference for wages (para. 1433).

IDENTIFYING THE QUESTION

Problems concerning loan capital are easy to identify in that they will have to indicate the nature of the different charges over the assets of the companies concerned. The question should be read carefully to ascertain the type of charges created and the assets covered by each charge. If the charges are over the same group of assets, which has priority? Does the problem state whether or not the charges have been registered and how will this affect priority? Is the company in receivership, liquidation or under an administration order? The answer to this last question will affect the possible remedies that you can suggest are available for increasing the assets of the company or avoiding charges. Are any goods that may be supplied subject to a 'Romalpa' clause, and if so is the clause stated to be 'legally effective', or does the question go into some detail about the content of the clause? In the former case the examiner is indicating that a discussion of the case law surrounding the interpretation of such clauses is not required, but that you must consider the clause and whether it is registrable when considering what assets would be available to the holders of floating charges or the preferential creditors. In the latter case you will need to identify whether or not, on the basis of the information supplied, the clause would be deemed effective by the courts.

Essay questions in this area can involve rather turgid discussions of the procedures surrounding administrative receivership or administration orders. More enlightened examiners will ask questions involving the implementation of the Cork or Diamond Reports, the Department of Trade and Industry review and the failure to implement the CA 1989, or the growth and treatment, both judicial and statutory, of 'Romalpa' clauses. This involves some knowledge of the statutory registration procedures and the procedures on receivership, although that knowledge needs to be applied from a different perspective.

QUESTION 1

Ash Ltd requires extra manufacturing capacity and stocks of steel to meet orders placed for its stainless steel ashtrays. To raise the necessary capital Ash Ltd approaches the Secure Bank plc which grants a loan for £10,000 on a debenture secured by a 'first and fixed charge over all book debts present and future'. The charge was created on 1 January 1995. The charge was registered on 5 February 1995, the date of the creation of the charge having been fraudulently altered to 30 January 1995. A certificate from the Registrar confirms the date of registration as 5 February 1995. On 1 January 1995 Flash, the managing director and majority shareholder of Ash Ltd, also lends the company £10,000. Three months later, after many of the orders have led to the company making losses, Ash Ltd is approaching insolvency. Flash obtains and registers a floating charge over all the assets of the company both present and future as security for his £10,000 loan.

One month after the floating charge is created Ash Ltd purchases a stock of steel for £10,000 from Forge Ltd under a contract which includes an effective reservation of property clause, property in the steel only passing to Ash Ltd after full payment for the stock has been made. It has not been registered as a charge. This is the only stock that Ash Ltd possesses. Two days after receiving the steel Ash Ltd goes into compulsory liquidation following a petition from an unsatisfied local authority creditor which hopes to rank as a preferential creditor of Ash Ltd.

The assets of Ash Ltd are:

	£
Book debts	8,000
Stock	10,000
Other assets	5,000

The liabilities of Ash Ltd are:

	£
Rates	3,000
Value added tax/national insurance contributions/ Pay As You Earn deductions all covering the previous three months	18,000
Secure Bank plc	10,000
Flash	10,000
Forge Ltd	10,000

Advise the liquidator.

The company's liabilities exceed its assets and, as in the vast majority of liquidations, the main issue concerns the priority of the creditors. The question can be broken down into various parts:

(a) The distinction between fixed and floating charges — what type of charge is held by the Secure Bank plc?

(b)   The procedure on registration of the bank's fixed charge — does the fraudulent change of date affect the validity of the registration?

(c)   The floating charge held by Flash was created after the debt had been incurred and could also be avoided as a preference.

(d)   Is the ordering of steel from Forge Ltd an example of fraudulent or wrongful trading?

(e)   Does the property in the steel reside with Forge Ltd or does Forge Ltd only have an unregistered charge on the steel?

(f)   Finally, having established what security each of the creditors possesses, advising the liquidator as to the order of priorities of repayment.

Fixed and Floating Charges

Every creditor is looking for the best possible security for his debt. The fixed charge provides this because on liquidation or receivership all the proceeds from the asset that is charged go to the chargee, whereas the proceeds from assets that are subject to a floating charge are first of all applied to any preferential debts that may exist (see points 4 and 5 in table 9.1). To what extent has the bank been successful in creating a fixed charge over book debts? Although the charging document describes it as a fixed charge this does not stop the courts from interpreting the clause so as to be effective in only creating a floating charge. This is an important issue for the bank, raising the possibility that it may not be able to get its hands on all of the £8,000 represented in the available assets by book debts, because the preferential creditors could dip into that fund if the charge was deemed to be of a floating nature.

The classic definition of a floating charge is to be found in the judgment of Romer LJ in *Re Yorkshire Woolcombers Association Ltd* [1903] 2 Ch 284, where he identified three characteristics which you must cite in any question involving floating charges:

(a)   it is a charge on a class of assets both present and future,
(b)   the class is changing in the ordinary course of business, and
(c)   it is contemplated that until the charge is enforced the company can carry on business in the ordinary way with regard to that class of assets.

It is this last characteristic that makes floating charges attractive to industry in that companies can raise money on stock, book debts and other assets of the company that are constantly changing. Until relatively recently the bank's charge on book debts would have been included in a general floating charge held over all the assets of the company. The attempt to create a fixed charge over this special group of assets is the banking response to the force of the preferential creditor, normally the government as tax collector, prevailing over the holders of floating charges, normally banks. This attempt was seen to be successful in *Siebe Gorman & Co. Ltd* v *Barclays Bank Ltd* [1979] 2 Lloyd's Rep 142, giving companies all the advantages of a floating charge and the chargee the knowledge that he can call in his security at any time and, on a winding up or receivership, have priority over preferential creditors.

It is important to cite the *Siebe Gorman* case when discussing the third characteristic of the floating charge identified by Romer LJ, although it should be noted that Romer LJ did not say that a floating charge must exhibit all three characteristics, only that where it did it was a floating charge. This uncertainty about the exact definition of a floating charge was taken up by Vinelott J in *Re Atlantic Medical Ltd* [1993] BCLC 386 where he stated (at p. 392) that Romer LJ's test in *Re Yorkshire Woolcombers Association Ltd*:

> was not attempting an exact definition of a floating charge. The characteristics he mentions are helpful tests or filters in deciding in a doubtful case whether a charge is fixed or floating.

It was argued in *Siebe Gorman* that the company would be free to deal with the book debts by barter or set-off against other debts owed to the company. Also, in that the debenture only required the company to pay the debts received into the bank account it had with the chargee, the company would be free to use those funds if in credit. Thus, the charge had all the characteristics of being of a floating rather than a specific nature. However, Slade J held that the charge was a specific one on the proceeds of the debts as soon as they were received. This prevented the company from disposing of the money without the chargee's consent and the bank could assert control over the account even if in credit. This is a crucial point because if Ash Ltd was free to deal with the money received as payment for debts owed to it, then Slade J agreed that the charge must be a floating charge, whereas the fact that debts could be negotiated in another form did not affect the intention of the parties and turn a specific charge into a floating one. The test of the validity of such a charge therefore appears to lie in the extent of freedom that the company has over the proceeds of the debts that are paid. If sufficient restrictions are placed on companies by the banks the charge will be a specific one (see *Re Armagh Shoes Ltd* [1982] NI 59; *Re Keenan Brothers Ltd* [1986] BCLC 242; cf. *Re Brightlife Ltd* [1986] 3 All ER 673). You will need to point out that the question is silent as to any such restrictions on Ash Ltd. The imposition of such restrictions could rebound on the banks. In *Re a Company, ex parte Copp* [1989] BCLC 13 it was argued that the extent of the restrictions could give rise to the bank becoming a 'shadow director' and, as such, possibly liable as a party to wrongful trading under IA 1986, s. 214, although no cases against banks on this ground have succeeded.

In *Re New Bullas Trading Ltd* [1994] 1 BCLC 485 the Court of Appeal decided that the intention of the parties was a key issue in deciding whether book debts were subject to a fixed or floating charge. In this case the uncollected book debts were held to be subject to a fixed charge and the proceeds of the debts that had been paid into a designated bank account over which the chargee could give instructions were subject to a floating charge. Goode calls this decision 'disappointing' (R. Goode, 'Charges over book debts: a missed opportunity' (1994) 110 LQR 592). He does not agree that you can divorce the characteristics of the charge over the book debts from the contractual provisions relating to the application of the proceeds. In *Siebe Gorman* the chargee's control over the proceeds was a crucial element of the decision which was re-emphasised in *Re Brightlife Ltd* where the charge was held to be a floating charge as there were no restrictions. At first instance in *Re New Bullas Trading Ltd* [1993] BCLC 1389, Knox J had not declared the charge on the uncollected book debts to be a fixed one drawing a distinction between having a power and exercising it, just as the power of intervention by a debenture holder does not crystallise a floating charge.

Registration

To retain priority, charges over corporate assets must be registered within 21 days of their creation (CA 1985, s. 395). Although the time-limit has not been adhered to in the question, a certificate of registration from the registrar is conclusive evidence that the requirements relating to registration have been satisfied (CA 1985, s. 401(2)(b)). You will need to discuss the effects of this statutory provision using the decisions in *Re C. L. Nye Ltd* [1971] Ch 442 and *R v Registrar of Companies, ex parte Central Bank of India* [1986] QB 1114. In *Central Bank of India* it was argued that the preclusive clause in s. 401 only excluded the admission of evidence regarding registration and did not exclude the jurisdiction of the court to grant judicial review against the decision of a public official like the registrar of companies where an error of law had been made. The Court of Appeal held that the certificate could not be called into question whether there was a mistake of fact or law, because that would involve looking at evidence regarding the registration which is prohibited under s. 401. However, there were some *obiter* comments relating to the willingness of the court to intervene if it could be proved that a certificate was obtained by fraudulent means, as in this question. Lawton LJ agreed with counsel for the registrar that judicial review may be available to quash the registrar's decision to issue a certificate if it could be proved that registration was obtained by some fraudulent means (at pp. 1169–70). However, Slade LJ disagreed preferring commercial certainty for those who are relying on the register (at p. 1177, see also *Re Eric Holmes (Property) Ltd* [1965] Ch 1052). Slade LJ went on to discuss the possibility of other remedies that may be available should such a fraud take place, and a brief mention of these would be relevant to your answer.

Flash's Floating Charge

Flash's floating charge secures a debt incurred before the charge was created. There are several restrictions on what property can be charged in such circumstances, including debts incurred before the charge was created, as in the question (see IA 1986, s. 245). Creditors are prevented from jumping the priority queue to secure a past debt when, as in this case, they think that the company is insolvent and in danger of going into receivership or liquidation. The charge will be void except to the extent that money is paid to the company 'at the same time as, or after, the creation of the charge' (see *Power* v *Sharp Investments Ltd* [1994] 1 BCLC 111). Flash is the managing director of Ash Ltd and is therefore connected with the company (defined in IA 1986, s. 249). The liquidator or an administrator could go back two years to challenge the floating charge because of this connection. Although this question concerns a person connected with the company, it could just as easily have involved someone not so connected when the period of time over which the liquidator or administrator can go back is reduced to one year. This would also have required a discussion as to whether or not the transaction led to the company being, or took place while the company was, unable to pay its debts (see IA 1986, s. 123, for the definition). This additional element does not apply if the person involved was connected with the company, as in this question.

The predecessors to IA 1986, s. 245 (CA 1948, s. 322 and CA 1985, s. 617) only applied 'where a company is being wound up' and any transactions effected under the authority of a charge before the commencement of a winding up were unaffected by the later application of the section (see *Mace Builders (Glasgow) Ltd* v *Lunn* [1987] Ch 191). This situation could lead to a race between the holders of floating charges to realise their security and other creditors to start the winding-up process. IA 1986, s. 245, only applies to floating charges created at a 'relevant time'. This period of time, two years, dates back from the 'onset of insolvency'. Just as a winding up was required before the old statutory provision came into effect, s. 245 now requires the 'onset of insolvency' which is defined as the date of presentation of a petition for an administration order that is subsequently granted or the date of the commencement of a winding up. The race is still on, but an additional finishing post for general creditors, the date of the presentation of a petition for an administration order, has been added. It is therefore important to note that a chargee whose floating charge could be avoided cannot veto the making of such an order (IA 1986, s. 9(3)(b)(ii)).

The floating charge could also be invalidated under the provisions relating to preferences. A liquidator can look at the two years prior to the company going into liquidation if the transaction concerned someone connected with the company, six months if it does not. He will seek to ensure that during that period, if the company was unable to pay its debts, no creditors were given preferential treatment over other creditors either in the repayment of their loans, discharge of guarantees or creation of charges over the company's assets. The previous statutory provisions were concerned with 'fraudulent preferences'. The provisions contained in IA 1986, s. 239, require that the company must be 'influenced' by the 'desire' to put a person in a better position than he would otherwise be in if the company went into liquidation. As we saw in chapter 3 this means looking at the state of mind of those in control of the company and, as it appears from the question that Flash both owns and controls the company, his state of mind could be taken to be that of the company. In *Re a Company, ex parte Copp* [1989] BCLC 13, the court identified a relationship between the proof required to show that a creditor was a 'shadow director' under the wrongful trading provisions (IA 1986, ss. 214, and 251) and that required under IA 1986, s. 239 (see also *Re Fairway Magazines Ltd* [1993] BCLC 643 where the motive in granting a director a debenture was held to be commercially proper although the finding on the timing of the grant of the debenture is overruled by *Power v Sharp Investments Ltd*). In this question the court could order the avoidance of the charge held by Flash over the company's assets.

The liquidator's willingness to pursue cases of voidable preferences and wrongful trading could be curbed by the decision in *Re MC Bacon Ltd* [1990] BCLC 607 that expenses incurred in such litigation do not carry priority as liquidator's expenses in realising the assets of the company. Liquidators may seek an indemnity from the creditors before pursuing such actions.

The Contract with Forge Ltd
The purchase of steel whilst insolvent or approaching insolvency raises the possibility of wrongful or fraudulent trading which are discussed in chapter 11. This could give rise to a court order against those knowingly party to any fraudulent trading requiring them to contribute to the company's assets, normally to the extent of the debts of the creditors who have been defrauded (i.e., Forge Ltd's £10,000). Any person made subject to such an order, or a similar order made under the wrongful trading provisions (IA 1986, s. 214), ranks as a creditor of the company and the court can order that they will rank in priority after all the other debts of the company (IA 1986, s. 215(4)). Although the liquidator can probably obtain such an order, the contribution towards the company's assets will not necessarily go towards satisfying Forge Ltd's debt. The contribution goes into the general pool of corporate assets to be distributed in order of priority.

The contract includes an effective reservation of property or *Romalpa* clause (under the Sale of Goods Act 1979, ss. 17 and 19). The question states that the reservation of property clause is 'effective'. The examiner is in some difficulty here in that the use of the word 'effective' or 'valid' could have two possible meanings: the clause is drafted in such a way as to retain property in the goods; or in addition to this the clause has been properly registered as charge. Given that the question also states that the clause has not been registered, the examiner must mean the former of these. It must therefore be an important part of the answer to respond to the issue as to whether or not a clause that is properly drafted so as to retain property in existing goods, with no extension to future or mixed goods or to all moneys owed by Ash Ltd to Forge Ltd, is registrable as a charge. This one word, 'effective', makes a considerable difference to the approach to this part of the question. If the question is silent about the effectiveness of the clause, then you would need to make an assessment regarding the amount of time you can spend on a discussion of the complexities of drafting such a clause. Care needs to be taken not to spend a disproportionate amount of time on what could comprise a small part of the question. A brief paragraph would be sufficient, concerning the effectiveness of such clauses being dependent upon evidence of a fiduciary relationship with strict controls as to how, for example, Ash Ltd could store and use the steel as evidence of Forge Ltd's ownership of the steel. You do need to concentrate on the registrable nature of such clauses. Registration is normally required in respect of claims to create rights over any future goods that the original material may be incorporated into (e.g., steel into ashtrays). There has been a large number of cases regarding these 'extended' clauses where the 'apparent impossibility of proving the fiduciary obligation of the buyer has defeated many such claims since the *Romalpa* case in which the obligation was admitted' (Hicks, 'Retention of Title — Latest Developments' [1992] JBL 398 at p. 409: see also *Ian Chisholm Textiles Ltd* v *Griffiths* [1994] 2 BCLC 291). However, the decision in *Clough Mill Ltd* v *Martin* [1985] 1 WLR 111 illustrates that registration is not required for 'simple' validly-drafted clauses where there is no such incorporation, the very nature of the clause being that the parties agree that the supplier still owns the goods; there is no charge on the assets of the company in that the goods do not comprise part of the company's assets. Successful clauses will also apply against sub-purchasers of the relevant goods (*Re Highway Foods International Ltd* [1995] 1 BCLC 209). 'All moneys' clauses, which state that property in the goods supplied does not pass until all debts due have been paid, have been recognised as effective and not requiring registration by the House of Lords in *Armour* v *Thyssen Edelstahlwerke AG* [1991] 2 AC 339.

Administrative receivers and liquidators must respect the valid title of goods held under such clauses; this is why companies like Forge Ltd see them as a useful method of protecting their interests. If Forge Ltd had such an effective clause it could reclaim its steel, as happened in *Romalpa* itself, rather than queuing as an unsecured creditor. Administrators trying to manage the company can apply to the court to seek permission to deal with charged property and goods subject to hire-purchase or conditional sale agreements, or goods that have been leased or are subject to retention of title clauses, but they must apply any proceeds that are recovered from disposing of those goods towards discharging the security or amount payable under the agreement (IA 1986, s. 15). Administrative receivers have a similar power to apply to the court under IA 1986, s. 43, but it only applies to charged property and not to property that is subject to a retention of title clause. The Department of Trade consultative document asks for opinions on whether the current common law should be codified or whether all clauses, both simple and extended, should be excluded from registration (paras 27–30).

Conclusion

A good conclusion for this question would bring all the points together by advising the liquidator as to who should be paid and how much. This may be subject to disclaimers arising from the various areas of difficulty that have surfaced during your answer, but this should not deter you from making some attempt to consolidate an opinion on the issue of priorities using the figures that the question gives you. The layout of the question, with the assets and liabilities given at the end, invites this sort of conclusion. We invite you to work it out by deciding what priority the various parties have and then dividing the available assets amongst them. This will include establishing what the preferential debts are (see point 4 in table 9. 1), with a comment on the wisdom of the local authority petitioning for a winding up; it appears to have been ill-advised and could have been better off seeking to recover the debt through other means.

The recommendation in the Cork Report that preferential status for rates should be abolished has been enacted (IA 1986, sch. 6). You could work through the groups of creditors one by one. If you do not have sufficient assets left to satisfy any one group of creditors falling within a priority band, treat each creditor in that group *pari passu* (i.e., you pay each creditor in the group the same proportion of his claim), and subsequent groups get nothing.

The proposals advanced in the Cork Report should be referred to throughout the answer, as suggested in the research and revision section of this chapter. Your conclusion could comment on the position of preferential creditors and the suggestion to curb their scope made in the Cork Report, as well as the proposal for a 10 per cent fund for unsecured creditors. If these proposals had been given statutory force, would it have altered your advice to the liquidator as to the distribution of assets?

QUESTION 2

You are the financial adviser to a company which is considering taking advantage of a government tax incentive encouraging the provision of loan capital to small companies. Advise your company as to any steps it should take to safeguard its investment. Include in your advice details of any procedures which could be adopted if the small companies to be invested in default in repayment of the capital sum or interest payable.

Every now and then you will come across a question that gives you enormous scope, including the scope to hang yourself. This question is on the edge of that category but not quite fully into it because, although it provides an opportunity to display a wide knowledge within a specific area of company law, it does not embrace the whole or a substantial part of the subject; this would be the hallmark of a true generalist question, e.g.:

Critically analyse the nature and scope of the statutory regulation of registered companies.

This example leaves you wondering where to start, whereas question 2 at least sets you off in the subject area of loan capital and even requests a treatment of topics within the area. This is the difference between open questions which leave the student substantial freedom as to how to tackle the answer, and closed questions, of which problems are one example, where the detailed nature of the content of the question determines the content and often the style of the response. Questions can vary in the extent to which they are open or closed, question 2 falling somewhere in the middle. The question itself concerns priorities and the remedies available to creditors of companies that get into financial difficulties, but there is plenty of freedom as to how the subject-matter can be developed within the answer. It is the style of the answer, and the ability to mould the substantive knowledge into a coherent and interesting framework that will boost an everyday 'this is all I know about loan capital' third-class mark into an upper-second and perhaps even higher.

The question contains three key words: 'adviser', 'advise' and 'advice'. The examiner is appealing to you to give advice to the company based on an objective appraisal of the legal situation. The answer could even be structured in the form of a report to the company including an introduction which would establish the various areas of difficulty that need to be considered, followed by an analysis of those areas, each analysis ending with a conclusion. The final part of the report would bring the various conclusions together in a general overview of the problem upon which advice was requested. The answer could be divided into headings and subheadings, as in a report; this is legitimate given the scenario that the examiner has portrayed. This question therefore provides an opportunity to demonstrate the answering technique that has been suggested throughout this book but in a more vivid and visual manner by adopting the 'report' style, a style that is particularly appropriate in the preparation of assessments or assignments. Some questions may even ask for the preparation of a report for the board of directors.

Some of the content of the answer has already been discussed in question 1, although its presentation would be different. The following areas would need to be covered bearing in mind that the elements selected should relate to the company's desire to protect itself whilst taking advantage of this hypothetical government incentive:

(a)   The power of the companies that are to be invested in to borrow money (see chapter 4).

(b)   The list of priorities as given in table 9.1.

(c)   The creation of fixed and floating charges and the extent to which more than one charge can be created over the same group of assets — how will this affect priority?

(d)   The crystallisation of floating charges — when do they crystallise and why is it important? This is an important area which can be revised by studying the decision in *Re Woodroffes (Musical Instruments) Ltd* [1985] 2 All ER 908, and attempting the following questions arising from the decision:

(i)   Why is the case being brought to court, and who is bringing the action?

(ii)   When and what type of charges were created over the company's assets?

(iii) Why is the date of the crystallisation of the bank's floating charge important?

(iv)   The bank has two main arguments in favour of crystallisation on 27 August. What are they?

(v)   Why is automatic crystallisation undesirable and when can it take place?

(vi)   Why is the result odd?

(vii) Would the decision still be the same if the facts occurred now (see IA 1986, s. 40(1), and *Re Brightlife Ltd* [1986] 3 All ER 673)?

(viii) Would the answer from (vii) be different if the floating charge crystallised prior to a winding up rather than prior to a receivership (see IA 1986, s. 175)?

(e)   The statutory registration of charges, including the power to apply for a rectification of the register (CA 1985, s. 404) — how does this affect reliance on the register by potential investors seeking to obtain security for their investment? The questions below test your knowledge of the effect rectification can have on priorities, and should be attempted after studying the terms of s. 404 and the decisions in *Watson v Duff Morgan & Vermont (Holdings) Ltd* [1974] 1 WLR 450, *Re Ashpurton Estate Ltd* [1983] Ch 110 and *Re Telomatic Ltd* [1994] 1 BCLC 90.

CA 1985, s. 404, only allows rectification with the leave of the court if the court is satisfied that the omission to register the charge in time was 'accidental or due to inadvertence or to some other sufficient cause'. Any rectification of the register will be subject to a *'Joplin'* provision which alters the register without prejudice to the rights of any person who has acquired rights between the date of creation of the charge that is the subject of the rectification application and the date of the registration of that charge. The Department of Trade consultative document proposes that, as part of the alterations to the core provisions of the CA 1985, the amendments in CA 1989, s. 95, should be introduced. This would allow for the late delivery of particulars without the involvement of the court, the charge only being protected from avoidance from the date of delivery of the particulars and remaining subject to avoidance against a liquidator or administrator if the company is unable to pay its debts at the time of delivery.

Who takes, or is likely to take, priority assuming that all the charges referred to are floating charges over the same group of corporate assets, the second chargee has no notice of the creation of the first charge and the company is and will remain able to pay its debts?

(i)   A's charge is created on 1 January 1991 but is not registered. B's charge is created on 3 January 1991 and registered five days later. A obtains rectification of the register under s. 404 on 5 February 1991.

(ii)   D's charge is created on 1 January 1991 but is not registered. E's charge is created on 28 January 1991 and registered on 6 February 1991. D obtains rectification of the register under s. 404 on 5 February 1991.

(iii)   F's charge is created on 1 January 1991 and registered five days later. G's charge is created on 5 January 1991 and registered five days later. This illustrates the problem of the current provisions on registration that do not reveal the existence of charges created but not yet registered but which may take priority. This is because a charge holder has a 21-day period to register the charge. During this period other, but later, charges over the same assets may be entered into and even registered before the first charge, but if the first charge is registered within 21 days it will take priority. The Department of Trade and Industry consultation document discusses the three options put forward in 1989 by Professor Diamond in *Review of Security Interests in Property*. They are: provisional registration of the fact that a charge may have been created (notice filing); an official certificate conferring priority on charges registered pursuant to it within a prescribed period; and provisional registration of a proposed charge that would give priority for 21 days. The Department of Trade and Industry appears to favour the latter option (paras 55–9).

(iv)   H's charge is created on 1 January 1991 and is not registered. J's charge is created on 5 January 1991 and is not registered. It is now 28 January 1991 and both H and J are applying for rectification under s. 404.

(f)   The powers of an administrative receiver (see IA 1986, sch. 1), the power of sale of a chargee under the Law of Property Act 1925 (ss. 101 and 103), and a brief mention of administration orders and the powers of administrators (IA 1986, ss. 8–27).

(g)   The power to wind up a company under IA 1986, s. 122(1)(f) — is this a realistic option given that the advice given should suggest some form of security over the company's assets? The inclusion of a power to appoint a receiver in any debenture will diminish the importance, and therefore time spent, on this power.

The question is directed at the provision of loan capital to small companies. Limited liability is often illusory for such companies in that substantial creditors will require personal guarantees from the individuals who control the company. This would be an option that should be included in the answer, for it is another illustration of how the essence of the separate corporate personality with limited liability can be introduced in varying degrees of depth into many answers (see chapter 3).

FURTHER READING

Department of Trade and Industry, *Company Law Reform: Proposals for Reform of Part XII of the Companies Act 1985* (URN 94/635) (London: DTI, 1994).
Goode, Roy, 'Charges over book debts: a missed opportunity' (1994) 110 LQR 592.

10 THE RIGHTS OF MINORITY SHAREHOLDERS

INTRODUCTION

This chapter deals with the issue of minority shareholder rights which has already been referred to in earlier chapters (in particular see chapter 5). The major issues in relation to the rights of minority shareholders, the rule in *Foss* v *Harbottle* (1843) 2 Hare 461, and CA 1985, s. 459 [CA 1989, s. 145 and sch. 19], will be looked at in isolation in this chapter despite the fact that the application of the rule is unlikely to appear on its own in an assessment question. Unfortunately this is yet another one of those topics which is a strong candidate for the dreaded 'mixed' question.

This chapter explores the problems associated with the law surrounding the rights of minority shareholders, discusses possible partnerships with other topics for examination questions and gives advice on how to tackle them. The rules governing minority rights are most likely to appear in questions dealing with directors' duties (see chapter 6), and the control and management of the company (see chapter 12).

MAIN ISSUES

The rule in Foss v Harbottle

This rule is certain to require discussion in at least one question on the examination paper. Regarded as a fundamental part of company law, the rule in *Foss* v *Harbottle* (1843) 2 Hare 461 illustrates the principle of majority control and its counterbalance of minority protection. The rule has two branches:

(a)   The corporate part of the rule which states that if a wrong is done to the company then the only proper plaintiff in an action to redress that wrong is the company and not a minority shareholder.

(b)   The partnership part of the rule which states that where the substance of the minority's complaint is that some act has been done wrongly which would nevertheless be lawful if there were an ordinary resolution in general meeting to authorise it, then the court will not interfere at the instance of a minority shareholder.

The rationale behind the rule is that control by the majority must prevail as control by unanimous consent of the shareholders would be impractical, and minority control unfair. Thus a minority shareholder who does not like a particular course of action authorised by the shareholders has the simple choice to accept it or sell his shares in the company.

The rule prevents multiple actions and the second branch shows that it is senseless for the court to entertain litigation at the suit of the minority if the majority do not wish it (per Mellish LJ in *MacDougall* v *Gardiner* (1875) 1 ChD 13).

The rule is subject to a number of exceptions which are instances where the court will hear a minority shareholder's action. Before examining these exceptions it's important for you to appreciate the basis upon which the minority shareholder brings the action if allowed to do so.

The plaintiff minority shareholder does not sue on his own behalf but either:

(a)   in a representative capacity where the member sues for all members affected by a breach of personal rights for relief against the other members, a member or the company; or

(b)   in a derivative capacity where the member seeks a remedy from a third party on the company's behalf. It is normal to join the company as a nominal defendant in a derivative action to allow the judge to award it a remedy which could include recovery of the company's property (see *Russell* v *Wakefield Waterworks Co.* (1875) LR 20 Eq 474). Additionally it is clear from Knox J's comments in *Smith* v *Croft (No 2)* [1988] Ch 114 at p. 189 that in any proposed derivative action it is the plaintiff's responsibility to show that the matter falls within one of the established exceptions to the *Foss* v *Harbottle* rule.

In addition to this a shareholder may sue in his own name, not joining other members as in a representative action, to enforce personal rights (see *Pender* v *Lushington* (1877) 6 ChD 70). This kind of action is brought to enforce the statutory contract contained in CA 1985, s. 14 (see chapter 5). However, it has already been made clear that the exact scope of the s. 14 contract is uncertain. If the shareholder can force the company to abide by *all* its articles by suing under s. 14 it will limit the occasions on which the rule in *Foss* v *Harbottle* will defeat him. However, the more accepted interpretation of the scope of the s. 14 contract is restricted to the enforcement of rights given to the shareholder in his capacity as a shareholder (see *Hickman* v *Kent or Romney Marsh Sheep-breeders' Association* [1915] 1 Ch 881). This interpretation ensures the continued vitality of the *Foss v Harbottle* rule. This is an occasion where the examiner may well require you to discuss the rule in *Foss* v *Harbottle* and to link it with the enforcement of the s. 14 contract.

The Exceptions to the Rule

The rule in *Foss* v *Harbottle* is a logical one. Because the wrong has been done to the company, the company is the only proper plaintiff. The exceptions cover situations where:

(a) actions cannot be put right by the company because they are not ratifiable by the general meeting; or

(b) the company is unable to act because those who perpetrated the wrong are in sufficient control of the company to prevent it from pursuing an action against them.

It is important to remember that the rule in *Foss* v *Harbottle* is a rule of procedure. It merely decides whether the action may be heard and who may represent the company at the hearing, i.e., either the majority, or the minority under one of the exceptions to *Foss* v *Harbottle*. The three established exceptions are listed below. It is possible that any of them may form part of an examination question, although the third one (fraud by wrongdoers in control) appears more frequently than the others because it raises most difficulties. The exceptions are:

(a) Where the acts complained of are *ultra vires* or illegal, the law allows the minority to sue because the acts cannot be ratified by the general meeting (see *Simpson* v *Westminster Palace Hotel Co.* (1860) 8 HL Cas 712).

This remains a valid exception even though CA 1985, s. 35(3) as amended, allows ratification by shareholders of the acts falling outside the company's objects. This is because ratification is by special resolution. However, it is suggested that this exception should properly be considered under (b) below.

(b) Where the act in question is one which can only be properly authorised by a special resolution the court will allow the minority to sue (*Baillie* v *Oriental Telephone & Electric Co. Ltd* [1915] 1 Ch 503 and *Salmon* v *Quin*

& *Axtens Ltd* [1909] 1 Ch 311). Otherwise this would allow something to happen by ordinary resolution (by way of ratification) where the company's own constitution required it to happen by special resolution.

(c)   Where the act complained of is a 'fraud' by wrongdoers in 'control' of the company (see *Burland* v *Earle* [1902] AC 83). This exception is the one which has attracted the largest amount of litigation and presents the greatest problems. Consequently it is the one that the examiner is most likely to assess, and therefore merits a more detailed treatment in this chapter. The problems centre around the meaning of the two words, 'fraud' and 'control'. The most obvious interpretation is that the exception will operate where the wrong-doers control the majority of the shares in the company and will not permit an action to be brought in the name of the company. However, the cases demonstrate that the exception may be wider in its application than this.

Control

The meaning of control is something that most examiners will require a discussion of in the examination. The accepted view was that control meant control of the votes in general meeting (see *Pavlides* v *Jensen* [1956] Ch 565). However, some recent cases suggest a more liberal interpretation of the word is acceptable. Vinelott J at first instance in *Prudential Assurance Co. Ltd* v *Newman Industries Ltd (No. 2)* [1981] Ch 257 was prepared to recognise that large public companies such as Newman Industries Ltd are in fact controlled by less than 51 per cent plus one of the votes in general meeting. In his view the court should take notice of *'de facto'* control as well as *'de jure'* control where the justice of the case demanded it. Unfortunately the Court of Appeal took a far more conservative view of control (see [1982] Ch 204). Although they recognised that many large public companies are in practice controlled by the holders of a simple majority of the shares they felt that Vinelott J's *'de facto'* control test was not a practical one to apply because it meant that where *'de facto'* control was argued the court would have to judge the substantive issue before deciding whether or not the minority shareholder was entitled to pursue the action in the company's name. This of course would mean that an allegation of *'de facto'* control would allow the issue to be adjudicated by the court and effectively side-step the rule in *Foss* v *Harbottle*. However, the observations of the Court of Appeal in *Prudential Assurance Co. Ltd* v *Newman Industries Ltd (No. 2)* [1982] Ch 204 on the meaning of control are interesting. They felt the term included, at the one end of the scale a simple majority of votes, moving to the other end of the scale where the majority of votes were made up of those likely to be cast by the delinquent himself plus those voting with him as a result of his influence and their apathy (at p. 219).

A further interesting development on this point appears in *Barrett* v *Duckett* [1995] 1 BCLC 73 where the shareholder suing on behalf of the company held

50 per cent of the company's shares and the other 50 per cent were held by the one other shareholder who was one of the directors. The result was that neither party was in a position to secure an ordinary resolution and satisfy the traditional control test. It was held that despite this the petitioner was entitled to bring a derivative action on behalf of the company. Sir Mervyn Davies explained (at p. 79):

> ... if the matter had been put to the board of the company, the board would have been equally split. There would therefore be no resolution to bring such an action and if the matter had been carried to the shareholders in general meeting, exactly the same result would have followed. Therefore as a practical matter, it would have been totally impossible for the plaintiff to set the company in motion to bring the action and it is under those circumstances that a minority shareholder's action will lie.

The issue of 'control' in this context appears to refer to the right to control litigation in the company's name. This links up to the discussion which takes place in chapter 12 on where the right to litigate in the company's name lies when the power of management is delegated to the board of directors by the articles.

This aspect of the rule in *Foss* v *Harbottle* is very uncertain and consequently a favourite area for examiners to set questions on. It all revolves around what is meant by 'fraud' and 'control' and it is up to you to exploit the uncertainty and display your knowledge of the problems and arguments which exist.

Next we consider 'fraud'.

Fraud

Fraud is used in the exception in two senses: common law fraud and equitable fraud. Fraud in the common law sense includes situations where directors steal their company's assets (*Cook* v *Deeks* [1916] 1 AC 554) or deceive the shareholders (*Prudential Assurance Co. Ltd* v *Newman Industries Ltd (No. 2)*). It also extends to situations where directors exercise their powers intentionally or unintentionally, fraudulently or negligently in a manner which benefits themselves (*Daniels* v *Daniels* [1978] Ch 406). Templeman J in *Daniels* distinguished *Pavlides* v *Jensen* [1956] Ch 565 on the basis that in that case the directors had not benefited themselves. Both cases involved the alleged selling of the company's property at an undervaluation, but in *Pavlides* the property was sold to a third party whereas in *Daniels* it was sold to a director.

A development in the decision in *Smith* v *Croft (No. 2)* [1988] Ch 144 may have reduced the effectiveness of this exception. Knox J held that even where the fraud by wrongdoers in control test is satisfied the court cannot allow the minority action to proceed if independent shareholders in the company (i.e., those not forming part of the majority in control or the minority seeking to bring the action) opposed the bringing of the claim.

The decision means that minority claims are less likely to succeed and is in keeping with the trend apparent in recent cases in making minority actions more difficult. You should note, however, that the harshness of *Smith* v *Croft (No. 2)* may be offset by the recent changes to the scope of actions available under CA 1985, s. 459 made by CA 1989 (see below).

Smith v *Croft (No. 2)* is a very important case in this area and is likely to feature in examination questions set on this topic. For further discussion of the likely effects of the decision see Stamp (1988) 9 Co Law 134 and Prentice (1988) 104 LQR 341.

Indemnity for the Costs of a Derivative Action

In *Wallersteiner* v *Moir (No. 2)* [1975] QB 373 the Court of Appeal recognised that a minority shareholder who brings a derivative action may have a right of indemnity from the company in respect of the costs incurred. The right to costs will depend on whether the minority shareholder acted in good faith in bringing the proceedings and an application of the 'independent board' test as stated by Buckley LJ in *Wallersteiner*. This decision should encourage minority shareholders to seek to right wrongs done to their company without the added worry of incurring substantial costs although a restrictive interpretation of the indemnity test in *Wallersteiner* was taken recently in *Smith* v *Croft* [1986] 1 WLR 580, where it was urged that a proportion of the costs of the action should normally be borne by the minority shareholder applying for the derivative action, Walton J commenting, at p. 598, that:

A spur of a mere 10 per cent to a genuinely poverty stricken individual may well be quite enough. To somebody merely hard up, much more money may be required. It must in the end all rest on the individual circumstances of each case.

Note the Court of Appeal's criticism of Vinelott J's approach at first instance in *Prudential Assurance Co. Ltd* v *Newman Industries Ltd (No. 2)* where because of his definition of '*de facto*' control, he had to hear the 30-day action before deciding whether the exception applied. As well as incurring tremendous costs in taking this approach, it also means that, if at the end of the hearing it is decided that the exception does not apply, the substantive matter has already been heard. What about the rule in *Foss* v *Harbottle*? The Court of Appeal in *Prudential Assurance Co. Ltd* v *Newman Industries Ltd (No. 2)* [1982] Ch 204 thought that a better method of dealing with this problem would be for the judge who is confronted with a minority shareholder trying to start a derivative action, rather than embarking on a lengthy action to see if there is 'fraud' by those in 'control' of the company, to establish first of all whether or not the action does fall within the proper boundaries of the exception to the rule in *Foss* v *Harbottle*. To do this,

> ... it may well be right for the judge trying the preliminary issue to grant a sufficient adjournment to enable a meeting of shareholders to be convened by the board, so that he can reach a conclusion in the light of the conduct of, and proceedings at, that meeting (p. 222).

Presumably if the meeting does not take any action about the alleged 'fraud', then it is open to the judge to hear evidence that this was because those who 'control' the company perpetrated the fraud or that it was a perfectly sensible management decision, the company deciding not to get embroiled in expensive litigation that could harm its public image. This would partly avoid the problem that the preliminary issue for a derivative action, the test of the shareholder's *locus standi*, is the same as the substantive issue that has to be fully tried and that if the court does go through a full hearing on the preliminary issue, the case has been heard and *Foss* v *Harbottle* has been effectively sidetracked.

Companies Act 1985, Section 459: Remedies for Unfairly Prejudicial Conduct

In 1980, CA 1980, s. 75 (now CA 1985, s. 459), replaced CA 1948, s. 210, as a statutory procedure to deal with problems experienced by minority share-holders. The most significant substantive change brought about by s. 459 is that the petitioner no longer has to prove 'oppression' only 'unfair prejudice'.

The section allows any member of the company to petition the court for a remedy on the ground that the affairs of the company are being conducted in a manner which is unfairly prejudicial to the interests of some part of its members (including at least himself) or the interest of its members generally; alternatively, that any proposed act or omission of the company (including an act or omission on its behalf) is or would be prejudicial.

Thus, for example, a minority shareholder is within the ambit of the section if he can show that the value of his shareholding in the company has been seriously diminished or at least seriously jeopardised by reason of a course of conduct on the part of those persons who have had '*de facto*' control of the company, which has been unfair to the member concerned (per Slade J in *Re Bovey Hotel Ventures Ltd* (unreported 31 July 1981) discussed in *Re R.A. Noble & Sons (Clothing) Ltd* [1983] BCLC 273). However, the conduct complained of must unfairly prejudice the member *qua* member (*Re a Company* [1983] 2 All ER 36 and *Re J.E. Cade & Son Ltd* [1991] BCC 360, but note Vinelott J's comments in *Re a Company* [1983] 2 All ER 854 on the application of s. 459 to the type of situation that existed in *Ebrahimi* v *Westbourne Galleries Ltd* [1973]

AC 360). Previously, if the loss was suffered by the company due to a director's breach of duty such as a diminution in the value of the company's assets rather than the members' shares, then no action would lie under s. 459 and the member would have to show that he fell within the ambit of the 'wrongdoer in control' exception to the rule in *Foss* v *Harbottle* because the wrong was done to the company and not to him personally (see *Prudential Assurance Co. Ltd* v *Newman Industries Ltd (No. 2)* [1982] Ch 204 and *Nurcombe* v *Nurcombe* [1985] 1 All ER 65). However, following an amendment introduced by CA 1989, s. 145 and sch. 19(II), if the unfairly prejudical conduct can affect the members *generally*. This amendment overrules decisions like *Re Carrington Viyella plc* (1983) 1 BCC 98, 951 and *Re a Company (No. 00370 of 1987)* [1988] 1 WLR 1068. Furthermore, the use of the word 'generally' in the section has been criticised as being imprecise (see Griffith (1992) 13 Co Law 83). It is arguable that the word 'generally' may not even mean the whole of the membership but merely the majority. If the latter is the case then presumably the court will still not be able to authorise civil proceedings to be brought in the name and on behalf of the company under CA 1985, s. 461(2)(c).

The main area of uncertainty, and therefore an issue likely to be raised by an examiner, is the meaning of 'unfairly prejudicial conduct'. You will need to look at some of the reported decisions under the section to illustrate the meaning of this phrase. In particular the Court of Appeal decision in *Re Saul D. Harrison & Sons plc* [1995] 1 BCLC 14 where although the court found the conduct complained of did not amount to unfair prejudice, Neill LJ's judgment contains a very useful discussion of the meaning of the term and a summary of the relevant case law at p. 28. This will be a useful starting point in understanding the term and identifying the most relevant cases to support your own discussion. See also, e.g. *Re R.A. Noble & Sons (Clothing) Ltd* [1983] BCLC 273, *Re a Company (No. 001761 of 1986)* [1987] BCLC 141, *Re Cumana Ltd* [1986] BCLC 430 and *McGuinness and another, petitioners* (1988) 4 BCC 161. See also Prentice (1988) 8 Oxford J Legal Stud 55. When discussing unfair prejudice it may also be helpful if you could identify circumstances which will not amount to unfair prejudice in order to demonstrate the boundaries of the rule. In this regard see *Re Saul D. Harrison & Sons plc* and *Nicholas* v *Soundcraft Electronics Ltd* [1993] BCLC 360.

One thing that was made clear in the decision in *Re London School of Electronics Ltd* [1986] Ch 211 was that s. 459 has to be construed without importing the test applicable under CA 1948, s. 210, of whether it was 'just and equitable' to grant the petitioner relief. Therefore, although the conduct of the petitioner could affect the relief which the court thought fit to grant under s. 459, there is now no independent or overriding requirement that it should be 'just and equitable' to grant relief or that the petitioner should come to court with clean hands.

You should also be aware of the remedies that are available under s. 459 which are more extensive than those which were available under s. 210 permitting the court to 'make such order as it thinks fit...' (CA 1985, s. 461(1). This includes the potential for authorising a derivative action on such terms, including payments for the action, by the company, as the court may direct (CA 1985, s. 461(2)(c)). To illuminate the thinking behind s. 459 you could usefully refer to the recommendations made by the *Jenkins Committee Report* (Cmnd 1749 (1962) paras 199–212) where a change in CA 1948, s. 210, was first proposed. This should give you an idea of the problems surrounding the application of s. 210 and the way in which the changes introduced in s. 459 are intended to deal with them.

Relationship between Section 122(1)(g) of IA 1986 and Section 459 of CA 1985

In some of the cases where s. 459 has been pleaded it has been used as a means of providing an alternative to a winding-up order under IA 1986, s. 1202(1)(g). IA 1986, s. 122(1)(g), provides that a company may be wound up by the court if the court is of opinion that it is 'just and equitable' to do so. Although the just and equitable ground is applicable to many situations, you should be principally concerned with the situation where a minority shareholder has a right to participate in the management of the company (on the grounds usually that it is a quasi-partnership) as well as its profits and is wrongfully excluded from so doing (see *Ebrahimi* v *Westbourne Galleries Ltd* [1973] AC 360). The exact relationship between the two sections is as yet unclear. There is obviously some overlap between the facts which will be actionable under IA 1986, s. 122(1)(g), and CA 1985, s. 459. The sections will in many instances offer alternative remedies. There will also be situations where only one of the sections will apply. For example a petitioner seeking a winding-up order under s. 122(1)(g) may be defeated because he must show clean hands (not a requirement under s. 459). Alternatively, it is possible to envisage conduct in a quasi-partnership which is not unfairly prejudicial and therefore not actionable under s. 459, but actionable under IA 1986, s. 122(1)(g) — see *Re R.A. Noble & Sons Ltd* [1983] BCLC 273.

The fact that an alternative remedy to an s. 122(1)(g) winding-up order is available to the petitioner need no longer be considered by the court (IA 1986, s. 125). However, the court may refuse the petition under s. 122(1)(g) if the petitioner is acting unreasonably in failing to pursue that alternative remedy (IA 1986, s. 125(2)). For what may amount to unreasonableness in these circumstances see *Re Ringtower Holdings plc* [1989] BCC 82; cf. *Re Abbey Leisure Ltd* [1990] BCC 60.

A further insight into the relationship between the sections may be observed from Warner J's judgment in *Re J.E. Cade & Son Ltd* [1991] BCC 360. Here the petitioner, T, was a shareholder in a company whose principal asset was a licence over a farm. T owned the freehold of the farm. An option to purchase the farm had been granted to the only other shareholder in the company J. J failed to exercise the option and T refused to extend the licence. T sought either an order that the other shareholder purchase his shares and the farm for £244,000 (the price at which the option was exercisable), possession of the farm or a winding-up order on the just and equitable ground arguing that the company's substratum had failed (the quasi-partnership ground was not argued). J's defence was that T was not seeking to protect his interests as a member of the company but as owner of the freehold. Warner J, striking out the petition, declared at p. 377: 'It would be quite illogical therefore to hold that a shareholder was entitled to seek a winding-up order on the just and equitable ground for the purpose of protecting a wider range of interests than he could seek to protect by means of proceedings under s. 459'.

Investigations by the Department of Trade and Industry

The Department of Trade and Industry has powers under Part XIV of CA 1985 [CA 1989, s. 58] to investigate the affairs of a company and if necessary bring proceedings on the company's behalf or petition for a winding-up order. In addition it has the power under CA 1985, s. 460, to apply for an order on the basis that the company's affairs are being conducted in an unfairly prejudicial manner. The powers of the Department are extensive, but are normally only used in the last resort. It is unusual for this topic to be the subject of a whole examination question although you should be aware of these provisions especially if your course has dealt with them during the year.

REVISION AND RESEARCH

Yet again, it appears that if you do not revise this area of company law you are going to seriously restrict your choice of questions in any examination. Failure to revise minority protection will not only mean that you cannot answer a question directly on the point, you may also be prevented from answering a question on directors' duties, or the relationship between the board of directors and the general meeting, or the s. 14 contract. You may find yourself in a situation where you cannot give a complete answer to several questions on topics which you would otherwise choose to answer. Consequently, can you really afford not to revise it?

One of the first things that you should clarify in your revision of the rule in *Foss* v *Harbottle* (1843) 2 Hare 461 is the procedure used by the minority shareholder in bringing the action on behalf of the company. What is a derivative action? How is it different from a representative or personal action? Who pays the costs?

The other aspects of the rule which are important are the exceptions, particularly the 'wrongdoers in control' exception. This is the one which has attracted most litigation and most readily links up to the other areas of company law mentioned earlier. We suggest that you concentrate your revision efforts here. It is important to sort out the cases and particular note should be taken of *Prudential Assurance Co. Ltd v Newman Industries Ltd (No. 2)* at first instance [1981] Ch 257 (Vinelott J's judgment), the Court of Appeal judgment [1982] Ch 204 and of *Smith v Croft (No. 2)* [1988] Ch 144 as well as *Barrett v Duckett* [1995] 1 BCLC 73 because the decisions illustrate the difficulties that exist for lawyers in their attempts to construe the boundaries of this exception.

As far as mixed questions are concerned we would again advise you to look at past examination papers to get ideas on possible combinations. In addition allow time in your revision programme to practise answering 'mixed' questions under examination conditions and hand them to your tutor for marking. This will give you practice at dividing your time between different areas of law in the same answer and at linking the areas together to produce a well-argued coherent answer.

You should not revise the rule in *Foss v Harbottle* and leave out s. 459. Although s. 459 essentially provides a minority shareholder with a personal remedy, since the amendment made by CA 1989 it may now be possible for a minority shareholder to obtain a remedy on behalf of the company under it. Following the decision in *Smith v Croft (No. 2)*, the section may prove popular with minority shareholders seeking to bring a derivative action.

Examiners may consider it quite legitimate to ask you to discuss s. 459 alongside the rule in *Foss v Harbottle* or as a means of providing an alternative to a winding-up order under IA 1986, s. 122(1)(g).

IDENTIFYING THE QUESTION

Because minority protection is likely to appear as only part of a problem or an essay, identification in the stressful conditions of the examination room becomes more difficult. The rubric of the question is the best starting-point to ascertain whether or not the examiner wants you to discuss the issue of minority protection. Although any enforcement of a corporate right will raise questions of *Foss v Harbottle* not all questions will require an in-depth discussion. In the questions where the examiner wants you to discuss minority protection in depth the rubric may be along the following lines: 'Advise Fred (a minority shareholder) on any remedies available to him or the company', or 'Discuss the liability of the directors and the problems facing Fred (a minority shareholder) in his attempts to force the directors to account to the company'. The fact that Fred is a minority shareholder may not be spelt out in the rubric; you will have to read the problem to ascertain whether he is or not.

In questions where the examiner wants a discussion of the rule in *Foss* v *Harbottle* the main issue is likely to centre around the 'wrongdoers in control' exception so look out for a situation where the wrongdoers are preventing corporate remedies being pursued. It is important not to forget that if the value of a member's shares are affected by the conduct of those in control of the company, a remedy may be available to him under s. 459 despite the fact that he cannot bring himself within any of the exceptions to the rule in *Foss* v *Harbottle*. But remember this remedy is a personal one not a corporate one. If the wrong is a corporate wrong then the action must be brought in the company's name.

QUESTION 1

The share capital of Loco Ltd is divided as follows: Peter and Chris 40 shares each and Mark 20 shares. Peter and Chris are the company's two directors. Loco Ltd owns three fairground sites and several fairground rides.

Slime, a friend of Peter's, owns several fairground rides and is looking for a permanent site on which he can set up a fairground. He and Peter agree that Peter will persuade the company to sell Slime one of its sites at £50,000 below a recent valuation and in exchange Slime agrees to appoint Peter as a director of his company at an annual salary of £10,000.

Peter manages to procure a false valuation of the site and uses it to trick the other shareholders into agreeing to the sale.

Mark transfers 10 shares to his son, Tim, but the directors refuse to register the share transfer.

Mark has recently discovered what Peter has done and wishes to sue to recover the £50,000 on behalf of the company. Chris refuses to support him in bringing the action as Peter has agreed to pay him one-half of the £10,000 salary from Slime's company.

Advise Mark and Tim.

Introduction

This problem raises several issues. The following comments will concentrate on the issues of minority protection, but where appropriate reference will be made to other areas of law to highlight possible areas of conflict and show how to link two areas together.

Breach of Directors' Duties

By selling the fairground to Slime at an undervaluation Peter is in breach of his duty to the company. He is clearly motivated by a desire to become a director of Slime's company and earn the extra salary. Thus Peter has made a secret profit by virtue of his position as director of Loco Ltd (see *Regal (Hastings) Ltd* v *Gulliver* [1942] 1 All ER 378 and *Industrial Development Consultants Ltd* v *Cooley* [1972] 1 WLR 443). He has also knowingly sold a corporate asset at a gross undervaluation. Mark seems to be in a difficult position as the only other substantial shareholder, Chris refuses to support him in his attempt to bring an action against Peter. Chris has also made a profit from the breach of duty by sharing in Peter's extra salary.

What can Mark as a minority shareholder do to prevent these directors keeping their ill-gotten gains and restore the company to health? At this point in your answer you should be prepared to discuss the operation of the rule in *Foss* v *Harbottle* (1843) 2 Hare 461. It will be necessary for you to explain how the rule normally operates to bar the minority shareholder's action, but be careful not to dwell too long on this part of your answer, as the main discussion should centre around the bringing of a minority action under one of the exceptions to the rule.

After discussing the rule in *Foss* v *Harbottle* you will need to consider which exception Mark will be most likely to fall within. From the facts it should be clear that the 'fraud by wrongdoers in control' exception presents the most likely possibility.

Normally, it is quite in order for directors who are also shareholders to ratify their own breach of duty (*North-West Transportation Co. Ltd* v *Beatty* (1887) 12 App Cas 589). However, if such a ratification would amount to a fraud on the minority of shareholders then any attempt to ratify will be invalid (*Cook* v *Deeks* [1916] 1 AC 554). In such a situation the minority shareholder will be able to bring a derivative action on behalf of the company to recover any loss it may have suffered, under the 'fraud by wrongdoers in control' exception to *Foss* v *Harbottle*.

Mark must therefore establish two things:

(a)   fraud,
(b)   by those in control of the company.

Meaning of fraud
The meaning of fraud in this context has attracted a great deal of judicial comment and therefore is worthy of particular attention in your answer.

To constitute a 'fraud' on the minority the wrongdoers must either have misappropriated the company's property or have committed an act which was actuated by an improper motive (see *Cook* v *Deeks*). It was at one time thought that only fraud in the common law sense would support an action under this exception and that certainly any allegation of mere negligence was not enough to constitute 'fraud' (*Pavlides* v *Jensen* [1956] Ch 565). However, in *Daniels* v *Daniels* [1978] Ch 406, Templeman J decided that fraud on the minority covered more than just common law fraud, so that where directors use their powers negligently to make a profit at the expense of the company a minority shareholder's action will lie provided the wrongdoers are in control. In this case it is unlikely that Mark will have any difficulty in proving fraud on the part of Peter and the knowing participation in that fraud by Chris. The valuation report was obtained in order to deceive the shareholders and this has been held to amount to fraud (see *Prudential Assurance Co. Ltd* v *Newman Industries Ltd (No. 2)* [1982] Ch 204). Having proved fraud, Mark must also establish that the wrongdoers are in control of the company.

Meaning of control
This aspect of the exception presents more difficulties. One question which may be asked is what do the wrongdoers have to have control of? If the answer is control of the corporate litigation, this immediately raises the controversy surrounding Table A, art. 70. Is it the general meeting or the board of directors who control corporate litigation (see chapter 12)? This area of company law is very uncertain and as can be seen in chapter 12, a definite answer is difficult to produce. In a question of this type you should not delve too deeply into the difficulties surrounding the relationship between this exception and art. 70 because you will simply not have enough time in the examination. However, you should raise the issue and at least outline the difficulties to the examiner. The traditional interpretation of 'control' is that the wrongdoers should control the votes in a general meeting — control *'de jure'*. However, Vinelott J was prepared to extend the concept of control to *'de facto'* control in the first-instance decision in *Prudential Assurance Co. Ltd* v *Newman Industries Ltd (No. 2)* [1981] Ch 257. He felt that a situation where the wrongdoers were in a position to manipulate the majority of the board of directors and prevent corporate litigation was sufficient to support a minority shareholder's action under the exception. The *'de facto'* control test was rejected by the Court of Appeal as being too uncertain to be regarded as a practical test especially as its application would necessitate a full hearing of the case. Such an approach would of course defeat the effect of the rule as a method of preventing minority actions.

In this particular problem the wrongdoers, Peter and Chris, control the board of directors and the votes in general meeting. Chris could not argue that he is an independent shareholder under *Smith* v *Croft (No. 2)* as he has participated in the wrongdoing. Instead he would form part of the majority seeking to prevent the action being brought. Consequently Mark should find no difficulty in bringing a minority action under the exception. Having decided this you should briefly mention the basis on which the action would be brought and who would bear the costs of the action if it were to prove unsuccessful. This will involve a discussion of the derivative action and an explanation of the decision in *Wallersteiner* v *Moir (No. 2)* [1975] QB 373. Be careful not to dwell too long on these points as they represent minor parts of your answer although they should not be omitted.

Failure to Register the Share Transfer

The failure by the directors to register the transfer of shares from Mark to Tim obviously effects Mark and Tim. Tim would be keen to have the matter sorted out to enable him to participate in the affairs of the company.

CA 1985, s. 459, would seem to offer Tim the most obvious chance of success. The section is designed to provide a procedure whereby minority shareholders who are unfairly prejudiced by the conduct of the company's affairs can petition the court for a remedy.

You will need to analyse the provisions of the section to be in a position to advise Tim as to his best course of action. This will involve you in breaking the section down into its component parts. We suggest the following plan of attack.

Who can sue?

Basically any member or group of members can sue. 'Member' in this context includes a person to whom shares have been transferred but not yet registered (see s. 459(2)). It is not sufficient to bring an action that there is only an agreement to transfer (*Re Quickdome Ltd* [1988] BCLC 370). The term 'agreement to transfer' has been construed as not requiring a bilateral element, but merely the agreement of a person to become a member — see *Re Nuneaton Borough Association Football Club Ltd* [1989] BCLC 454. However, it appears that there has been a transfer rather than merely an agreement to transfer here. This means that Tim would be in a position to take action under the section. The remedy which he would seek is a personal one unlike the situation where a minority shareholder brings a derivative action to recover a remedy on behalf of the company.

What does the minority shareholder have to prove?

The minority shareholder has to show that he is being 'unfairly prejudiced' by the conduct of the company's affairs. The meaning of 'unfair prejudice' is not defined by the Act and reference must be made to the decided cases for some guidance. Cases decided under the previous stricter provision of CA 1948, s. 210, where the petitioner was successful will obviously fall within the wider scope of CA 1985, s. 459. It is the wider meaning of 'unfair prejudice' which will cause problems. Just as with s. 210 the 'unfairly prejudicial' conduct in s. 459 must affect the petitioner qua member and this can include a situation where there has been an effect on the value of the member's shareholding (see *Re R.A. Noble & Sons (Clothing) Ltd* [1983] BCLC 273 and Lord Grantchester in *Re a Company (No. 004475 of 1982)* [1983] 2 All ER 36).

In this particular problem the conduct of the directors in refusing to register the transfer to Tim has obviously affected the value of Tim's shares because it means he cannot exercise any rights attached to them. Therefore, it is likely that Tim will be able to bring a successful petition under CA 1985, s. 459. The forms of relief available under the section are wide and include an order requiring the company to carry out an act which the petitioner has complained it has omitted to do which would be appropriate in this situation.

Summary

This mixed problem requires you to discuss a number of issues. We would again wish to emphasise the need to divide your time up carefully between the various issues raised and not to deal with the issues in isolation. One of the examiner's main reasons for setting a 'mixed' problem is to test your ability to link and relate different areas of company law and identify any conflict that may exist between the different rules.

QUESTION 2

The articles of Luxor Ltd include a provision that the company's main asset, freehold land at Karnak, shall not be sold without the unanimous agreement of the company's three directors, Tom, Dick and Harry. The three directors own the following shares: Tom 26, Dick 34 and Harry 40.

Phoarah Ltd approaches Dick and Harry with an offer for the land at Karnak. Dick and Harry wish to accept the offer but Tom feels it is too low because a recent valuation valued it at £5,000 above the offer. Nevertheless, Dick and Harry go through with the sale because they have been promised annual holidays for the rest of their lives on Nile cruisers owned by Phoarah Ltd. Tom wishes to prevent the sale and tries to enforce the article against the company. Dick and Harry call a general meeting to ratify the sale.

Dick and Harry at the same meeting of shareholders vote together and dismiss Tom from the board to prevent him causing further trouble. They have not declared any dividends since, but pay themselves large salaries as directors.

Prior to forming Luxor Ltd the three men operated the business as partners.

Advise Tom, the minority shareholder.

Introduction

This is another example of a problem which asks you to discuss and interrelate several areas of company law. It represents a typical combination which may confront you in an assessment. The following topics will need to be discussed in your answer:

(a) The s. 14 contract.
(b) The rule in *Foss* v *Harbottle* (1843) 2 Hare 461.
(c) CA 1985, s. 459.
(d) Winding-up orders available under IA 1986, s. 122(1)(g), and the principle in *Ebrahimi* v *Westbourne Galleries Ltd* [1973] AC 360.

The Section 14 Contract and its Relationship with the Rule in Foss v Harbottle

This is fully explored in chapter 5 so we are only going to look at the last three issues here. If s. 14 no longer means what it says, and only those rights which affect a member *qua* member are enforceable what alternative course of action is available to Tom?

His other option would be to bring a derivative action under an exception to the rule in *Foss* v *Harbottle*. First of all he must be in a position to argue that by selling the land a wrong has been done to the company. For example, in this case he would probably be able to show that the land was sold at an undervaluation and the company has suffered a loss as a consequence.

The next step would be to prove that he falls within the scope of one of the exceptions to the rule in *Foss* v *Harbottle*. The most likely exception is 'fraud by wrongdoers in control'. Tom will have to prove fraud and control which we looked at in question 1. Refer to this question for an explanation of the meaning of the concept of fraud in this context.

Dick and Harry have gained a holiday from this transaction and have benefited themselves. It would also seem that the company has suffered a loss as it would probably have been able to get a higher price for the land had it been sold to someone else.

Therefore, you should be able to conclude that Tom can establish fraud in the equitable sense on the part of the directors as they have benefited personally (*Daniels* v *Daniels* [1978] Ch 406).

In this problem Dick and Harry control the board meetings especially in the light of Tom's removal from office and they also control the votes in general meeting. Hence, Tom would be able to show that there has been a 'fraud by wrongdoers in control of the company'. In these circumstances you should advise him that he will be unlikely to succeed in his attempt to enforce the article against the company but would probably be successful in a derivative action against Dick and Harry.

CA 1985, Section 459, Winding-up Orders under IA 1986, Section 122(1)(g), and the Principle in Ebrahimi v Westbourne Galleries Ltd

The directors' actions in dismissing Tom from office and failing to declare dividends on his shares affect him in his capacity as a member and cannot be considered wrongs done to the company. This aspect of the problem invites you to consider the remedies that may be available to Tom under CA 1985, s. 459. You must consider what Tom will have to prove to bring a successful petition under the section.

From the facts of the problem it is clear that the repeated failure to declare dividends affects Tom in his capacity as a shareholder and that this conduct could be considered unfairly prejudicial. It obviously has had an adverse effect on the value of his shares.

However, will s. 459 apply to Tom's dismissal as director? This conduct affects him in his capacity as a director rather than as a shareholder. Given that the parties originally worked together as partners should Tom instead seek the ultimate sanction of a winding-up order under the just and equitable rule in IA 1986, s. 122(1)(g), as in *Ebrahimi* v *Westbourne Galleries Ltd* [1973] AC 360, or will a remedy be available to him under s. 459? What is the relationship between these two statutory provisions?

There is an apparent conflict in the authorities on this point. In *Re a Company (No. 004475 of 1982)* [1983] 2 All ER 36 Lord Grantchester QC held that the prejudice must affect the member qua member. The approach taken in this case would therefore clearly exclude an '*Ebrahimi*'-type situation. However, in the later *Re a Company (No. 002567 of 1982)* [1983] 2 All ER 854, Vinelott J felt that s. 459 would apply to an '*Ebrahimi*' situation where a shareholder was wrongly excluded from participating in the management of the company. He said (at p. 859):

> It seems to me unlikely that the legislature could have intended to exclude from the scope of [CA 1985, s. 459] a shareholder in the position of Mr Ebrahimi in *Ebrahimi* v *Westbourne Galleries Ltd*.

This approach was followed in *Re Bird Precision Bellows Ltd* [1984] 3 All ER 444 where exclusion from management was the basis of a successful petition under s. 459. In this case it was eventually ordered by consent that the respondents should jointly and severally purchase the shares of the petitioners (see also *Re Stewarts (Brixton) Ltd* [1985] BCLC 4).

It is likely that Tom would be able to establish a right to a remedy under s. 459 for the failure to declare dividends and his wrongful exclusion from management. Unfair prejudice includes conduct which affects the value of the member's shares — *Re a Company (No. 004475 of 1982)* [1983] 2 All ER 36. The repeated failure to declare dividends will obviously have an effect on the value of Tom's shares, but what about the act of excluding him from taking part in the management of the company? If you take a simplistic view of whether the value of Tom's shares are affected by such conduct the answer must be no. However, if the company is considered to be a quasi-partnership with all members entitled to participate in the management of the company, then surely the right to manage must be considered to be a shareholder right? If this reasoning is correct then Tom should be entitled to a remedy under s. 459 for the failure to declare a dividend and the wrongful exclusion from the management of the company. It is now clear that the court will not grant the drastic remedy of a winding up petition under s. 122(1)(g) if there is an alternative remedy available under s. 459 and the petitioner has acted unreasonably in not pursuing that alternative remedy — see *Re Ringtower Holdings plc* [1989] BCC 82 and cf. *Re Abbey Leisure Ltd* [1990] BCC 60. Thus Tom may be more likely to get a remedy under s. 459 than a winding-up order under s. 122(1)(g).

Remedies

Section 461 gives the court a wide power to grant relief if the petition under the section is granted. The court can regulate the conduct of the company's affairs in the future and provide for the purchase of the shares of the member by either other members or the company itself. The latter remedy was awarded in *Re Bird Precision Bellows Ltd* [1984] 3 All ER 444 where the court found that the petitioner had been wrongfully excluded from the management of the company and gave a winding-up order. The parties eventually agreed that the petitioner's shares would be bought by the remaining shareholders and the price paid was fixed on a pro rata basis, without any discount to reflect the fact that the shares constituted a minority holding. The court added *per curiam* that where shares were acquired as an investment without any intention on the part of the holder of participating in the management of the company's affairs, it might well be fair that the shares be bought out on the same basis if an order for their purchase is made under s. 461(2)(d).

The remedy that the court is likely to award Tom is an order that Dick and Harry purchase his shares in Luxor Ltd. As Tom seems to have purchased the shares with a view to participating in the management of the company the valuation should be on a *Bird Precision Bellows* basis.

Many of the reported decisions under s. 459 have centred around the basis of valuation of the shares to be bought out (see *Re OC (Transport) Services Ltd* [1984] BCLC 251). However, it is unlikely that the examiner will require a detailed discussion of the various methods of valuation. But you should mention that different methods of valuation have been used particularly when the order has been granted in an *Ebrahimi* situation.

SUMMARY

The issues raised in this problem are complex in their own right besides being 'mixed' with other topics. Do not avoid the problems involved because they are difficult and remember that they should not be considered in isolation. In a question of this type it is important that you try to interrelate matters to present the examiner with a clear overview of the law and how the issues are linked to each other.

FURTHER READING

Boyle, A. J., 'The Prudential, the Court of Appeal and *Foss* v *Harbottle*' (1981) 2 Co Law 264.

Fox, D. W., 'Valuing minority holdings in private companies' (1985) 129 SJ 456.

Prentice, D. D., 'The theory of the firm: minority shareholder oppression: sections 459–461 of the Companies Act 1985' (1988) 8 Oxford J Legal Stud 55.

Rider, B. A. K., 'Amiable lunatics and the rule in *Foss* v *Harbottle*' [1978] CLJ 270.

Riley, Christopher A., 'Contracting out of company law: section 459 of the Companies Act 1985 and the role of the courts' (1992) 55 MLR 782.

11 WINDING UP

INTRODUCTION

A company is created by law and can be killed off only by law. The killing-off process is known as dissolution. However, prior to dissolution the company must go through a winding up or liquidation (the terms are interchangeable). This latter process allows a company's property to be distributed to its creditors, rather like the administration of a deceased person's estate except that the winding up of a company (distribution of assets) takes place before dissolution (death). This chapter is concerned with the process of liquidation and the problems experienced by liquidators where trading irregularities on the part of the directors, or others involved in the management of the company, are exposed.

When a company in winding up is solvent, the procedure is relatively straightforward. However, if the company is insolvent and cannot satisfy the demands of its creditors a number of complex problems regarding the distribution of the assets that the company possesses arise. The law which regulates this distribution is found largely in the Insolvency Act 1986 and has undergone a substantial recent review. This factor alone is likely to make the topic popular with examiners, although the ending of a company's life is an area which is important in its own right, and it merits a separate chapter.

MAIN ISSUES

This chapter will concentrate on three main issues which are essential to the proper understanding of the winding-up process and the common problems associated with it:

(a) the role of insolvency practitioners,
(b) modes and the legal effect of winding up,
(c) irregularities exposed by the winding up and their investigation.

Insolvency Practitioners

One of the major reforms contained in the IA 1985 was the introduction of minimum qualifications for insolvency practitioners. These apply to people acting as receivers (see chapter 9) or liquidators. Prior to 1985 neither liquidators nor receivers had to possess any qualifications. This factor undoubtedly contributed to some very dubious practices by a small minority of liquidators in the case of a small number of liquidations. The losers were inevitably the creditors of the insolvent company.

The rules regulating the qualification, competence and appointment of insolvency practitioners, including liquidators, are now contained in the IA 1986, ss. 388 to 393. These provisions determine who is qualified to be an insolvency practitioner and specify the people who are disqualified from acting in that capacity. Remember that these rules also apply to the appointment of receivers and should be noted when revising the subject-matter contained in chapter 9. Although these rules are unlikely to form the major part of a question, they are new and therefore likely to attract the examiner's attention, and it is quite probable that an examiner will test your awareness of these rules if the topic forms part of your taught syllabus.

Modes and the Legal Effect of Winding Up

Three modes exist by which a company may be wound up. These are:

(a) A members' voluntary winding up.
(b) A creditors' voluntary winding up.
(c) A compulsory winding up by the court.

The rules which regulate the various methods of winding up are very tedious and therefore can be difficult to learn for examinations. We feel that for the purposes of explaining the rules, and from a revision point of view, the easiest way to deal with them is in tabular form. At the bottom of each table points of interest or difficulty are noted for you to follow up as part of your revision programme.

Voluntary Winding Up

Table 11.1   Members' voluntary windingup

---

1. Trigger
Members pass a special resolution under IA 1986, s. 84.

2. Conditions
The company must be in a position to pay its debts within one year of the passing of the resolution. Its directors must make a declaration of solvency to this effect. It is an offence to make a false declaration of solvency (IA 1986, s. 89). Failure to make such a statutory declaration automatically renders the winding up a creditors' voluntary winding up (IA 1986, s. 90).

3. Appointment of the liquidator
Where the statutory declaration has been made by the directors and the winding up remains a members' voluntary winding up the general meeting has power to appoint the liquidator (IA 1986, s. 91).

4. Powers of the liquidator
See table 11.2.

Table 11.2   Creditors' voluntary winding up

---

1. Trigger
If the directors fail to make a statutory declaration of solvency in the five weeks preceding the meeting which resolves to wind up, then the liquidation will become a creditors' voluntary winding up under IA 1986, s. 90, or if the liquidator appointed by the members forms the opinion that the company will not be in a position to pay its debts within the time period specified by the directors, then the winding up becomes a creditors' winding up under IA 1986, s. 95.

2. Conditions
The company is unable to pay its debts in either of the circumstances described above.

3. Appointment of the liquidator
Both the creditors and the members are entitled to appoint a liquidator, but if they nominate different people then it is the creditors' choice that is appointed, subject to a right of appeal by the directors or members (IA 1986, s. 100).

In addition to a liquidator a liquidation committee may be appointed to assist the liquidator. The creditors may appoint up to five persons to act for them. If they do this then the members may also appoint up to five persons to represent their interests on the committee. However, creditors may veto all the members' nominees unless the court orders otherwise (IA 1986, s. 101).

The functions of this committee are set out in IA 1986, ss. 101, 103 and 165.

4. Powers of the liquidator in either type of voluntary liquidation
Once the liquidator has been appointed he effectively takes over the day-today running of the company. Statute sets out the powers of the voluntary liquidator under the following main headings:

(a) Notification of appointment: IA 1986, s. 91; CA 1985, ss. 42 and 375.

(b) Effect on directors' powers: IA 1986, s. 103.

(c) Duties to the creditors: IA 1986, s. 165; see also the cases of *Pulsford v Devenish* [1903] 2 Ch 625, which shows that the liquidator may be sued for breach of statutory duty if he has not distributed the company's assets properly to creditors who proved in the liquidation, and *James Smith & Sons (Norwood) Ltd v Goodman* [1936] Ch 216.

(d) Meetings and reports to be made by the liquidator: IA 1986, ss. 93 and 192 (members' liquidation); (final report in a members' liquidation); IA 1986, s. 192 (creditors' liquidation); IA 1986, s. 66 (final report in a creditors' liquidation).

(e) Control of the liquidator by the courts: IA 1986, ss. 112, 167, 168, 173, 187, 212, and the case of *Re Home & Colonial Insurance Co. Ltd* [1930] 1 Ch 102 where the liquidator was liable to the company in misfeasance proceedings under what is now IA 1986, s. 212, because he wrongly admitted a claim by a creditor.

Points to Note

In a creditors' voluntary winding up the creditors, in theory at least, have the right to appoint the liquidator, although this has not always happened. The decision in *Re Centrebind Ltd* [1966] 3 All ER 889 demonstrated that it was possible for members of an insolvent company to appoint a liquidator who could then dispose of assets rapidly and cheaply, usually to the controllers of the insolvent company. This would allow the controllers of the insolvent company to start up in business again quickly and cheaply. This loophole has been stopped up by IA 1986, s. 166, which makes it an offence for a liquidator nominated by the members in a creditors' voluntary winding up to exercise any powers except to preserve property until a creditors' meeting has been held. The fact that all insolvency practitioners now have to be qualified people should also reduce the risk of similar unacceptable practices occurring in the future.

You will need to look out for questions which appear to involve a members' voluntary winding up where the company turns out to be insolvent. The winding up will, of course, then become a creditors' voluntary winding up and be subject to different rules.

Table 11.3   Compulsory winding up

---

1.   Trigger
The presentation of a petition by a person envisaged by IA 1986, s. 124.

2.   Conditions
The company may be wound up by the court if the petitioner can satisfy one of the grounds contained in IA 1986, s. 122.

3.   Appointment of the liquidator
At any time after the presentation of the petition the court may appoint a provisional liquidator (it is usual to appoint the official receiver as provisional liquidator in England and Wales) (IA 1986, s. 135).

   In circumstances where the court grants a petition to wind the company up the official receiver attached to the court becomes the liquidator of the company (IA 1986, s. 70). At the first meeting of creditors and contributories a liquidator may be appointed to replace the official receiver; it is the creditors' choice that will prevail. However, if the creditors fail to appoint a liquidator then the members will be entitled to appoint one (IA 1986, s. 139).

4.   Powers of the compulsory liquidator
   (a)   Effect on the powers of the directors. Although the IA 1986 does not specifically state that the powers of the directors cease on the making of a winding-up order, the liquidator's powers are so wide that the directors will have very little scope to act (see IA 1986, ss. 144 and sch. 4).
   (b)   The rest of the liquidator's powers are the same as those given to the voluntary liquidator with some additions. We suggest you refer to your text book for a detailed account of these.

Points to Note

This mode of winding up represents the one most likely to be the subject of a question because the grounds which the court will require to be made out indicate that the company has or is experiencing problems of either a financial or managerial nature.

The majority of petitions are brought under IA 1986, s. 122(1)(f) and (g). Both these grounds are considered in detail in questions 1 and 2.

The court will not grant a petition as of right. The order will be granted at the discretion of the court and it may consider awarding a number of other orders instead (IA 1986, s. 125). You should also note that the court will restrain or strike out a petition which would amount to an abuse of process or is bound to fail or where a petition has already been presented. The most common reason for striking out a petition occurs where the petitioner and the company are in dispute over a debt.

Remember that it is quite likely that a company that has gone into a compulsory liquidation has at some stage in its history been guilty of a trading irregularity and you should always bear this in mind when dealing with a question in this area (the main irregularities are discussed below).

Irregularities and their Investigation

In any examination question dealing with either loan capital or liquidations you will need to be aware of the avenues available to the liquidator by which he will be able to increase the assets available for distribution to the creditors. These avenues revolve around certain irregularities which may have occurred at some stage during the company's lifetime and which will invalidate some acts carried out in the company's name particularly with regard to loan agreements — see chapter 9.

The main ones to look out for are:

(a) Fraudulent trading. This will occur where a company in a winding up appears to have been carrying on its business with an intent to defraud its creditors or potential creditors (see *R* v *Kemp* [1988] QB 645, CA). The court may on application by the liquidator order persons who were knowingly parties to the fraud to contribute to the company's assets. In *Re a Company (No. 001418 of 1988)* [1990] BCC 526, the judge limited the compensatory sum for which the director was declared liable to the amount of the trading loss during the period of fraudulent trading. The director was also declared to be liable to contribute a further sum by way of punishment. If the grounds are proved then a criminal offence has also been committed (IA 1986, s. 213). This is discussed in detail in question 1 below.

(b) Wrongful trading. This is not a criminal offence and therefore does not require the criminal standard of proof to be satisfied or fraud to be proved. Instead the court will make an order if it is satisfied that a director, a *de facto* director or shadow director knew or ought to have concluded that the company had no reasonable prospect of not going into insolvent liquidation (*Re Hydrodam (Corby) Ltd* [1994] 2 BCLC 180). Civil liability is imposed by requiring those found liable to contribute to the company's assets (IA 1986, s. 214), see *Re Produce Marketing Consortium Ltd* [1989] 1 WLR 745. In question 1 the relationship between fraudulent and wrongful trading is discussed further.

(c) Transactions at an undervalue and preferences. A transaction at an undervalue can be reversed by the liquidator if it prejudices claims or potential claims of others against the company. Where the company is in liquidation it is the liquidator's job to apply for reversal. Transactions subject to the rule are any which satisfy the definition in s. 238(4) and were entered into within two years of the date of winding up. In line with the rule on preferences a transaction at an undervalue cannot be called into question unless it can be shown that at the date of the transaction the company was unable to pay its debts.

There are a number of defences available to the company, persons transacting with it and sub-buyers (ss. 238(5) and 241) which will prevent the court granting an order in favour of the liquidator.

The rule on preferences tries to ensure that all creditors are treated on the same basis. This is particularly important if the company is insolvent. IA 1986, s. 239, allows a company's liquidator to examine all payments to creditors for the six months prior to the winding up of the company to ensure that if the company was insolvent at any time during that period no creditor was treated any better than he would have been in a winding up. IA 1986, s. 239(4) states what amounts to the giving of a preference. You should note that prior to 1986 this used to be known as a fraudulent preference: the new wording does not require proof of fraud. However, under s. 239(5) intent still has to be proved to show that the company in deciding to give a preference desired to prefer one creditor over another — see, e.g., *Re M. Kushler Ltd* [1943] Ch 248. You should be aware of the orders that a court may make if it is satisfied that a creditor has been preferred over another — see IA 1986, s. 241.

(d) Misfeasance proceedings. A person may be liable in misfeasance proceedings if he has misapplied or retained or become accountable for any money or other property of the company in breach of a fiduciary or any other duty (IA 1986, s. 212). This section will apply to both directors and the liquidator of the company — see, for example, *Re Home & Colonial Insurance Co. Ltd* [1930] 1 Ch 102 discussed above. You should note that the section will apply to a wide range of activities carried out by directors or a company liquidator and additionally the phrase 'breach of fiduciary or any other duty'

could include common law negligence, although the position is far from clear
— see *Re Welfab Engineers Ltd* [1990] BCC 600.

REVISION AND RESEARCH

This is not one of the easiest topics to revise due to the fact that much of the
material centres around the different procedures by which a company may
be wound up. The majority of this material is nothing more than a mass of
rules which simply have to be committed to memory as it is clearly important
that you are aware of the grounds and major steps involved in each type of
winding up. All questions on winding up will be set in the context of one type
of winding-up process. However, the real nitty-gritty of the question will
centre around issues that have attracted the attention of the legislature and
the judiciary recently. A number of areas are clearly identifiable:

(a)   Ground (g) in IA 1986, s. 122 — winding up on just and equitable
grounds. It is quite possible to see whole questions dealing with this ground
alone — see question 2. It will be essential for you to be conversant with the
decision in *Ebrahimi* v *Westbourne Galleries Ltd* [1973] AC 360 and other cases
on the subsection as a detailed discussion of the case law is likely to be
required.
(b)   Irregularities associated with securing loans and winding up are also
very popular with examiners. You will see from question 1 and some of the
comments we have made in chapter 9 that it would be advisable to revise loan
capital alongside liquidations as the chances of the dreaded mixed question
here are very high! Added to this is the fact that much of this area of law has
recently been the subject of a detailed review by the Cork Committee (see
chapter 9), some of whose recommendations have found their way into the
IA 1986, and is therefore likely to attract the attention of the examiner. One of
the difficulties in revising irregularities is the different time-limits within
which a transaction must be challenged.

A sensible strategy would be to ensure that you are aware of the procedures
and the grounds for the various types of winding up, the legal consequences
of each and the powers of the two types of liquidator. However, you should
concentrate your efforts in terms of detailed revision on the three areas
specified above, remembering that it would be sensible to revise this section
of the course alongside the section on loan capital.

IDENTIFYING THE QUESTION

Problem questions concerning liquidations are easy to identify as the
question will normally indicate that the company has passed a resolution to

wind up or that a petition has been presented to the court asking for a winding-up order to be granted. However, beware: read the question carefully to ensure you are clear about what type of winding up the company is in and look for additional problems which the examiner may have raised. For example, are there any outstanding debentures? Are all the debentures valid? Have they been duly registered? Is it possible that any irregularities mentioned above have occurred?

Essay questions can range from rather turgid discussions of the procedures surrounding the winding up to fairly involved consideration of the scope of a particular ground which will require a detailed knowledge of the relevant case law, see question 2.

QUESTION 1

Grotty Ltd, a company formed to produce whiskey from potatoes using a special formula, is not in a position to pay its debts as they fall due. Three of its major suppliers are pressing for payment.

Poto Ltd, its supplier of potatoes, is owed £15,000. Chem Ltd, the supplier of processing chemicals, is owed £10,000. Crunch Ltd, the supplier of equipment, is owed £12,000.

Drinky Ltd approaches Grotty Ltd's managing director, Nicky, with a view to purchasing 1,000 crates of whiskey. Nicky offers a 10% discount so long as 50% of the selling price is paid in advance. Drinky Ltd agrees to this and pays Grotty Ltd £22,500.

Nicky immediately uses this money to pay off Poto Ltd completely and a large proportion of Chem Ltd's debt with the balance. He realises that there is no hope of ever producing Drinky Ltd's order because it will be impossible to obtain raw materials on credit. Shortly after these payments are made Crunch Ltd petitions the court to have Grotty Ltd wound up because it has still not received payment of its debt. Drinky Ltd has discovered that Grotty Ltd is insolvent and there is no prospect of receiving its order or the return of its money.

Advise the following:

(a) Crunch Ltd on the procedure involved and the legal effects of its petition.
(b) Drinky Ltd on its chances of recovering its money.

Introduction

The first thing to do with a question of this type is to break it down, isolating the parts which will require detailed discussion. The following major issues can be identified:

(a)   The procedure and legal effects of the petition:

(i)   What type of winding up is it?
(ii)   If it is a compulsory winding up, on what ground is the petition presented and is the petitioner qualified to present such a petition?
(iii)   You should then be in a position to discuss the procedure and legal effects of the petition. Remember to do this from the point of view of Crunch the petitioner.

(b)   Advice to Drinky on the chances of recovering its money:

(i)   Status of Drinky as a creditor?
(ii)   Is there anything Drinky can do to improve its status or the assets available for distribution?

Type of Winding Up

The question tells you that Crunch has petitioned the court for a winding-up order, so it is clear that Grotty has not resolved to wind itself up voluntarily. This should tell you that Crunch has petitioned for a compulsory winding up.

Grounds and Status of the Petitioner

This is where a detailed knowledge of IA 1986, ss. 122 and 124, will prove to be important. From your knowledge of these sections you should know that Crunch is a creditor and that he may be entitled to bring a petition on the ground that the company is unable to pay its debts (s. 122(1)(f)). To succeed, Crunch will have to show the court that Grotty is in fact unable to pay its debts. This should lead you straight into a discussion regarding the procedure which Crunch will have to go through before the court will grant a winding-up order.

Procedure and Legal Effects of the Petition

A court will only grant an order under s. 122(1)(f) if the creditor can show first that he is a creditor under s. 123(2) in that he has a financial claim for a definite amount which is presently due and payable — see *Re Equitable Bond & Mortgage Corp. Ltd* [1910] 1 Ch 574 — and secondly that his debt is not disputed by the company. (You should also be aware of other obstacles which may stand in the way of Crunch and its ability to obtain an order such as (a) the court being satisfied that the order is for the benefit of the majority of creditors as the petitioner is not entitled to the petition as of right; or (b) that the company is subject to an administration order under IA 1985, s. 30, in which case the court will strike out a petition for a winding-up order. Neither of these situations seem to apply in this question but you must be aware of their existence for the examination.

In addition Crunch must also show that the company is unable to pay its debts. The court will only grant the petition if the debt is sufficiently large to demonstrate the company's inability to pay its debts. Consequently the creditor will have to show that he is, or that he and others petitioning jointly are, owed more than £750 and that this debt has been left unpaid for more than three weeks. The exact procedure to be followed is laid down in IA 1986, s. 123(1) and (2).

If Crunch successfully demonstrates to the court that the company is unable to pay its debts and the court grants the winding-up order you will have to advise Crunch of the legal effects of the granting of such an order. The legal effects should be examined from Crunch's point of view and it will primarily be concerned with the preservation of the assets of the company and its priority as a creditor. In the case of a compulsory winding up you will need to consider two periods of time:

(a)   the period between the presentation of the petition and the granting of the order and,

(b)   the period after the granting of the order.

Period between presentation of the petition and making the order
This is a bit of a limbo period for the company. This is because the date of presentation of the petition is classed as the date the winding-up order commenced, though it is still not certain that an order will be granted. However, to ensure that the assets of the company are preserved for the benefit of the creditors, restrictions are placed upon the directors' ability to deal with the company's property and an outsider's ability to bring actions against the company with a view to seizing its assets. The IA 1986 sets out the legal effects as follows: s. 126 requires that any legal proceedings commenced against the company are stayed, s. 127 prevents any dispositions of assets or transfers of shares and s. 128 avoids any sequestration, distress or execution put in force against the assets of the company after the petition has been presented. In addition to this the court may appoint a provisional liquidator to do such things as he sees fit (IA 1986, s. 135).

Period after granting the order
The first thing that happens is that the official receiver becomes the liquidator of the company and his first task is to inquire into the extent and type of assets the company possesses and if there are any affairs of the company that require further investigation, e.g., the possibility of fraudulent trading (see below for an account of Drinky's position).

From Crunch's point of view the two important legal effects after the granting of the order are the appointment of a liquidator to take over from the provisional liquidator (see IA 1986, s. 139) and the ability of the creditors and contributories to appoint a liquidation committee (IA 1986, s. 137). This committee performs similar functions to those performed by the committee appointed in a creditors' voluntary winding up but IA 1986, ss. 160 and 167 set additional special functions and you should be aware of these. The other is the effect the order has on the directors' powers to act. IA 1986, s. 144, allows the liquidator to take into his custody all property and things in action to which the company appears to be entitled. Consequently the directors' powers will cease to be effective because of the width of the liquidator's powers. It is fair to say that the liquidator can do anything that the directors could have done so long as it is beneficial to the winding-up. Liquidators are however subject to the control of the court. In this sense Crunch is better off because the directors may have acted in their own or shareholders' interests rather than the creditors' interests, whereas the liquidator's task is to collect the assets to pay off the company's debts.

Advice to Drinky on the Chance of Recovering its Money

Status of Drinky as a creditor
From the facts of the question Drinky would appear to be an unsecured creditor as the company has not given any security for its payment to them of £22,500. In these circumstances Drinky would not come very high up on the list of creditors as far as priority for payment is concerned (see chapter 9). In this case the company appears to be insolvent and the chances of Drinky being repaid the full amount of its debt appear to be poor.

Is there anything that Drinky can do to improve its status or increase the assets available for distribution?
It is easy to understand why Drinky feels aggrieved at having lost £22,500 as it has only just paid the company this money. Grotty, by incurring this liability at a time when it was insolvent or approaching insolvency, could have been trading wrongfully or fraudulently. It is clear from the facts of the question that Grotty was being pressed for payment by its creditors and that it did not seem to be in a position to pay them. This means that the company was probably insolvent. This is a question you must determine in each case as not all questions will be as clear-cut as this one. Here it is probably fair to conclude that the company was insolvent as it could not pay its debts as they fell due. If Drinky, via the liquidator, could establish that the company had been trading fraudulently this could give rise to a court order against those knowingly a party to it requiring them to contribute to the company's assets, normally to the extent of the debts of the creditors who have been defrauded — in this case Drinky's £22,500.

However, you should make clear in your advice to Drinky that even if the liquidator could obtain such an order the contribution towards the company's assets will not necessarily satisfy Drinky's debt. This is because the contribution will go into the general pool of assets to be distributed to creditors in order of their priority (see chapter 9 for the order of priority).

The next question you must consider is whether the liquidator could establish a case of either fraudulent or wrongful trading. You will need to consider the two together as the only essential differences between them are the type of knowledge and standard of proof required.

Under IA 1986, s. 213, any person who is *knowingly* a party to the carrying on of a fraudulent business can be declared by the court to be liable to make such contributions to the company's assets as the court thinks fit. In addition such a person is guilty of a criminal offence (CA 1985, s. 458) and may as a result be disqualified from holding office (CDDA 1986, s. 10).

The major obstacle facing the liquidator (and therefore Drinky) is the proof of fraud. One question you will have to consider by referring to the relevant case law is what amounts to fraud for the purposes of the section? Maugham J's definition in *Re Patrick & Lyon Ltd* [1933] Ch 786 is a good starting point. He felt fraud was 'actual dishonesty involving, according to current notions of fair trading among commercial men, real moral blame'.

In addition to this the liquidator must show that Grotty's business was carried on with an *intent* to defraud its creditors. In an important recent decision, *R v Grantham* [1984] QB 675, the Court of Appeal reviewed the phrase 'intent to defraud' by referring to an *obiter* comment by Lord Radcliffe in *Welham* v *DPP* [1961] AC 103: 'it requires a person as its object: that is, defrauding involves doing something to someone'.

You should note further that the court in *Re William C. Leitch Brothers Ltd* [1932] 2 Ch 71 pointed out that where a company carries on a business and incurs debts at a time when, to the knowledge of the directors, there is no reasonable prospect of the debts being paid the court will normally infer that it was intended to defraud creditors.

Applying these tests to the question you should have no difficulty in concluding that the directors of Grotty were intent on defrauding Drinky. However, the question only deals with one transaction: is that sufficient to be considered to be carrying on a business? A good case to look at here is *Re Gerald Cooper Chemicals Ltd* [1978] Ch 262 where it was held that carrying on a business for the purpose of the section can include a single transaction designed to defraud a single creditor.

It would seem quite likely that the liquidator could make out a case under the section; however, there is still something further for you to consider. The section provides that an order can be made against those who are parties to the carrying on of the business. Who are the parties for the purposes of this question? The best authority to use here is *Re Maidstone Buildings Provisions*

Ltd [1971] 1 WLR 1085 where Pennywick V-C's comments are helpful: ' ... in order to bring a person within the section you must show that he is taking some positive steps in the carrying on of the company's business in a fraudulent manner' (cf. *Re Augustus Barnett & Son Ltd* [1986] BCLC 170). In the light of these comments, if the court made an order it would only be against Nicky, the managing director.

Although fraud was not difficult to establish in this question you might not always be in such a fortunate position in other questions. Prior to 1985 problems surrounding the proof of fraud led to a number of cases failing. The Cork Committee on Insolvency Law and Practice (Cmnd 8558, 1982) found that the present situation was undesirable and recommended the creation of a civil wrong requiring a civil standard of proof to be known as wrongful trading. This recommendation was acted upon and the new wrong is now contained in IA 1986, s. 214. Instead of having to prove fraudulent intent on the part of the directors before making an order, the court can now make an order if it is satisfied that a director or shadow director knew or *ought to have concluded* that the company had no reasonable prospect of not going into insolvent liquidation and did not take every step he ought to have taken to minimise the potential loss to creditors.

Like fraudulent trading the section only comes into operation if the company goes into insolvent liquidation and it is the liquidator's job to apply to the court for an order.

The standard of care and behaviour required on the part of the director is different to that required by s. 213. Failure to meet the standard set out in s. 214 will found liability. The test that the court will apply is set out in s. 214(5): this states that wrongful trading occurs where a company has gone into an insolvent liquidation and at some time before the commencement of this winding-up, a director or shadow director *knew or ought* to have *concluded* that there was no reasonable prospect that the company would avoid going into an insolvent liquidation and you should familiarise yourself with it. Knox J in *Re Produce Marketing Consortium Ltd* [1989] 1 WLR 745 set out guidelines to the future application of the section:

(a)   The objective/subjective elements of the test. The court will judge the director by the standards of what could reasonably be expected of a person fulfilling his functions and showing reasonable diligence in doing so — the objective element of the test. But the test will be related to the particular company business and director — the subjective element of the test. So the test will vary to some extent from company to company. Consequently each case must be decided on its own merits.

(b)   'Ought to know'. Knox J stated that the section would not apply to factors which the director 'ought to have known' from the factual information available *but also* to facts which he ought to have ascertained from the factual information available. This imposes an obligation on directors to be diligent and to *ascertain* possible consequences from the factual information available even though s. 214 does not mention the word 'ascertain'. This apparent extension of the ambit of the section will certainly give the 'honest, incompetent and unjustified optimist something to fear' (see Finch (1992) 55 MLR 179).

Indeed recent cases demonstrate that directors who fail to keep proper accounting records allowing them to implement some form of accounting control (*Re DKG Contractors Ltd* [1990] BCC 903) and directors who allow a company which is woefully undercapitalised to commence trading, have much to fear from the section (*Re Purpoint Ltd* [1991] BCC 121).

Re Sherborne Associates Ltd [1995] BCC 40, gives a further insight on the term 'ought to know'. The company was run by three directors none of whom had experience of the company's business as an advertising agency, but one of whom, S, was a cost accountant. The business was established early in 1987. Proper books of account and board minutes were kept. By January 1988 it had become obvious that insufficient business had been generated and the company was in serious financial difficulty. S convened a board meeting to consider whether to continue trading. A decision was taken to implement tighter financial controls and to continue trading. In August 1988 the bank withdrew its support because of the company's poor trading record. Banking arrangements were made with another bank but in February 1989, following advice from insolvency practitioners, the company was put into liquidation.

The liquidators asserted that in January 1988 the directors ought to have concluded that there was no reasonable prospect of the company avoiding insolvent liquidation. On the facts the judge was not satisfied of this. It was clear that the fact that proper books of account were kept, and board meetings were held and properly minuted helped the directors in their defence. The line between a realistic and fanciful financial forecast is a difficult one to draw, but clearly where inadequate financial and associated records are kept it is likely that any judgment made regarding the company's future is likely to be regarded as fanciful.

(c)   Relief under CA 1985, s. 727, is not available for liability proved under s. 214. This is because the subjective test applied to relieve liability under s. 727 could not be applied in a consistent fashion to the essentially objective test of liability under s. 214.

Conclusion

The question has asked you to advise two parties, Crunch Ltd and Drinky Ltd, and your discussion of the law above should contain the law applicable to each party. Your conclusion should bring these points of law together to form a coherent piece of advice for the parties concerned. Remember if the question tells you to advise — advise!

Advice to Crunch Ltd

It would appear from the facts of the question that Crunch Ltd would have grounds to present a petition under s. 122(1)(f) and that it would have the *locus standi* to petition. You should go on to point out that the procedure which Crunch will have to comply with is explained above. You should also point out to Crunch that if its petition is granted and the company goes into insolvent liquidation, it is unlikely that its debt will be satisfied in full if at all.

Advice to Drinky Ltd

You should advise Drinky to inform the liquidator of the circumstances in which the £22,500 was parted with and ask him to petition the court for an order under IA 1986, s. 213 or 214, although this will not necessarily ensure that Drinky is repaid his £22,500 it will at least provide more assets for the general pool and increase Drinky's chances of being paid. You should also point out that such an order will in turn also increase Crunch's chances of being paid.

QUESTION 2

The effect of IA 1986, s. 122(1)(g), is to enable the court 'to subject the exercise of legal rights to equitable considerations; considerations, that is, of a personal character arising between one individual and another, which may make it unjust, or inequitable, to insist on legal rights, or to exercise them in a particular way' (per Lord Wilberforce in *Ebrahimi* v *Westbourne Galleries Ltd* [1973] AC 360 at p. 379).

What effect did this statement have on the scope of the court's power to make a winding-up order under the section on the basis that the company is a quasi-partnership?

Introduction

The statement is taken from a case which has become regarded as *the* authority on quasi-partnership as a ground for winding up. However, the question asks you to discuss the effect the decision has had on the scope of the court's power to make a winding-up order on this ground, not merely to examine the case from which the statement was taken. It is obvious that you will need to refer to the *Ebrahimi* decision because it is important and central to your answer, but take care to answer the question rather than merely discuss the *Ebrahimi* decision. If you analyse the statement further it becomes obvious that four issues require analysis and discussion in order to answer the question:

(a)   The origins and rationale of the just and equitable winding-up ground.

(b)   The scope of the court's power before the *Ebrahimi* decision.

(c)   The effect the *Ebrahimi* decision had on the court's power.

(d)   The post-*Ebrahimi* situation.

The Rationale of the 'Just and Equitable' Winding-up Ground

Section 122(1)(g) of IA 1986 provides a minority shareholder who has been subject to some form of oppressive treatment by the majority with the opportunity to seek relief by having the company compulsorily wound up by the court as long as the court feels it is just and equitable to do so.

The courts have consistently refused to create categories of situations which would justify a winding up on the just and equitable ground-see *Re Blériot Manufacturing Aircraft Co. Ltd* (1916) 32 TLR 253 per Neville J: 'The words 'Just and equitable' are words of the widest significance, and do not limit the jurisdiction of the court to any case. It is a question of fact, and each case must depend on its own circumstances.'

Despite this attitude the reported decisions on the ground do divide themselves into categories and are referred to and discussed, by academics and lawyers alike, by reference to these categories. One such category involves cases in which the courts have treated the company as a partnership.

The theory was that when a company is a quasi-partnership, i.e., it is in substance a partnership although it is operating with a corporate form, it should be wound up if the facts put before the court would give grounds for dissolution of partnership under partnership law. The principle seems to have originated in the Scottish case of *Symington* v *Symingtons' Quarries Ltd* (1905) 8 F 121 but the first reported English case is the Court of Appeal's decision in *Re Yenidje Tobacco Co. Ltd* [1916] 2 Ch 426. The judgment of Lord Cozens-Hardy MR is extremely important to explain the partnership analogy and you should familiarise yourself with it to explain the rationale of the ground.

Having explained and examined the origins and rationale of the ground you will need to move on to deal with the heart of the question.

The Scope of the Court's Powers before the Ebrahimi decision

Two issues are prominent if you look at the cases decided before 1973:

(a)   the fact that the courts were having some difficulty in deciding what characteristics a small private company had to possess before it could be considered to be a quasi-partnership for the purposes of the section; and

(b)   whether or not *mala fides* on the part of the majority was necessary before a winding-up order would be granted.

Characteristics of a quasi-partnership
One of the major difficulties here is that partnerships come in all shapes and sizes. It is difficult if not impossible to define a typical partnership. So what have the courts used as their model partnership? You will have to look at the cases reported before 1973 to be in a position to discuss this. The cases suggest that the courts have looked for characteristics which they regard as essential or fundamental to the concept of partnership. However, this approach has in itself caused problems because it is difficult to distinguish between essential and non-essential characteristics. It is clear from the cases that a degree of uncertainty existed. You should look at an article by Chesterman (1973) 36 MLR 129 on this point, especially the cases he cites at p. 132. Despite a degree of uncertainty a number of points are clear from the cases: the company should only possess a small number of members with four probably representing the maximum; there should be a right to participate in the day-today management of the company; the members should have become associated pursuant to an agreement involving the creation of a personal relationship between them (see *Re Wondoflex Textiles Pty Ltd* [1951] VLR 458). One matter that does emerge is the importance of the right to participate in the management of the company; it was this point that ensured the petitioner failed in *Re Leadenhall General Hardware Stores Ltd* (1971) 115 SJ 202.

Is mala fides *on the part of the majority necessary before a winding-up order will be granted?*
This issue relates to the type of conduct required to give rise to circumstances which would justify the granting of a petition. One matter which has troubled the courts is a clash between a fundamental rule of company law and a rule of partnership law. It is a well-established rule of company law that a shareholder owes no duty to anyone when exercising the voting rights attached to his shares and may vote even in his own selfish interests (see *North-West Transportation Co. Ltd* v *Beatty* (1887) 12 App Cas 589). However, a partnership is based on considerations of good faith, trust and confidence between members: a member, therefore, who acts in his own selfish interests may be acting perfectly properly according to principles of company law but may find that he has infringed a principle of partnership law which may ultimately result in the company being wound up. Should the courts make adjustments when applying partnership law to take account of the provisions of the Companies Act and the company's articles? If so an act which is done *mala fide* but in accordance with the company's constitution and the law would not necessarily give rise to a winding-up order on the quasi-partnership ground but might give rise, for example, to a successful petition under CA 1985, s. 459.

The other matter you will need to consider is whether or not the courts have made the proof of bad faith essential to the granting of an order. Two cases illustrate the conflict on the point. In *Re Cuthbert Cooper & Sons Ltd* [1937] Ch 392 where the court refused to grant an order because bad faith was not established, despite the fact that there was evidence of a lack of trust between the parties. In *Re Lundie Bros Ltd* [1965] 1 WLR 1051 where Plowman J granted an order without requiring bad faith to be shown. He expressly based his decision on the broad considerations of good faith appropriate between partners. It is clear that a great deal of uncertainty existed about what type of company would fall within the scope of the court's jurisdiction to grant an order and the type of conduct which would justify the granting of an order. It is for this reason that the House of Lords decision in *Ebrahimi* assumes such importance.

The Effect the Ebrahimi *Decision Has Had on the Court's Power*

When is a company to be treated as a quasi-partnership?
A good starting point is Lord Wilberforce's comment in *Ebrahimi v Westbourne Galleries Ltd* [1973] AC 360 at p. 380 where he makes it clear that although it may be convenient to refer to companies as quasi-partnerships it may also be confusing. This is because the parties who were once partners and are now shareholders have accepted new obligations in the eyes of the law. Despite the fact that it may be desirable to treat the company as a quasi-partnership, the parties have nevertheless chosen to form themselves into a company and the courts will not ignore this fact with impunity. However, it seems from the tone of Lord Wilberforce's judgment, that the rules of company law will only be disregarded to 'enable the court to subject the exercise of legal rights to equitable considerations', and that it would be undesirable to define all the circumstances where this will occur. Nevertheless, after reviewing all the authorities he suggested that one or more of the following factors should be present:

(a)   that it be an association formed or continued on the basis of a personal relationship, involving mutual confidence;
(b)   that there be an agreement that all or some of the shareholders shall participate in the management of the business; and
(c)   that there be restrictions on the transferability of the members' interest in the company.

This statement represents an improvement on the old law inasmuch as it lays down the factors that the court will require to be present before granting an order under the section. In addition Lord Wilberforce urges that this area should be developed as a branch of company law in its own right rather than continuing to be tied to partnership law. From this statement you should be in a position to determine when a company will be treated as a quasi-partnership with a great deal more certainty than before.

Does bad faith have to be present?
The House of Lords found as a matter of law that the other shareholders had acted within their rights, within the provisions of the Companies Acts and within the articles in removing Ebrahimi from office. Nevertheless, the power under the section was not limited to proven cases of bad faith, and the legal correctness of the shareholders' conduct would not prevent the court interfering where it felt it was unjust or inequitable for a party to insist on his strict legal rights or to exercise them in a particular way. The House of Lords went even further: they stated that a petitioning shareholder was not required to show that the conduct complained of affected him in his capacity as a member of the company, but was entitled to rely on any circumstances of justice or equity which affected him in his relationship with the company or the other shareholders.

Therefore you can conclude that the effects of the *Ebrahimi* decision are threefold:

(a)   it clarifies the factors relevant in deciding whether a company is a quasi-partnership,
(b)   it clarifies the position regarding the requirement of bad faith, and
(c)   it does not limit the availability of the remedy to conduct affecting the petitioner in his capacity as a shareholder and thus broadens the scope of the rule.

Post-Ebrahimi *situation*

Perhaps one of the best examples of the application of the *Ebrahimi* principle is to be found in *Re Zinotty Properties Ltd* [1984] 3 All ER 754 which features elements of most of the old categories which were subsumed by the *Ebrahimi* decision. See also *Re A & BC Chewing Gum Ltd* [1975] 1 All ER 1017 where the shareholder's right to participate in the management of the company was laid down in the articles and the majority refused to give effect to that right: the shareholder was granted an order.

The most interesting use of the *Ebrahimi* principle is to be found in *Clemens* v *Clemens Bros Ltd* [1976] 2 All ER 268. Where Foster J applied the principle as a means to restrain an abuse of power by a controlling shareholder. However, this use of the rule was questioned in *Bentley-Stevens* v *Jones* [1974] 2 All ER 653. One thing that is clear is that any course of dealing or conduct which produces a breakdown in mutual confidence may well suffice to justify an order under the section (see *Jesner* v *Jarrad Properties Ltd* [1993] BCLC 1032).

Conclusion

Your conclusion should attempt to do two things:

    (a)   summarise the immediate effect of the *Ebrahimi* decision; and
    (b)   summarise its impact as evidenced by subsequent cases. It is fair to say that the decision has increased the scope of the court's power while at the same time it lays down much clearer and more well-defined principles as to when an order will be granted. The former aspect of the decision is illustrated by the subsequent cases and it would be fair to suggest that the rule has become wide enough to encompass all the pre–1973 decisions.

SUMMARY

The law relating to winding up is vast. It is beyond the scope of this book to undertake a thorough review. All we have done is to highlight those aspects we feel are likely to attract the attention of the examiner, either because of the degree of difficulty involved or because they have attracted the recent attention of Parliament.

FURTHER READING

Chesterman, M. R., 'The "just and equitable" winding up of small private companies' (1973) 36 MLR 129.
Hicks, Andrew, 'Advising on wrongful trading' (1993) 14 Co Law 16, 55.
Prentice, D. D., 'Winding up on the just and equitable ground: the partnership analogy' (1973) 89 LQR 107.
Wheeler, Sally, 'Swelling the assets for distribution in corporate insolvency' [1993] JBL 256.

12 GOVERNANCE AND MANAGEMENT OF THE COMPANY

INTRODUCTION

The topic of this final chapter lends itself to a discussion of questions that cover various areas of company law. This can be the students' nightmare in an examination — the 'mixed' problem that requires a knowledge of various areas of company law. Or, it could be an assessment essay question, the content of which also covers an array of company law issues. Although students usually dread such questions, examiners see them as a useful way of testing a candidate's ability to draw from and relate different areas of company law. The governance and management of the company link quite readily with other areas of company law, particularly the rule in *Foss* v *Harbottle* (1843) 2 Hare 461 (see chapter 10) and directors' duties (see chapter 6). This topic also takes us into an area that will be an increasingly important part of your studies: corporate governance, which spans a wide range of company law and also involves non-legal issues.

There are three main organs that are responsible for the management of the company: the company in general meeting, the board of directors ('the board') and managing director. There are other organs of the company that may also possess management powers including the liquidator, receiver and any special body or person who has powers vested in them by the articles or memorandum.

The allocation of governance or control of the company and its management functions is governed by the company's constitution, usually the articles, and the various Companies Acts. In a small private company the members of the company and the board will usually be the same people. In a large public company with a wide ownership of shares, a heavy proportion of which could be institutional investors, the board and the general meeting will be distinct entities. However, prudent management and control of the proxy voting machinery will usually ensure that general meetings rarely intervene in management decisions. Even at board level, the board will often be led down the various commercial paths prepared by the executive directors and the expert personnel within the company who have access to the corporate information. Thus, for large public companies it has been suggested that:

(a) There is a divorce of 'ownership' from 'control' of the company. (See Berle and Means, *The Modern Corporation and Private Property* and E.S. Herman, *Corporate Control, Corporate Power*. For a management perspective see P.F. Drucker, *Managing in Turbulent Times*, pp. 177–95.) Herman puts forward the theory of the market for corporate control which is supposed to reduce the risks of managers engaging in non-profit maximising behaviour (see Bradley (1990) 53 MLR 170 and the comments by Harman J in *Re a Company, ex parte Glossop* [1988] 1 WLR 1068 at p. 1075).

(b) The control is not necessarily vested in the board but in a group of 'technocrats' who have access to corporate information and expert knowledge. They may be found in various parts of the corporate network. Galbraith calls this the 'technostructure' (J.K. *Galbraith, The New Industrial State*, chs 6 and 7; see also 'Bored directors', *The Economist*, vol. 314 (27 January 1990), p.84).

Despite the differences that exist between different sizes of company, these companies are all regulated by the same principles of company law concerning the allocation of power between the different organs of management although company law does recognise that there should be differences in procedures in the way that some of those powers can be exercised (e.g., CA 1985, ss. 381A and 80A [CA 1989, ss. 113 and 115]). Unfortunately, just as we saw with the *Salomon* principle with regard to groups of companies (see chapter 3), legal theory does not necessarily coincide with commercial reality. It is an indictment of company law, and perhaps also the way that it is taught, that the student is often asked to discuss problems, particularly on the management of companies, that bear little relationship to the way the vast majority of public companies, and especially public listed companies, are actually run. One way of overcoming this is to analyse the management of the company from a 'corporate governance' perspective rather than just a strict legal perspective, and this is dealt with in question 2.

MAIN ISSUES

The Allocation of Functions between the General Meeting and the Board via the Articles and Companies Acts

The articles normally allocate management functions to the board. To what extent can the general meeting intervene with the exercise of this power by the board? Does this management power extend to include control over the litigation of the company?

Problems will often ask for advice as to the possibility of legal action by the company in response to a wrong done to the company, and will therefore involve a discussion as to which organ of the company has the power to commence the litigation.

The exception to the rule in *Foss* v *Harbottle* (1843) 2 Hare 461 which appears most frequently in examinations concerns whether a fraud has been perpetrated by those who control the company. Does this mean those who control the general meeting, the board of directors or both? In that the rationale of the exception is to alleviate injustices that might arise from those who perpetrated the fraud failing to authorise litigation against themselves, it is perhaps logical to assume that the organ of control referred to in the exception is the same organ of the company that controls the corporate litigation. Therefore there is a link between the allocation of management power (does it include the power to commence litigation?) and this important exception to the rule in *Foss* v *Harbottle* (for a detailed discussion of treatment of the rule see chapter 10).

If the provisions of the Draft 5th EC Directive (COM (90) 629) are incorporated into national law, art. 16 provides for the enforcement of directors' liabilities under art. 14 when the general meeting resolves that legal action should be taken or holders of 10 per cent of the subscribed capital so resolve to bring proceedings on the company's behalf, although in this latter example of a breach of the rule in *Foss* v *Harbottle* the courts may require that if unsuccessful, the minority shareholders pay the costs of the action.

Alteration of Management Power via the Articles or Dismissal

Alteration of the articles was discussed in chapter 5. The dismissal of directors involves several procedural problems. An answer could involve a quick citation of CA 1985, s. 303, or a more involved discussion of the procedures involved depending on the depth the question requires. The dismissal of directors is going to come up somewhere on the examination paper and in coursework assessments. It is one of the main weapons in the armoury of a majority shareholder, so look out to see where the majority shareholding lies in any given problem.

Role of the Managing Director

Table A allows for the appointment by the directors of a managing director (art. 72). The relationship between the board and the managing director is governed by the articles and any executive contract between the managing director and the company. The two main issues that could arise in an examination concerning the office of managing director are:

(a)   the extent of the managing director's authority and the power to alter that authority, and

(b)   the 'managing director' who has not been formally appointed under the articles.

A power to appoint a managing director is normally included in the articles (Table A, art. 72), the directors being allowed to delegate their management powers conferred by art. 70 to some person or persons holding the post of managing director. Under art. 72 such a delegation can be made 'subject to any conditions the directors may impose, and either collaterally with or to the exclusion of their own powers and may be revoked or altered'. Article 84 already provides that the appointment of a managing director holding an 'executive office under the company' terminates on failure to continue as a director of the company, but the managing director can still claim any damages that might be payable for breach of the contract of service between the executive director and the company.

It is important to indicate in any answer involving a managing director that the office usually involves the holding of two positions in the company:

(a)   as an elected director of the company, and

(b)   as an executive director holding an 'executive office' under a contract of service with the company (i.e., an employee of the company — note the definition of 'employment' in CA 1985, s. 319(7), which also includes employment under a contract 'for services' — see chapter 6).

Remuneration is also governed by art. 84 being determined by the directors as they think fit (*Re Richmond Gate Property Co. Ltd* [1965] 1 WLR 335 — see chapter 5). An informal agreement about the role of managing director may relate to both the appointment and to the terms of the service contract. If a question is unclear on this, and it may be deliberate or just poor drafting of the question, you must point out the lack of clarity and comment in the answer on the possible alternative meanings. Informal assent will be accepted by the courts in some cases, but would it apply, for example, to approval of a 10-year service contract? CA 1985, s. 319(3), requires that such a term be 'first approved by a resolution of the company in general meeting'. Where an informal appointment has been made the *Duomatic* principle could be applied whereby an informal appointment can nevertheless be accepted as a formal appointment (discussed *post*). Alternatively, the rule in *Royal British Bank* v *Turquand* (1856) 6 E & B 327 could always be invoked by innocent third parties (see chapter 4). There could, however, be a more explicit statement in a problem that would clearly require greater detail in the answer on the application of *Turquand*, e.g.:

Flash, who had never been properly elected as managing director of the company, entered into contracts on behalf of the company to . . .

Where Flash is concerned it needs to be ascertained whether the third parties involved in the contracts can use *Turquand* to cure the admittedly defective appointment (see *Freeman & Lockyer* v *Buckhurst Park Properties (Mangal) Ltd* [1964] 2 QB 480). For *Turquand* to apply there must be some form of appointment or acceptance of a managing director, albeit a defective one. It will not protect third parties if Flash got out of bed one morning and suddenly decided to act as managing director (see *Rama Corporation Ltd* v *Proved Tin & General Investments Ltd* [1952] 2 QB 147).

There are therefore three possible situations involving the appointment of a managing director:

(a)   Where the managing director is properly elected under the articles and he has actual authority to bind the company.

(b)   Where there is some defect in the appointment, but the person is being held out by those in actual authority as having some ostensible authority to act on the company's behalf. In this situation a third party relying on that representation can invoke the rule in *Turquand's* case to cure the defective appointment as long as the third party does not have constructive or actual notice that the managing director has not been appointed properly, or is not put on suspicion that something is wrong (see *Freeman & Lockyer* v *Buckhurst Park Properties (Mangal) Ltd* and *J. C. Houghton & Co.* v *Nothard, Lowe & Wills Ltd* [1927] 1 KB 246). An outsider is also given additional protection under CA 1985, s. 285, which provides that: 'The acts of a director or manager are valid notwithstanding any defect that may afterwards be discovered in his appointment or qualification' (see also Table A, art. 92).

(c)   Where a director gets out of bed one morning and decides to play 'managing directors' for the day. In this case there is no 'holding out' by those in authority and there is no defective appointment which an application of *Turquand's* rule can be used to cure: there has been no appointment at all. For the same reason CA 1985, s. 285, and Table A, art. 92, will also not apply because this is not just a procedural defect, it is a total lack of any appointment (see *Morris* v *Kanssen* [1946] AC 459).

The status of the managing director is usually linked to the ability of that officer of the company to enter into contracts on behalf of the company, and any problem question could then link that to a consideration of which officers within the company have the capacity to bind the company in contracts (see chapter 4).

A question in this area could involve the revocation or variation of the powers of the managing director. This is permitted under art. 72 (see *Harold Holdsworth & Co. (Wakefield) Ltd* v *Caddies* [1955] 1 WLR 352). However, beware of questions which state that there is a special article giving independent status to the managing director with specific powers as in *John Shaw & Sons (Salford) Ltd* v *Shaw* [1935] 2 KB 113, where certain permanent directors were given powers of management by the articles. In this situation the powers can only be altered by alteration of the articles.

The position of managing director and the authority of the person holding that position has led to a body of case law. This means that students will often forget another important position within the company that is rarely at the forefront of legal disputes: the chairman of the board of directors. In *El Ajou* v *Dollar Land Holdings plc* [1994] 2 All ER 685, it was the non-executive chairman who was deemed by the Court of Appeal to be the 'directing mind and will' of the company. The formal (contractarian) position of the chairman within the company under the company's constitution is not the only factor that the courts will look at. This is often the case with the position of chairman: their actual authority and position within the company exceeds their formal legal position. This applies particularly in larger public limited companies and quoted companies. In smaller private companies the position of chairman may not even have been recognised or appointed to. For the formal position you should analyse arts 88 and 91 of Table A, the provision of a casting vote at board meetings often being one of the articles that private companies choose to remove if there is a need to build a deadlock into the control of the company. The role and position of the chairman requires closer consideration as corporate governance reforms highlight the changing role of the board of directors. In the foreword to Sir Adrian Cadbury's book, *The Company Chairman*, Sir John Harvey-Jones comments on the actual position of the chairman:

> If a company is successful it is due to the efforts of everyone in it, but if it fails it is because of the failure of the board. If the board fails it is the responsibility of the chairman, notwithstanding the collective responsibility of everyone. Despite this collective responsibility, it is on the chairman's shoulders that the competition and performance of that supreme directing body depends.

Management Power of All the Shareholders Acting Together other than in a General Meeting

When can the actions of all the shareholders acting informally be deemed to be the actions of the company?

The *Duomatic* principle (*Re Duomatic Ltd* [1969] 2 Ch 365) provides that, except where the Companies Acts specifically require a general meeting to be held, all the corporators acting together informally and unanimously giving their assent can do anything that a formal resolution at a general meeting could have achieved. For private companies this procedure now has effect in respect of all company resolutions regardless of any requirement in the CA 1985 to call a meeting (CA 1985, s. 381A [CA 1989, s. 113]). The more restricted *Duomatic* principle still applies to public companies. This was applied in *Re Duomatic Ltd* itself in respect of ratification of the payment of directors' salaries, although it appears that a different conclusion was reached on the application of the principle to CA 1985, s. 312. No payment can be made to a director by way of compensation for loss of office without 'the proposal being approved by the company' under s. 312, which Buckley J interpreted as meaning 'by the company in general meeting' in *Re Duomatic Ltd* at p. 374. However, the *Duomatic* principle has been applied to alteration of the articles in *Cane v Jones* [1980] 1 WLR 1451 (CA 1985, s. 9: 'a company may by special resolution alter its articles'), and to the sanctioning of negligence by directors in *Multinational Gas & Petrochemical Co.* v *Multinational Gas & Petrochemical Services Ltd* [1983] Ch 258. However, it does not mean that when there is only one registered shareholder, that shareholder can bind the company to anything in his private thoughts (*Re New Cedos Engineering Co. Ltd* [1994] 1 BCLC 797 per Oliver J at p. 813).

The majority decision in *Multinational* found that all the shareholders consented to the directors' actions and therefore the company could not complain, the shareholders' action being deemed to be the company's action even if this consent was not given at a formal meeting. There was a dissenting judgment from May LJ which throws an interesting perspective on the nature of the company as a separate legal entity. May LJ declared that if the directors of the company act negligently, albeit with the knowledge of the company, the company still retains a right to sue for breach of duty because the company is a separate entity. Although the members are unlikely to start any legal action, there could come a time, within any limitation period, when another organ of management could pursue the action (e.g., the liquidator upon a liquidation of the company as occurred in *Multinational*).

Therefore, the approval of all the shareholders acting together informally could arise in many different areas of company law. Assessment questions, especially problems, should be closely read to see whether this is one of the issues that is raised and whether or not, in the case of a private company, the written resolution procedure in CA 1985, s. 381A, has been complied with.

The *Duomatic* principle was not necessarily confined to small private companies with individual shareholders; it can also apply to companies that have a few corporate shareholders undertaking large ventures, as in *Multinational*.

Corporate Governance

The main issues discussed so far relate to specific legal topics in this area. However, the legal aspects surrounding the management of corporations provides an opportunity to raise wider issues which come under the heading of 'corporate governance'. This is dealt with in detail in question 2.

Corporate governance is a topic where illustrations of a wider perspective and a range of background reading are necessary to achieve anything other than a poor mark.

REVISION AND RESEARCH

If you do not revise this area of company law you are cutting yourself off from giving complete answers to a large number of possible questions.

A suggested revision technique is to go through past examination papers and assessment questions, and look at the problems where you are asked to 'Advise' either a member or a director or the company. What practical legal remedies are there? Are these possible remedies aimed at the management of the company and, if so, what are they: dismissal, alteration of management power, an action for damages or recovery of property? What procedure needs to be undertaken to initiate these remedies? In any question where you might be advising litigation by the company, which organ of the company can authorise its commencement or prevent its authorisation?

In many cases you will need to know and be able to cite the relevant articles from Table A concerning the management of the company, in particular arts. 70 to 72 and 84. You will also need to revise the various procedures imposed by statute and the articles regarding: the calling and conduct of annual and extraordinary general meetings (CA 1985, ss. 366–71, arts. 36–53), the methods of proposing and passing the different types of resolution (CA 1985, ss. 376–9, arts. 46–53) and the procedure for dismissing directors (CA 1985, s. 303). Also include some revision of the proxy-voting machinery (CA 1985, ss. 373–5, arts. 59–63) and the right of representation by companies at meetings (CA 1985, s. 375). These procedural formalities are sometimes tedious to learn, but they provide good practical legal advice that can be given to support an answer. An answer which simply states that X can be dismissed as director by the majority of shareholders, under CA 1985, s. 303, ignores the possibility that the annual general meeting might be 11 months away, that X might not be on the agenda for re-election at the next general meeting, and that X might have a five-year rolling contract and be on an annual salary of £150,000. You can use these various procedures to supplement the substantive element of your answers in any area of company law.

A topic that is mentioned in this chapter but not expanded upon in great detail involves the use of the derivative action. You need to revise what the derivative action is, who can bring the action, how it differs from a personal action brought by a member, when the action can be brought, and who pays for the cost of a derivative action (see Gower on the enforcement of corporate duties and *Wallersteiner* v *Moir (No. 2)* [1975] QB 373; see also *Prudential Assurance Co. Ltd* v *Newman Industries Ltd (No. 2)* [1982] Ch 204 at p. 212, where the Court of Appeal criticised Vinelott J because he had not asked himself the 'all-important question: "Ought I to be trying a derivative action?"', and chapter 10).

It is advisable to read the newspapers on a regular basis to keep informed of the most recent commercial scandals and any changes that they may prompt in the area of directors' duties or the structure of companies and their management.

IDENTIFYING THE QUESTION

Where the control and management of the company appear as only part of a problem or essay, identification of the issue is more difficult, particularly when under the stress of sitting an examination. However, the management issue is likely to be raised in nearly all problem questions, the only difficulty being in identifying the depth to which you are expected to go. Whenever asked in a question to 'Advise Bert', 'Advise the company' or 'Advise the minority shareholders', consideration will need to be given to the methods by which Bert, the company, the minority or even the majority of share-holders can exercise any right they may have. A right is not much use without a remedy; this might involve alteration of the management powers, litigation by the company either directly or through a derivative action, or dismissal of the directors. There may also be other remedies available, particularly statutory remedies, but the above three all require some knowledge concerning the control of the management of the company. In particular, any possibility of litigation by a company will require an analysis of which organ of the company can sanction the litigation. If it is the same organ of the company that actually perpetrated the wrong on the company then what remedies or procedures have to be invoked to get the litigation off the ground, because presumably the wrongdoers are not going to sanction litigation against themselves even if they are the Greater London Council (see *Estmanco (Kilner House) Ltd* v *Greater London Council* [1982] 1 WLR 2, discussed *post* in question 1). But you need to identify that the question is establishing that scenario: the wrongdoers themselves preventing the pursuit of corporate remedies in respect of their actions. Logically, to prevent the pursuit of any remedy the company may have, the wrongdoers must be in a position within the company to stop litigation by the company. What is that position? How does it match with the position the wrongdoers occupy in any problem that you are confronted with?

This is a difficult area but it does help if you clearly identify the wrongdoers in a company and establish whether they control the board of directors or general meeting, or both. This then gives you a platform from which to launch any advice you may have about the corporate pursuit of these wrongdoers. It helps if you have some idea as to who does control the corporate litigation, and this is looked at in question 1. Unfortunately, as you will see, it is difficult to reach any firm conclusion on the present authorities.

Question 1 concentrates on the treatment of the 'mixed' problem. The difficulties of dealing with such questions revolve around identification of the issues involved, and ensuring that the topics you revise are suitably chosen so as to be able to cope with most 'mixed' problems. Question 1 is a complete problem which requires the identification of several company law issues, one of which is the relationship between the different organs of management. Also included are extracts from problems illustrative of the type of statements that examiners may include in problems when a discussion of management powers is required. Where necessary the relevant part of the problem is highlighted in the text.

QUESTION 1

James is one of four directors of Roadhog plc, a specialist motor car manufacturer. Roadhog's articles are in the form of Table A, as prescribed by the Companies (Tables A to F) Regulations 1985. *All the directors own a small number of shares in the company.*

Roadhog plc is offered a profitable opportunity by Niki to build a racing car. James recommends the project to the board of Roadhog plc for he is anxious to enhance his prestige as an expert designer of racing cars. Roadhog plc offers to build the racing car but is doubtful as to whether it would be completed within three years. Niki would prefer a shorter completion period.

James is one of two directors of, and a shareholder in, Speed Ltd. Moss, a major shareholder in Roadhog plc, is the other director. Niki approaches James with a view to Speed Ltd building the racing car. Speed Ltd is offered and accepts the contract to build the racing car within one year and makes a large profit from the contract.

The board of Roadhog plc decides to takes legal proceedings against James. At a properly summoned annual general meeting of Roadhog plc James resigns as director. Moss and James secure a properly proposed resolution by a bare majority which declares that: 'Roadhog plc shall take no legal proceedings against James or Moss arising out of any events connected directly or indirectly to the racing car contract with Niki'.

Advise the directors of Roadhog plc.

In this problem there are several issues. The following comments concentrate on the relationship between the directors and the general meeting which is illustrated in the highlighted parts of the question as a clash over the control of the corporate litigation. This also affects the protection of minority shareholders via the exception to the rule in *Foss v Harbottle* (1843) 2 Hare 461 regarding the perpetration of a fraud on the minority by those who control the company. Note that the directors whom you are asked to advise are also minority shareholders.

Control of the Corporate Litigation

In the question the general meeting is seeking to overrule the board decision to commence legal action, but a problem could quite as easily reverse this situation, e.g.:

> The board of Roadhog plc decides not to pursue any legal action against James, so as to avoid lengthy and expensive litigation that could harm the company's public image. Tom, a major shareholder, wants legal action to be taken against James. Advise Tom.

The starting point for any discussion of the allocation of powers between the board and the general meeting must lie in the articles where art. 70 of Table A states that: '... the business of the company shall be managed by the directors who may exercise all the powers of the company'. The exercise of these powers is subject to:

(a) the provisions of the Companies Acts,
(b) the memorandum and articles of the company, and
(c) 'any directions given by special resolution'.

The phrasing of this third restriction on the exercise of powers by the directors was introduced into the model set of articles in 1985. Prior to this the meaning of the equivalent restriction in the old Table A (art. 80) was unclear in that it provided that the power of the directors to manage the company was subject to 'such regulations, being not inconsistent with the aforesaid regulations or provisions, as may be prescribed by the company in general meeting'. Elsewhere in the old art. 80, 'regulations' had clearly meant 'articles', but to accept this meaning in the last phrase would have been tautologous. It was accepted by some academics that this phrase in the old Table A carried little weight and could be virtually ignored, referring only to the power that deed of settlement companies used to have to make by-laws governing procedural matters, which are now largely overtaken by statute (see Pennington, *Company Law*, 6th ed., pp. 574–5).

The new restriction as expressed in art. 70 is clearer. The phrase, 'any directions given by special resolution', indicates that the company can pass a special resolution to issue directions to the directors as to the exercise of some part of their management powers. Although special resolutions of public limited companies should be passed in general meetings (see CA 1985, s. 378(2)), this has not prevented the courts applying the *Duomatic* principle (*Re Duomatic Ltd* [1967] 2 Ch 365) to votes requiring a special resolution (as in *Cane* v *Jones* [1980] 1 WLR 1451, alteration of the articles under CA 1985, s. 9). It would be odd if an alteration of the articles could be subject to such a principle yet 'directions' issued under art. 70 could not, as they have virtually the same effect including the requirement of disclosure to the Registrar under CA 1985, s. 380, although 'directions' do not need to be disclosed under CA 1985, s. 18, as such 'directions' do not constitute 'an alteration in the company's memorandum or articles'. Such 'directions' are presumably also not subject to the common law restriction that any alteration of the articles must be made bona fide in the best interests of the company (see chapter 5), as there is no alteration of the articles. Therefore, be on the look-out in problem questions for the *Duomatic* informal acceptance by all the shareholders being used to impose 'directions' on the directors without a formal meeting.

Therefore, if art. 70 is applicable, the directors have the power of management of the company and this can only be taken out of their hands by alteration of the articles, by directions given under art. 70 or by removal of the directors under CA 1985, s. 303. Thus, unless one of these restrictions is applied, the general meeting cannot, for example, force the sale of the company's property as this is part of the management powers of directors as in *Automatic Self-Cleansing Filter Syndicate Co. Ltd* v *Cunninghame* [1906] 2 Ch 34, where the management powers of the directors could not be controlled except upon the passing of an extraordinary resolution (see also *Re Emmadart Ltd* [1979] Ch 540). The general meeting cannot require the board to override a veto that was vested in a managing director (*Quin & Axtens Ltd* v *Salmon* [1909] AC 442).

Any 'special power given to the directors by the articles' (art. 70), is also subject to the three restrictions. You will need to establish in any problem question concerned with the management of the company whether any special powers have been given to a director or the directors and whether or not 'directions' have been made under art. 70 as to the exercise of that power.

This question is directed specifically at the extent to which control over the management of the company includes control over the litigation the company can commence. An attempted answer to this question can rarely be avoided in any examination in company law.

In *John Shaw & Sons (Salford) Ltd* v *Shaw* [1935] 2 KB 113, the general meeting was unsuccessful in its attempt to get a writ that had been issued by the board withdrawn. The court applied the principle of *Automatic Self-Cleansing Filter Syndicate Co. Ltd* v *Cunninghame*. Does this mean that the board controls the litigation of the company as part of their management function, or does it only mean that the general meeting cannot stop legal action once it is taken by the board? In *Marshall's Valve Gear Co. Ltd v Manning, Wardle & Co. Ltd* [1909] 1 Ch 267, where there was an article that bore a marked similarity to the old art. 80, the directors decided not to commence litigation, but the dissenting directors included the majority shareholder who was allowed to bring proceedings in the company name, and the approval of a formal general meeting by ordinary resolution could be sought later.

Neville J commented (at p. 274) that under the articles:

> ... the majority of the shareholders in the company at a general meeting have a right to control the action of the directors, so long as they do not affect to control it in a direction contrary to any of the provisions of the articles which bind the company.

The last part of Neville J's statement is crucial and is now covered by the third restriction in art. 70, as any attempted control of the power of management of the directors outside of the scope of art. 70 would be an attempt to 'control it in a direction contrary to ... the articles'. It still leaves the problem, however, as to what is meant by the management of the 'business of the company'. Does this mean that the power of management includes the commencement of litigation, or is it a dual initiative or parallel power that is exercisable by both the board and the general meeting? Or, is it a residual power of the general meeting exercisable only if the board refuse or are unable, for example, through a deadlock situation, to start litigation (see Lord Hailsham's judgment in *Alexander Ward & Co Ltd* v *Samyang Navigation Co. Ltd* [1975] 1 WLR 673, *Barrett* v *Duckett* [1995] 1 BCLC 73 per Sir Mervyn Davies at p. 79 and the statutory residual power in CA 1985, s. 385A(4) [CA 1989, s. 119]).

The case of *Breckland Group Holdings Ltd* v *London & Suffolk Properties Ltd* [1989] BCLC 100 confronted Harman J with this 'difficult point of law' at 4.20 pm on a Friday. He concluded that only the board of directors could adopt unauthorised legal proceedings and it was not a matter where the general meeting could intervene; they were precluded from doing so by the articles (art. 80 in this case). This 'contractarian' approach to management power within the company also received support in *Re Saul D. Harrison & Sons plc* [1995] 1 BCLC 14, where the Court of Appeal considered a complaint by an aggrieved shareholder under CA 1985, s. 459, about the way the company had been managed by the directors. The court looked to the articles to see if the directors were being 'unfair' in the context of this contractual arrangement and any understandings that existed between the directors and the shareholders, as in *Ebrahimi* v *Westbourne Galleries Ltd* [1973] AC 360. The court held that:

... in the absence of 'something more', there is no basis for a legitimate expectation that the board and the company in general meeting will not exercise whatever powers they are given by the articles of association (per Hoffmann LJ at p. 20).

The control of corporate litigation is one of those areas of company law where a definitive answer is hard to come by. The problems are caused partly by some of the companies in the authorities cited having sets of articles that did not correspond to the old art. 80. However, any problem that you will be confronted with will normally require an application of the current art. 70, and any essay question will certainly require you to apply art. 70. The only conclusion that you may be able to reach as to where the power to control litigation lies is an inconclusive one but that the strict 'contractarian' approach of applying the contract (art. 70) between the directors and shareholders appears to be prevailing. The issue is of fundamental importance. However, it does provide an opportunity to illustrate a knowledge of the conflicting judgments involved (see further, Wedderburn (1976) 39 MLR 327). What is clear is that if the control of litigation is a management power, the clarification of the third restriction in art. 70 could now lead the judiciary to question the general meeting's power to act by ordinary resolution regarding this aspect of management, as art. 70 now clearly lays down when a general meeting can intervene. If the control of corporate litigation is seen as a management power then the prevailing 'contractarian' approach would be that interventions by the general meeting in the exercise of this power can only be carried out in accordance with art. 70, that is, by special resolution to alter the articles or to give 'directions'. Unless the courts impose restrictions on voting rights when such 'directions' are given, as they have done in other areas (e.g., *Clemens* v *Clemens Bros Ltd* [1976] 2 All ER 268) and could be said to have done in respect of a vote to compromise the company's litigation (see *Estmanco (Kilner House) Ltd* v *Greater London Council* [1982] 1 WLR 2), then a majority shareholder who is able to gather more than 75 per cent of the votes cast at a general meeting would be advised to seek a 'direction' to the directors to stop any litigation against himself rather than an alteration of the articles which must be made bona fide for the benefit of the company and could be challenged on this ground.

It has already been commented that the debate over the control of litigation links to the fraud exception to the rule in *Foss* v *Harbottle*. The cases discussing the fraud exception appear to accept that the control of litigation lies wherever the alleged fraud takes place be it at the board meeting or general meeting. There is no judicial analysis as to where the control of litigation lies. For example, in *Estmanco (Kilner House) Ltd* v *Greater London Council* [1982] 1 WLR 2 the shareholders, the Greater London Council (GLC), told the directors not to commence legal action against the GLC. Sir Robert Megarry V-C commented (at p. 11) that:

Where the majority shareholders genuinely believe that it is in the best interests of the company as a whole that an action by the company should not be brought, that is decisive, unless no reasonable shareholder in their position could hold this belief.

Thus, according to Sir Robert Megarry V-C, the decision not to litigate is ultimately one for the general meeting. If it is not a genuine decision — in *Estmanco* it stultified the purpose for which the company was established — then the minority shareholders can seek redress via the fraud exception to *Foss* v *Harbottle*. Consideration should perhaps have been given to whether or not the general meeting actually had the power to overrule the board who had decided to take legal action against the GLC. There would then have been no need to invoke *Foss* v *Harbottle* or any of its exceptions. There is a great deal of judicial confusion which you can exploit. We have already seen one extract from Sir Robert Megarry V-C in *Estmanco*; in an earlier part of the judgment there appear some interesting comments which you can dissect. He states at p. 10:

If a wrong is done to a company, then it is the company alone which can decide whether or note [sic] to sue in respect of that wrong;

All right so far: this is just a restatement of the rule in *Foss* v *Harbottle*. He continues:

and that decision, like all company decisions, must be made by the appropriate body,

It appears that we are now going to get an answer to the question of which body controls the litigation of the company:

either the directors or the company in general meeting, acting by a majority if necessary.

Is this a statement of the parallel power theory? It might appear to be, but Sir Robert Megarry V-C carries straight on to cede dominance to the general meeting commenting that:

Even if the minority is profoundly convinced that a decision not to sue is wrong, the minority is a minority and not the majority. In the present case, not a single vote was cast against discontinuing the action, and that is that.

Perhaps the courts are assuming that the control of litigation lies wherever the fraud or misconduct has taken place, the main concern in *Estmanco* being whether a derivative action could be brought in respect of alleged fraudulent conduct on the part of the general meeting.

In *Prudential Assurance Co. Ltd* v *Newman Industries Ltd (No. 2)* [1982] Ch 204, the Court of Appeal appeared at times to be supporting the parallel power theory rather than ceding dominance to the general meeting when commenting (at p. 221) that:

> ... a judge might have reached the considered view that the prosecution of this great action should be left to the decision of the board *or* of a specially convened meeting of the shareholders. (Emphasis added.)

To summarise, the control of corporate litigation is a legal minefield but one into which you have got to tread because it can arise in so many different forms wherever a problem question asks you to advise a shareholder, director or the company itself. It is also possible that an essay question could be asked on the control of litigation or on the 'fraud' exception *to Foss* v *Harbottle*. A restyled conclusion from Wedderburn's article, (1976) 39 MLR 327, could give rise to the question:

> 'The courts have clarified the secure standing of the derivative action brought on the company's behalf by the shareholder but have yet to clarify who has the authority to initiate action by the company'. Discuss.

Apart from simply signifying agreement with the statement, it is possible to bring in other authorities to supplement the above discussion including *Danish Mercantile Co. Ltd* v *Beaumont* [1951] Ch 680 and *Re Argentum Reductions (UK) Ltd* [1975] 1 WLR 186. Indeed it would be permissible to see whether the residual power argument was applied in circumstances other than the control of litigation (e.g., *Barron* v *Potter* [1914] 1 Ch 895 and *Bamford* v *Bamford* [1970] Ch 212).

Alteration of Management Power

If the general meeting are unhappy with the exercise of managerial power by the board the ultimate sanctions are either to alter the articles (see chapter 5) or dismiss the directors. However, any newly appointed directors will still have a duty to act in the best interests of the company and that will not necessarily mean following the instructions of the general meeting (see *Lonrho Ltd* v *Shell Petroleum Co. Ltd* [1980] 1 WLR 627). Similarly, directors cannot, by entering into a management agreement, take away the powers of new directors. Regard must be made to the constitutional division of powers within a company for '. . . the function of the directors is to manage, but the appointment of the directors who are to do the managing is constitutionally a function of the shareholders in general meeting' (per Dillon LJ in *Lee Panavision Ltd* v *Lee Lighting Ltd* [1992] BCLC 22 at p. 30).

The question asks for advice to be given to the directors of Roadhog plc. Even if they were successful in any attempt to ignore the resolution passed at the instigation of Moss and James they could lay themselves open to dismissal by the general meeting and they would need to be advised of this possibility and any procedural methods by which they might frustrate this attempt. It is the procedural areas that cause most problems with dismissal. Many a candidate asserts that a director can be removed by a bare majority of a general meeting under CA 1985, s. 303, but then fails to highlight the practical and procedural problems of:

(a) Getting a meeting convened — note that the annual general meeting has just been held in the question. CA 1985, ss. 366–8, lay down the requirements for convening annual and extraordinary general meetings. CA 1985, s. 368(4), provides that the directors must 'proceed duly to convene a meeting' within 21 days of the requisition being deposited and this requirement is not satisfied unless the meeting takes place within 28 days of the notice convening the meeting (CA 1985, s. 368(8) [CA 1989, Sch. 19, para. 9]).

(b) Placing the resolution on the agenda of an annual general meeting: note that the resolution passed in the question was 'properly proposed' (see CA 1985, s. 376, and *Pedley* v *Inland Waterways Association Ltd* [1977] 1 All ER 209).

(c) The financial disincentive of CA 1985, s. 303(5), as well as the special procedures laid down in CA 1985, ss. 303(2) and 304. Directors' contracts of service should be disclosed (CA 1985, s. 318) and any such contract requires the approval of the general meeting if it is to include a term under which the directors' employment is to exceed five years (CA 1985, s. 319).

There are other procedural difficulties that could be encountered relating to dismissal of directors. For example you could find that part of a problem question provides that:

The articles of association are in the form of Table A, apart from a provision that, on any resolution to remove a director, the director to be removed will have five votes per share.

This is a clause calling for discussion of *Bushell* v *Faith* [1970] AC 1099. Also, in a 'quasi-partnership' type of company where the majority shareholders remove a director from office, a petition could be made by the removed director under IA 1986, s. 122(1)(g) (see *Ebrahimi* v *Westbourne Galleries Ltd* [1973] AC 360). It is therefore necessary to observe whether or not a 'quasi-partnership' situation has been established in the question to be answered. This situation does occur in the next question to be looked at.

The other issues raised in this problem are:

(a)   Breach of directors' duties (see chapter 6):

(i)   James, through his directorship of Roadhog plc, has taken advantage of a corporate opportunity that was offered to Roadhog. Is this allowed? Are there any situations in which James could take up the contract to build the car? Does it matter that it is not James taking the contract, but Speed Ltd? Is it relevant that Niki might not have awarded the contract to Roadhog anyway? There are a host of questions that need to be asked, and hopefully answered, in connection with the taking of a corporate opportunity.

(ii)   James is a director of two competing companies; is this allowed? If James does not do all he can to get the contract for Roadhog he may have broken any duties he owes to Roadhog, but if he does not try to get the contract for Speed hasn't he broken his duties that he owes to Speed? It is not that often you can quote the Bible at an examiner, and even less the words of Jesus Christ when he said: 'No man can serve two masters: for either he will hate the one, and love the other; or else he will hold to the one, and despise the other' (Matt 6, 24 — see also Christie (1992) 55 MLR 506).

(iii)   Should there have been any declaration of interests in the contract, and what are the consequences of any failure to declare?

(b)   Voting restrictions. Are there any restrictions on voting power at the general meeting where the resolution is passed. Note, however, that this is not a 'quasi-partnership'-type company (*Clemens* v *Clemens Bros Ltd* [1976] 2 All ER 268, cf. *North-West Transportation Co. Ltd* v *Beatty* (1887) 12 App Cas 589 and *Northern Counties Securities Ltd* v *Jackson & Steeple Ltd* [1974] 1 WLR 1133).

(c)   Statutory protection for minority shareholders. The directors are also minority shareholders of Roadhog and could try an application under CA 1985, s. 459 (see chapter 10).

QUESTION 2

Prepare a presentation for the seminar on the following:

'What constitutes good corporate governance?'

Notes:

(a)   The presentation should be accompanied by a written assignment of no more than 3,000 words. Your assignment must state the number of words contained in it.

(b)   The marks for this assignment will comprise 50 per cent of the total marks available for this module and will be added to your examination mark with equal weighting.

(c)   The presentation will account for 10 per cent of the total marks available for this assignment.

(d)   The presentation should last no longer than 20 minutes, excluding any questions or discussion that may be prompted by your presentation.

(e)   Your attention is drawn to the university regulations on plagiarism and cheating.

(f)   The assignment must be handed to the tutor at the seminar. University penalties for late submission apply if this deadline is not adhered to.

General Points

The notes to the assessment question indicate the information that you will need to be aware of even if this is not expressly stated. This is a coursework assignment with a presentation element, a not unusual combination. The question is very wide and provides substantial scope for your research skills. A strict legal approach would be inappropriate as the topic of corporate governance crosses various disciplines including strategic management and accountancy.

The Question

The question is really two questions: what is corporate governance and what is good corporate governance? The first requires an objective analysis of the current debates on the definition and content of corporate governance; the other requires a more subjective appraisal leaving you free to develop your own thoughts on the topic with appropriate authority to support your arguments. You will need to research wider than the traditional legal texts if you want to achieve anything other than a bare pass.

'Corporate governance' is a phrase that has come into modern use relatively recently following a succession of well-published scandals (e.g., Maxwell, Polly Peck, Guinness and BCCI), and concern about the pay levels of executive directors, particularly of the recently privatised industries. In response to the financial scandals, in May 1991 the Committee on the Financial Aspects of Corporate Governance (chaired by Sir Adrian Cadbury) was established by the Financial Reporting Council, the London Stock Exchange and the accountancy professions to address the financial aspects of corporate governance. The remit of the Committee was confined to financial aspects of corporate governance and this undoubtedly affected the scope of its definition of corporate governance. A second 'Cadbury-style' committee has been established under the chairmanship of Sir Ronald Hampel to review the reforms that have been introduced so far as a result of the Cadbury Report and the Greenburg Report on executive pay, and to establish how they can be improved upon. The Cadbury Report was published in May 1992 and it defined corporate governance as 'the system by which companies are directed and controlled' (para. 2.5). In *International Corporate Governance* (1994) Tricker defines corporate governance in a wider way. He focuses on the processes of management at the top level of company structures but also incorporates the need for conformance at all levels within the organisation through management supervision and accountability:

> Corporate governance ... is concerned with the way corporate entities are governed, as distinct from the way businesses within those companies are managed. Corporate governance addresses these issues facing boards of directors, such as the interaction with top management, and relationships with the owners and others interested in the affairs of the company, including creditors, debt financiers, analysts, auditors and corporate regulators. Concern about corporate performance through involvement with strategy formulation and policy-making, and corporate conformance through management supervision and accountability to the stakeholders fall into the field of governance. (p. xi.)

This definition allows for the processes of corporate governance to vary according to the particular situation of the company. The 'issues facing boards of directors' will not be the same for the board of a subsidiary company compared to the board of an entrepreneur company where one person holds the majority of shares and is also Managing Director and Chairman. Monks and Minow in *Corporate Governance* (1995) also adopt a wider perspective on the individuals who are involved in the determination and implementation of corporate governance issues, defining corporate governance as:

> the relationship among various participants in determining the direction and performance of the company (p. 1).

These definitions raise the issue of the wider accountability of the company, leaving the question for you to research and follow up later in your assignment: to whom is the company accountable? A similar consideration is provoked by the definition in the *Financial Times*, 6 April 1992:

> Corporate governance is all about finding ways to make companies run better.

What are the criteria for determining whether a company is being run better? Is it share value, growth, consideration for employees or customers, a good environmental record, contribution to the local or national economy, compliance with the law or a host of other potential ways of determining whether a company is run better? The Tricker definition incorporates the regulation of companies. You will need to assess the relative merits of self-regulation, promoted in the Cadbury Report, and statutory intervention. We have already seen in chapter 3 that one of the major problems of national company laws is their apparent inability to regulate multinational enterprises. There is an international dimension of corporate governance (see Saunders (1982) 30 AM J Comp Law 241, which looks at some of the self-regulating codes that apply to multinational enterprises.

Process or Substance
It is possible to interpret corporate governance in a very simple process-orientated way, looking at the mechanisms for governance or control within the company including an analysis of the composition and structure of the board of directors. This approach and a good analysis would receive a moderate mark. For a better mark you can widen the scope of the definition and therefore your answer. Concern about how companies are governed must bear some relationship to the question: in whose interests should a company be run? The response to this question has a direct bearing on the way a company should be run or the way the company should be directed or controlled. This is not a new concern. In the 1930s, Berle and Means in *The Modern Corporation and Private Property* (1932) identified a shift in the property relationship which was as momentous as the shift from feudalism to capitalism. The divorce of ownership from control raised concern about the freedom of action of senior managers who it had been previously assumed were operating under the control and direction of shareholders. The extent to which there was ever really true freedom for senior managers is debatable. Various pressures and influences have always affected their decision-taking and these have changed over time with a different emphasis. It is the identification of these trends that sets the modern agenda for corporate governance.

The question, 'For whom are corporate managers trustees?' was debated in articles by Berle and Dodds in the *Harvard Law Review* (1932) 43 Harv L Rev 1049; (1932) 45 Harv L Rev 1145), by Herman (*Corporate Control, Corporate Power* (1981)) and by Robinson, with regard to multinationals (*Multinationals and Political Control* (1983)). The answer requires continuous re-evaluation in light of changing circumstances. In particular a current concern is the accountability of senior managers to shareholders contrasted with their accountability to the legitimate wider company interest, partly as payment for the privilege of operating as a corporation, including limited liability. This has led to the identification of a wider group of 'stakeholders' in companies; other interests to which the company, and therefore the managers of the company, should have regard. Carl Hahn, the chairman of the board of management of Volkswagen AG, has stated:

> A company is duty-bound to safeguard the interest not only of the stockholders — its owners, but also those of the environment, of the workforce and of society. A balance must be constantly struck between these interests. (*The Ethics of Capitalism* (1994) Institute of Directors Annual Convention, Director 13.)

Carl Hahn's agenda for the 1990s was the environment, the workforce and the countries of Central and Eastern Europe. The stakeholders are wider than just the shareholders of the company. This can be reflected in a much wider definition of corporate governance which first of all identifies the wider context of the interests that companies may have regard to and then assesses if the processes within the company are sufficient to deliver recognition and action with regard to those interests. Therefore, an extended definition of corporate governance is:

(a) the social and ethical responsibilities and obligations of corporations and of individuals within the corporation; and

(b) the management philosophy, structures and decision-making processes that ensure harmonisation with and the furtherance of those responsibilities and obligations.

Corporate governance, as defined above, would embrace how directors and managers within companies balance sometimes competing social, ethical, legal, professional and commercial responsibilities and reflect this in their different corporate structures and the decision-making process throughout the company.

Having established the range of definitions of the subject of your assignment, the next stage is to make an assessment of the various proposals that have been put forward relating to the 'process' aspect of corporate governance. This will be followed by an analysis of the wider context of corporate governance and then an attempt to bring the two aspects together.

The Cadbury Report

The starting point for the process content of your answer must be the Cadbury Report and the Code of Best Practice that accompanied it. The broad contents of the report should be outlined:

(a) the number, selection, calibre and role of non-executive directors and the support that they need through audit committees of the board of directors (Code of Practice, paras 1.3, 2, 4.3 and notes 7 and 11);

(b) the respective roles of the chairman and managing director who should not normally be the same person so that 'no one person has unfettered powers of decision' (Code of Practice, para. 1.2);

(c) shareholders should approve directors' service contracts that exceed three years; there should be full disclosure of total emoluments and directors' pay should be subject to the recommendations of a remuneration committee of the board comprised wholly or mainly of non-executive directors.

The Committee recommended that all listed companies should comply with the report and publish a compliance statement in their annual reports. The penalties for non-compliance with the report are hard to see as the Stock Exchange would be reluctant to harm shareholders by delisting any recalcitrant company. This is therefore a voluntary code, the main sanction being the threat of government intervention if non-compliance is widespread or, more likely, if there is another series of commercial scandals. Research published by Conyon shows that between 1988 and 1993 there has been a 'massive reorganisaton in corporate governance structures of UK companies' through implementation of many of the Cadbury proposals (see M. J. Conyon (1994) 2 Corporate Governance 87; A. Belcher [1995] JBL 321).

The Greenbury Report
The Greenbury Report on executive pay published in July 1995 re-emphasised some of the Cadbury Report's proposals following the considerable controversy over some recent pay awards to directors, particularly of the privatised utilities (*The Times*, 18 July 1995, p. 28). It will be interesting to see how the extensive privatisation of utilities will affect the perception of the nature of all companies. There is a blurring between the public and private organisations with a movement from the public sector into the private sector and with some private-sector organisations taking on public-sector characteristics as they undertake 'public' activities. Indeed Robinson claimed that this blurring had already occurred with regard to multinational companies:

With its impact on investment, and indeed on the economy in general, the multinational company has, in turn, begun to be perceived less as a private organisation and more as a quasi-public international institution but one operating largely free of public controls (*Multinationals and Political Control*, p. 48).

In the regulation of corporate behaviour the public and private divide will be difficult to maintain. In this way the wider interests of the company will be recognised even more as governments seek to impose constraints on the way that all companies are managed, under the banner of good corporate governance, to protect the legitimate public interest. The Greenbury Report highlighted the fundamental principles of accountability, transparency and performance. It recommended a Code of Best Practice on directors' remuneration which should apply to all listed companies, monitored through publication of another compliance statement and an alteration of the CA 1985 to require companies to make a remuneration report to shareholders. Conyon, op. cit., found that chief executive officers of companies were on the remuneration committees of the company in 41 per cent of occasions. This is criticised by Conyon, Gregg and Machin who concluded in an analysis of executive pay that the relationship between executive pay and stock market performance is very weak and that by the 1990s there was no relationship (see M. Conyon, P. Gregg and S. Machin (1995) 105 The Economic Journal No. 430, 704).

Linking Process and Substance

During this analysis of the 'process' issues concerning corporate governance you can comment on what the various reports and writers consider to be 'good' corporate governance structures and how far they reflect reality. The next part of the answer takes the discussion further. It raises the question: for whose benefit are these processes operating? You can argue that this must be ascertained before you can decide whether or not the processes are 'good'. In this way we can make a link between the Cadbury process-driven debate on corporate governance and the wider issue of the nature of companies and corporate responsibility. This broader definition of corporate governance finds it impossible to separate the key process issues such as the composition of the board and the presence of independent renumeration committees from the prior concern about whose interest the company is operating for. This should be reflected in the direction and control of the company and the factors that managers take into account in their day-to-day decision-making. How do the structures at the top of the company affect the real decisions that companies make every day? Corporate governance, like total quality management, must flow through the organisation and cannot be isolated at the top of the company, although this is where most of the reports and writers focus their attention. This becomes more important as corporate structures are continually streamlined (through flattening, delayering or resizing!). One of the reasons for developing missions and strategic plans for the corporation is to provide a focus and reference point for decision-making. This focus can be transmitted down the managerial lines so that it impinges on all decision-making within the corporation and all staff share in the delivery of the accepted corporate strategy. Indeed, they would have been involved in its creation. The mission needs to be clear and understood by all staff for it to have an impact on daily decision-making. The objective is to have a focused effect from all staff towards the delivery of the mission and the associated strategic plan, in the same way as total quality relies on the acceptance of the concept and actions by all staff in support of it. Decision-makers in companies could be spread all over the world and will be confronted with issues that raise legal, ethical, social, professional and commercial concerns. The route that the decision-maker takes will depend on a number of factors including:

(a) ignorance of the wider context of the issue,
(b) personal prejudices,
(c) personal perceptions of how the company will want the decision-maker to act,
(d) the corporate mission and strategic plan so far as they refer to the wider legal, moral, social and professional aspects of corporate governance.

If we leave decisions to personal prejudices then individuals will apply their own individual ethical stances to the problem, their own views of what is in the best interests of the company, just as they did in the Indian factories which served the Union Carbide group in Bhopal.

The application of different aspects of corporate governance will need to be adjusted according to the different nature of the company. The Cadbury Committee concentrated on large listed companies, although it expressed the desire that all other companies would embrace the principles inherent in the report. We have seen that the vast majority of companies are small or medium-sized enterprises (SMEs), and the vast majority of company directors are directors of such enterprises. In these companies there is an added complexity as quite frequently the role of shareholder, employee, director and creditor may all be located in one person or a small group of people. The question of the divorce of ownership from control has not yet occurred, but it soon will, as only the company has the potential to live for ever. As the company grows or succession is implemented the 'hands-on' approach which the shareholder-director(s) will usually have undertaken cannot continue. Decision-making has to be devolved within an organisation. How do boards of directors ensure that their view of the mode of corporate behaviour that is in the best interests of the company mirrors the actual decision and behaviour of the company as the company starts to grow and devolution increases?

The application of corporate governance, although relevant to all companies, must vary in content and depth according to the nature of the company. In a similar vein, the Department of Trade and Industry estimate that 66 per cent of the registered companies are subsidiary companies of one form or another has a considerable impact on the way in which corporate governance principles will be applied with regard to a large number of companies and directors. The issue of corporate governance is not confined to the large companies; it affects every company, but it will do so in different ways according to the nature of the company.

Future Legal Developments

Because responsibility for decisions is devolved within corporations it is important to consider how this affects the wider legal aspects of corporate governance. From a legal perspective the cynic might predict that as personal liability on directors and officers increases they may wish to ensure that the decisions that give rise to that liability are made lower down the organisation (V. Finch (1994) 57 MLR 880 at p. 882). Increasingly, national legislation is imposing liability on directors and senior managers as well as the companies that they run. This is referred to as 'gatekeeper liability'. As a consequence in the United Kingdom there has been a substantial increase in directors' and officers' liability insurance. This is encouraged by the CA 1989, s. 137, which amended the CA 1985, s. 310, so that companies may now purchase and maintain insurance for their directors and officers against liability for negligence, default, breach of duty or breach of trust in relation to the company. Finch raises the issue of how insurance will affect the balance between enterprise and individual liability. Based on experience from the USA, the advent of insurance may lead the courts to hold directors and officers more frequently liable for the actions of their corporations, and possibly increase the areas of corporate liability so as to enable compensation and loss spreading to take place. Finch states there is a relationship between the enhanced personal liability of directors and corporate responsibility, as personal liability may serve to distance the director from management. But it may also encourage directors to monitor the actions of others within the company affecting the nature of corporate governance within companies in a devolved environment.

Insurers may also demand changes in the internal structure of the corporation with more audit committees and non-executive directors strengthening the gatekeeper role of directors. Gatekeeper liability, and the extension of areas of such liability, is likely to be extended throughout the European Union as a tool whereby the enterprise can be encouraged to uphold certain corporate responsibilities and this will inevitably extend to the holding company as the gatekeeper for its subsidiaries (see *Dairy Containers Ltd* v *NZI Bank Ltd* (1995) 7 NZCLC 96–609).

The European company provisions and the draft 5th EC Directive (COM (90) 629) also provide for the ability of 10 per cent of shareholders to commence an action on behalf of the company when directors have committed a misfeasance. Individual directors can escape liability if they prove no fault is attributable to them, but the general thrust is to increase the potential liability of those who govern companies. This is a breach of the normal rule in company law that only the company can initiate action except where the wrongdoers control the company (*Foss* v *Harbottle*). The Law Commission is also looking at derivative actions as part of the Department of Trade and Industry's overall review of company law announced in December 1992. Another option open to legislators confronted with corporate misfeasance, other than direct regulation or opening avenues for minority shareholders to take action, has not yet been considered. Compulsory insurance could be required for directors. Lawyers, accountants and medical practitioners already have this. This could be a mechanism for enhancing the gatekeeper role of directors, pushing the burden onto insurance companies to develop techniques of quantifying the risk of insuring directors in return for a compulsory market.

This is a wide-ranging topic that gives you plenty of scope to illustrate your research and contextual skills. You will need to reach your own conclusions about what constitutes good corporate governance. When you are making the presentation it would be advisable to type the different definitions on to a sheet of paper and distribute this as a handout. An acetate (overhead projector slide) could categorise the differences between the definitions, ranging from the Cadbury definition, which was interpreted as an analysis of the top management processes and structures, to the much wider definition that demands the prior establishment of the nature and mission of the company before any structures can be analysed to see if they are good enough to meet these aspirations. You could use acetates to outline the main recommendations of the Cadbury Report and to portray the rise in director and officer insurance liability premium. You would need a final acetate to state what you think are the attributes of good corporate governance. Questions to direct at your audience could include:

(a)   Which of the definitions do you prefer? Why?

(b)   Do you think that processes and structures alone will lead to good corporate governance? If not, why not?

(c)   Should government, or combinations of governments, intervene or should government leave these issues to self-regulation?

(d)   Is this a national or international issue? If it is international what is the international model for regulation?

FURTHER READING

Belcher, Alice, 'Regulation by the market: the case of the Cadbury Code and compliance statement' [1995] JBL 321.

Blake, A., 'Suing in the company name: who decides' (1987) 5 Company Law Digest 19.

Blake, A., 'Company law and employees' (1989) Kingston L Rev 69.

Conyon, M. J., 'Corporate governance changes in UK companies between 1988 and 1993' (1994) 2 Corporate Governance 87.

Conyon, M. J., Gregg, P., and Machin, S., 'Taking care of business: executive compensation in the United Kingdom' (1995) 105 (No. 430) Economic Journal 704.

Finch, Vanessa, 'Personal accountability and corporate control: the role of directors' and officers' liability insurance' (1994) 57 MLR 880.

Monks, Robert A. G., and Minow, Nell, *Corporate Governance* (Oxford: Blackwell, 1995).

Sanders, Pieter, 'Implementing international codes of conduct for multinational enterprises' (1982) 30 Am J Comp Law 241.

Titus, R. B., 'Limiting directors' liability: the case for a more balanced approach — the corporate governance project alternative' (1989) 11 W New Eng L Rev 1.

Tricker, R., *International Corporate Governance* (Singapore: Prentice-Hall, 1994).

Wedderburn of Charlton, Lord, 'Trust, corporation and the worker' (1985) 23 Osgoode Hall LJ 203.

CONCLUSION

At the beginning of this book we said that company law can be dry and boring. If you have managed to get this far then we hope that we have at least partially alleviated that condition. You may have modified your approach to some of the basic areas of company law so that they appear clearer as well as even identifying how some of the different topics weld together, particularly in the final chapter. At times, attempts to understand the subject are frustrated, not only by the volume of statutory and common law authorities involved as well as the numerous academic attempts to interpret them, but also by the problem that every area of company law seems to be interrelated in one way or another. The question you come to ask when revising for an examination is which areas can I afford to leave out, rather than which topics shall I revise? We have tried to avoid suggesting that you should revise all of company law, but only just. That would be the ideal situation, but examiners are well aware that most students, quite legitimately, will be selective in their choice of revision topics. Hopefully, that process of selection will have been facilitated by reading the preceding chapters and some of your marks will have been achieved in good assignment answers.

Having read the substantive chapters, it would now probably be a good idea to return to chapters 1 and 2 so as to establish how the material dealt with in those chapters could be put into a programme of research and revision and actually used in your assignments examinations.

Finally, good luck in your studies and enjoy them.

BIBLIOGRAPHY

Berle, A. A., and Means, G. C., *The Modern Corporation and Private Property* (New York: Macmillan, 1933). 2nd ed. (1967).

Boyle, A. J., and Birds, J., *Company Law*, 3rd ed. (Bristol: Jordans, 1995).

Cadbury, A., *The Company Chairman* (Cambridge, Director Books, 1990).

Committee on the Financial Aspects of Corporate Governance, *Report* (London: Gee, 1992).

Company Law Committee [Chairman: Lord Jenkins], *Report* (Cmnd 1749) (London: HMSO, 1962).

Department of Trade, *The Law of Insider Dealing* (Consultative Document, 1990).

Department of Trade and Industry, *Company Law Review: the Law Applicable to Private Companies, A Consultative Document* (URN 94/529) (London: DTI, 1994).

Drucker, P. F., *Managing in Turbulent Times* (London: Heinemann, 1980).

Easterbrook, Frank H., and Fischell, Daniel R., *The Economic Structure of Corporate Law* (Cambridge Mass: Harvard University Press, 1991).

Farrar, J. H., Furey N., and Hannigan, B., *Farrar's Company Law*, 3rd ed. (London: Butterworths, 1991).

Galbraith, J. K., *The New Industrial State*, 2nd ed. (London, 1972).

Gower, L. C. B., *Principles of Modern Company Law*, 5th ed. (London: Sweet & Maxwell, 1992).

Hadden, T., *The Control of Corporate Groups* (London: Institute of Advanced Legal Studies, 1983).

Herman, E. S., *Corporate Control, Corporate Power* (Cambridge: Cambridge University Press, 1981).

Insolvency Law and Practice: Report of the Review Committee (Cmnd 8558) (London: HMSO, 1982).

Mayson, S. W., French D., and Ryan, C., *Mayson, French and Ryan on Company Law*, 12th ed. (London: Blackstone Press, 1995).

Parkinson, J. E., *Corporate Power and Responsibility* (Oxford: Clarendon Press, 1993).

Pennington, R. R., *Company Law*, 6th ed. (London: Butterworths, 1990).

Rider, B. A. K., *Insider Trading* (Bristol: Jordans, 1983).

Robinson, John, *Multinationals and Political Control* (Aldershot: Gower, 1983).

Samuels, J. M., and Wilkes, F. M., *Management of Company Finance*, 2nd ed. (London: Nelson, 1975).

Tindall, R., *Multinational Enterprises* (1985).

Wedderburn, K. W., 'The legal development of corporate responsibility', in European University Institute, *Corporate Governance and Directors' Liabilities* (1985).

Wedderburn of Charlton, Lord, *The Worker and the Law*, 3rd ed. (London: Sweet & Maxwell, 1986).

Wheeler, S. (ed.), *The Law of Business Enterprise* (Oxford: Clarendon, 1994).

Wooldridge, F., *Groups of Companies: The Law and Practice in Britain, France and Germany* (London: Institute of Advanced Legal Studies, 1981).

INDEX

OTHER TITLES IN THE SERIES

SWOT Constitutional and Administrative Law
SWOT Law of Evidence
SWOT Company Law
SWOT Law of Contract
SWOT Family Law
SWOT Land Law
SWOT Criminal Law
SWOT Equity and Trusts
SWOT Commercial and Consumer Law
SWOT A Level Law
SWOT Law of Torts
SWOT Jurisprudence
SWOT Employment Law
SWOT English Legal System
SWOT EC Law
SWOT Conveyancing
SWOT Law of Succession
SWOT Intellectual Property Law
SWOT International Law